LITERARY TRANSLATION AND THE
REDISCOVERY OF READING

The act of translation is perhaps the ultimate performance of reading. By translating a text, translators rework the source text into a reflection of their reading experience. In fact all reading is translation, as each reader incorporates associations and responses into the reading process. Clive Scott argues that the translator needs new linguistic resources to do justice to the intricacies of the reading consciousness, and explores different ways of envisaging the translation of a literary work, not only from one language to another, but also from one form to another within the same language. With examples drawn from different literatures, including English, this exciting new departure in translation theory has much to offer to students of literature and of comparative literary criticism. It also encourages all readers of literature to become translators in their turn, to use translation to express and give shape to their encounters with texts.

CLIVE SCOTT is Professor Emeritus of European Literature at the University of East Anglia.

LITERARY TRANSLATION AND THE REDISCOVERY OF READING

CLIVE SCOTT

CAMBRIDGE
UNIVERSITY PRESS

CAMBRIDGE
UNIVERSITY PRESS

University Printing House, Cambridge CB2 8BS, United Kingdom

Cambridge University Press is part of the University of Cambridge.

It furthers the University's mission by disseminating knowledge in the pursuit of education, learning and research at the highest international levels of excellence.

www.cambridge.org
Information on this title: www.cambridge.org/9781107507654

First published 2012
First paperback edition 2015

A catalogue record for this publication is available from the British Library

Library of Congress Cataloguing in Publication data
Scott, Clive, 1943– author.
Literary translation and the rediscovery of reading / Clive Scott.
pages   cm
Includes bibliographical references and index.
ISBN 978-1-107-02230-0 (hardback)
1. Translating and interpreting.   2. Literature – Translations – History and criticism.
3. Reading, Psychology of.   I. Title.
PN241.S36   2012
418′.04 – dc23   2012020255

ISBN 978-1-107-02230-0 Hardback
ISBN 978-1-107-50765-4 Paperback

*In memory of
Malcolm Bowie
late Master of Christ's College, Cambridge
'an interdisciplinarist
beyond the dreams
of the modern university'*

Contents

Illustrations

Acknowledgements

I offer my sincerest thanks to the Master and Fellows of Trinity College, Cambridge, for inviting me to give the 2010 Clark Lectures, and for their unstinting hospitality. I owe particular debts of gratitude to Boyd Hilton, Adrian Poole and Eric Griffiths for their support and guidance during the course of the lectures, and for the warmth of their care. These lectures make up the first four chapters of this book.

Chapter 1 was first published, in a slightly shorter version, in *Translation Studies* (4/2, 2011, 213–29); Chapter 5 first appeared in *The Australian Journal of French Studies* (47/1, January–April 2009, 46–59), also in a shorter version; Chapter 6 first appeared in the electronic journal *Thinking Verse* (1, 2011, 67–101); Chapter 7 is a reworked version of the Malcolm Bowie Memorial Lecture, delivered in Oxford in March 2008 and first published, in revised form, in Antoinette Fawcett, Karla L. Guadarrama García and Rebecca Hyde Parker (eds), *Translation: Theory and Practice in Dialogue* (London: Continuum, 2010), 109–27; the Epilogue was first published in *Comparative Critical Studies* (7/2–3, 2010, 381–93). I would like to thank the editors and publishers concerned for their kind permission to reprint these pieces.

I would also like to thank the University of California Press, for permission to reproduce C. F. MacIntyre's translation of Rilke's 'Voller Apfel, Birne und Banane' (*Die Sonette an Orpheus*, Part I, 13); Scribner Publishing for the US rights to reproduce Yeats's 'Leda and the Swan' (*The Tower*, 1928); Éditions Gallimard, for permission to reproduce Jules Supervielle's 'L'Errant' (*Les Amis inconnus*, 1934); Random House Group Ltd, for permission to reproduce J.B. Leishman's 'The Reader', a translation of Rilke's 'Der Leser' (*Neue Gedichte*, 1907/8), originally published by the Hogarth Press (1964); Anvil Press Poetry, for permission to reproduce Oliver Bernard's translation of Apollinaire's 'Marizibill' (*Guillaume Apollinaire: Selected Poems*, new edn, 2004); *The Sun*, for permission to reproduce a page from their issue of 23 July 2001; and Veer Books, for permission to reproduce Sean Bonney's translations of Baudelaire's 'À une passante' (*Baudelaire in English*, 2008). Every effort has been made to track down all copyright holders and secure necessary permissions; any omissions of acknowledgement derive from failure of contact, and will be rectified on notification.

Finally, I would like to express my lasting gratitude to my editor, Linda Bree, upon whose advice and creative thinking I have heavily relied in preparing this book for publication; and to Maartje Scheltens and Jodie Hodgson for overseeing the progress of the book to production, with such patient and resourceful understanding.

All translations are my own, unless otherwise specified.

Introduction

This book is primarily a vehicle for the 2010 Clark Lectures. These lectures constitute Chapters 1 to 4 and appear, aside from minor revisions, very much as they were delivered. They bring in their train further chapters on some of the issues addressed by them, issues which the lectures could only touch upon and which, by their very nature, deserved much fuller critical consideration. Indeed, we are here confronted by topics whose significance far exceeds the bounds of this book. Before embarking on a fuller description of the structure and contents of the book, I would like to outline, in their bare bones, the arguments underlying the lectures, and the polemical positions from which they spring.

The task of the lectures, put in its simplest form, was this: to develop a mode, or rather modes, of translation which would capture reading as a phenomenological, rather than as an interpretative, activity. To achieve this switch-over from the interpretative to the phenomenological, one must abandon hermeneutic habits of reading and listening and adopt what these lectures call 'constructivist' ones. What is the back-argument of this enterprise?

Currently, translation is principally understood as the translation of a source text (ST) in one language into a target text (TT)[1] in another language, for the benefit of readers who are not conversant with the language of the ST (interlingual translation). But if it is translation's business to increase the circulation of languages and to sharpen our awareness of the inbuilt problematics of language and of linguistic transfer (transtextuality), then clearly the current model, as I have defined it, does not work. Indeed, it is a form of translation which, by encouraging the continuing linguistic ignorance of the reader, acts directly against what I take to be translation's principal concern. If, then, we insist that translation should preoccupy itself with readers *familiar* with the source language (SL), what kind of translation should we envisage, and what should its function be? What we can immediately say is that interlingual translation should forfeit its present monopoly, and that our engagement with intralingual translation (translation of a language into a different version of itself) and intermedial translation (translation across media) should become correspondingly more conspicuous.

Let us start from another point. The chief concern of literary criticism, as at present constituted, is the interpretation and evaluation of literary works. The discourse of interpretation is a public discourse, constituted of shared disciplines, modes of analysis and critical language. Interpretation is a post-textual operation. It tends to assume that a text, once properly established by scholarly means, remains constant to itself, whatever its mode of presentation or delivery, and, however much interpretations of it vary as time unfolds, in something approaching an a-temporal state. What literary criticism wishes to lock out of interpretation are the personal idiosyncrasies of the reader, the associative mechanisms, the memories, the unpredictable intertexts, in short, the *autobiographical* input, on the grounds that it does not transcend the anecdotal and the impressionistic. Also included in this outlawed autobiographical input is the realisation, or enactment, of text by the individual reader's voice, the elements of paralanguage (speed, loudness, pausing, intonation, tone, differing degrees of stress), since the voice is the instrument whereby the reader actualises or embodies his/her individual experience of the text, of the reading process. In canvassing the importance of this autobiography of reading, I am therefore arguing for two basic shifts of emphasis: from textual examination to readerly consciousness, and from post-textual, post-reading, critical retrieval of text to in-textual, in-reading readerly response. It is with the latter components of these shifts that translation should concern itself. And these shifts make it desirable to envisage translation not just as an in-textual act, but also as a pre-textual act (i.e. the ST is an inadequate transcription of an oral performance by the reader that has already taken place) and as a post-post-textual act (i.e. translation should not just be the translation of a reading of a text, but also, possibly, the translation of the *memory* of reading a text).

Immediately we speak of 'in-textual reading', of a view of the text from an ongoing, developing inside, from a constructivist position, we must abandon 'standard' translation's dedication to textual stasis, to the textual immobilisation of the ST. By this we do not mean that meaning *within* the ST has achieved stasis, since evidently polysemy, connotative range and interpretative variation, are part of the ST's literariness. No, we mean rather that the ST is deemed to have achieved *textual* stasis, has authority as a text, so that the TT can safely mount itself on that ST and aim at the same completeness, the same achieved condition. But the ST, as we have it before us, is in fact not in a suspended state, but at the intersection of three durations: the process of the work's composition and revision, a process which has within it the dimension of potentially infinite extension; the process of the ST's post-publicational life, in the minds of countless readers, in different editions, imitations, adaptations, merchandising, and so on; the process of the ST's existing and becoming in the mind of any *individual* reader.

We must be careful, then, not to disparage this autobiographical input, not to regard it as the accidental, the decorative, the whimsical; it is, after all, that by which a reader assimilates himself/herself bodily into text and, conversely, that by which text is enriched by a reader and absorbed into a life. Autobiographical input is best understood as a creative force, a creative force which can be harnessed, 'respectabilised', textualised, by translation, fed back into the ST as part of translation's own creative project. In other words, translation is in a peculiarly *privileged* position to give expression to what literary criticism, for professional reasons, for reasons of critical integrity, must push to one side: the contingencies of linguistic association and of vocal realisation.

And if the translator is properly to become the reader we describe, and vice versa, we must move on from the partial view of the translator, as someone with a particular translational competence, to a holistic view of the translator, as an unconscious, a subjectivity, a writerly metabolism. That is, we must move on from translation as a linguistic activity necessitated by the non-translatedness of a particular text to translation as an existential need and condition of reading. We need, correspondingly, to distinguish between a TT which generates an audience for itself by virtue of its connection with an otherwise unreadable ST, and the TT which is part of the audience of the ST; and to distinguish between a translation which purports, in some form or another, to be 'Baudelaire', and translations which seek, thanks to the continuing activity of the ST, either to co-author with Baudelaire (dialogue/communion), or to produce a not-Baudelaire, where Baudelaire is still present in the 'notness'.

The empirical languages now go their own ways, neither as perfect nor as failed languages, but as languages which have come into their own and have the wherewithal to expand and evolve. Translation attempts neither to reconcile languages nor to demonstrate their differences as inalienable, as measures of cultural identity or indelibility. Is it translation's function to act out, again and again, the right-thinking ethnic ritual whereby one understands and imaginatively inhabits the 'other' and seeks to preserve it, even in one's own linguistic sphere? I think not. More important is the entirely personal enterprise of alterity: I confront another to become myself; this is neither the concealment of other in self, nor the preservation of other in self, but the transformation of other into self, where the transformative process itself is what counts, is what must remain visible, is both process and project. It is for this reason that there is no difference between intra-lingual and interlingual translation.

Properly to conduct this process of transformation, the translator must have at his/her disposal every resource of language, and every resource of verbal and visual paralanguage. We may regret that the experimental and the avant-garde, for all the local enthusiasms they may have engendered, have generally been marginalised, so that we have signally failed to learn from their imaginative leaps, and have consequently failed to incorporate their findings into our own middle-of-the-road practices. In my own translations, I feel I am engaged in an endless process of catching up with the expressive possibilities that the experimental and the avant-garde have long made available to us. This book tirelessly, if implicitly, argues that translation should, by definition, be a form of experimental writing, by definition (a) because its material, what we are loosely calling 'the autobiographical input of reading', is unstable, shifting, varied, metamorphic, multi-lingual and multi-sensory – that is to say, its parameters are difficult, if not impossible, to establish; and (b) because it is translation's business to put the ST at the cutting edge of its own progress through time, to open up for the ST its possible futures, its strategy of textual self-regeneration. We at present lack a language able to capture the phenomenology of reading, and experimental writing offers us the best hope of finding one.

The autobiographical input of reading/translating, as understood in this book, has two faces: one turned towards the reader's encounter with the language of text itself, as a set of somatic, associational triggers, and towards the ways in which translation can textualise this encounter, can make it textually significant; the other is turned towards the environment, the ambience within which the act of reading takes place, and towards the ways in which, through translation, the text-internal and the text-external might find a route to fruitful co-habitation and interaction. But these two faces do belong to the same figure: deepening readerly response, particularly the reader's auditory capacity, through verbal and visual paralanguage, not only extends the range of readerly consciousness, but opens up new channels of communication between the text and the world outside.

The first two chapters explore the former of these faces, the way in which a reader inhabits text, and that in two senses: first, in terms of psycho-physiological and kinaesthetic responses to the materials and structures of

language itself – phonemes, morphemes, parts of speech, syntactic constructions; and second, in terms of vocal and rhythmic inputs into text, the
paralanguage of the reading consciousness. To capture these responses in
all their complexity, translation's own language must expand: in the development of visual paralanguage (typography, page layout, bibliographical
design, readerly gestures and postures) and of alternative graphics (handwriting, doodling in pen and paint, crossing out), so that translation is
actively engaged in textual performance, both performance *in* the text, and
performance *of* the text.

The first chapter is entitled, simply, 'Reading and translation'. It begins
by reviewing some of the sources and objectives of the book as a whole,
and of this chapter in particular. A principal concern is the clarification of
what is to be meant by literary translation. It then elaborates a distinction
between hermeneutic and constructivist reading, before adopting the constructivist position as a reading/translational strategy in relation to Edward
Thomas's 'Adlestrop'. The consideration of this poem, with an emphasis
on the perceptual experiences communicated by linguistic structure (enumeration) and parts of speech (proper noun, co-ordinating conjunction),
leads to a two-part translational development, the second part of which
also incorporates the notion of radial reading. This is followed by an exploration of one of Rilke's *Sonnets to Orpheus*, focusing on the ways in which
textual acoustics use the body of the reader to make the poem's sense and
to inculcate an intensified aural receptivity. This analysis, in its turn, generates a translation, and a detour into doodling. The chapter closes with
a brief reflection on textual exactitude and its relation to the written and
the oral.

Resuming the constructivist mode of reading, the second chapter ('Reading: voice and rhythm') considers readerly input into text in two related
aspects: voice and rhythm. It opens with a differentiation between the phys-
iological/pronunciatory and the expressive/articulatory versions of voice,
and with an examination of voice in the speech-indicators of popular fiction. It assesses the injustices that criticism, and particularly the criticism
of poetry, has done to the voice, and suggests possible ways out of that
predicament. Voice and its paralanguage are central to the constitution
of rhythm, whereas metre is peculiarly neglectful of them. The chapter
argues that metre and rhythm have deeply divided interests, and briefly
explores the translation of the metrical into the rhythmic in a treatment
of Yeats's 'Leda and the Swan'. A section of W.E. Henley's *In Hospital*
cycle is the occasion of a further translation, a pre-textual translation,
in which vocal performance is incorporated into text, in anticipation of

its achieving textual status. Themes touched on at the close of the first chapter – handwriting and doodling – return as important features of translational practice. The chapter ends with an investigation of voice and rhythm in a tabular, as opposed to a linear, text – in this instance, a translation of the translation by Philip Cranston of a short poem by Jules Supervielle ('L'Errant').

Correspondingly, Chapters 3 and 4 are concerned with the relationship between text and the outside world, reading and the ambient, and with the ways in which translation might express or facilitate that relationship. The third chapter ('Translating the textual environment (1)') addresses the incorporation of the environment into the reading experience, the infiltration of world into text. The image of reading which our art favours is that of the reader absorbed in the world of the book, to the exclusion of all else. But there is an equally instructive thematics of looking up from the page, of interrupted reading (Woolf, Bonnefoy, Barthes), and this looking up helps us to distinguish between two kinds of ambience: one connected with radial reading, with the activation of the reader's own associations and memories, embodied here in a photographic translation of Apollinaire's 'Marizibill'; the other connected with the absorption into text of the world beyond the text. The development of this latter aspect necessitates both a reappraisal of collage (in relation to Shakespeare's Sonnet 71) and an elaboration of the ways in which we think about onomatopoeic and ideophonic devices (graphic novel, Futurism, anthropology), and culminates in a 'multilineal' translation of a sentence from Maupassant's 'La Femme de Paul'.

The fourth chapter, as its title indicates ('Translating the textual environment (2)'), picks up where the previous chapter left off: where the third chapter was principally interested in the infiltration of text by environment, the fourth considers the exfiltration of text into the environment. But before embarking on this reversal of direction, we pay a last visit to infiltration, by re-examining Shakespeare's Sonnet 71, in a version in which it is overrun by environment. The investigation of exfiltration follows two lines: that of performance, and that of text projected into the wider environment. We are familiar with the opportunities offered by performance for wrenching text from the page and enlarging and diversifying its area of operation. But we do not sufficiently attend to the opportunity to develop new kinds of listening, nor do we sufficiently consider how performance studies might interact with translation studies and literary criticism. The projection of text into the ambient looks into the possible applications of R. Murray Schafer's World Soundscape Project and Henri Lefebvre's 'rhythmanalysis', and explores how a translation of Thomas Nashe's 'Song' might be used as a rhythmic component in a larger soundscape. As a further model of exfiltration, we briefly visit translation as a destabilising insertion of text into the status quo. The chapter goes on to a further reconsideration of the relationship between the written and the oral, before concluding with reflections on survival translation (as opposed to transmissional translation). Survival translation encapsulates many of the aspirations identified in the opening sequence of chapters.

One of the book's underlying arguments is the case for the redemption of the paralinguistic from the linguistic, the performed text from the silently read, the dict from the script. But within the paralinguistic, as Chapter 2 has already demonstrated, there is a potential, and potentially destructive, 'rivalry' between the two aspects of the paralinguistic, the physiological/pronunciatory and the expressive/articulatory, between timbre and delivery. It might be claimed that these two aspects belong to different 'ages' of the voice, the prelapsarian (geno-vocal) and the postlapsarian (pheno-vocal); at all events, the latter tends to exist at the expense of the former. Chapter 5 ('Translating the acousticity of voice') investigates this distinction in relation to a translation of Baudelaire's 'Causerie'. This translation is based on a thorough metrical and acoustic exploration of the poem and an examination of the ways in which it invites the reading voice to invest the text with the voice's own idiosyncrasies. The translation attempts to release the Baudelairean poem from its vocal quandaries, an enterprise given a different kind of significance in a second translation, an 'overwritten' version of the same texts. Overwriting, the closing argument runs, is a model of the naturally 'redemptive' function of all translation.

The opening question posed by Chapter 6 ('Free verse and the translation of rhythm') is: what part should metrical considerations play in the translation of verse? Translators often make them paramount. But this is to drive translation off course, particularly if one believes that it is translation's business to capture the perceptual experience of reading/performing one text into another. Metre has no interest in paralinguistic values, and, accordingly, it obstructs the translator's capacity to reconcile texts, to cross back and forth between languages, in endless acoustic and dictional explorations. Rhythm is the proper instrument of such transactions, and it is so because, in relation to metre, it is potentially so inclusive a paralinguistic category. The pursuit of this argument entails an enquiry into assumptions made by English and French metrical analysis about verse-constitutive features, an assessment of the advantages of free-verse and tabular translation, and the detailed investigation of two examples: a translation of the first line of Baudelaire's 'Chant d'automne', and a translation of the first stanza of Valery Larbaud's 'Ode'.

This book is dedicated to the memory of Malcolm Bowie,[2] not only to mark the passing of a peerless scholar and a critic of inspiriting breadth and subtlety; not only to express by this memorial some of the gratitude owed to him by the worlds of French Studies and Comparative Literature for the magnificent way in which he nourished them; but also, and perhaps presumptuously, to suggest that many of the ideas and argumentative threads pursued in this book lie within the purview of his own convictions. Accordingly, Chapter 7 ('The reinvention of the literary in literary translation') is largely the text of the Malcolm Bowie Memorial Lecture delivered in Oxford in March 2007, in which I addressed more fully a topic only touched on in Chapter 4, but central to an approach to translation that wishes translation to be the record of the phenomenology of reading, namely literary translation's constant reinvention of the literary. Standard attitudes hitherto have tended to assume that a literary text is literary by virtue of qualities which inhere in it, in its printed language, and that, therefore, translation should seek to keep these qualities in place as best it can – this means that, ideally, one translates metaphor by metaphor, ambiguity by ambiguity, alliteration by alliteration. If, however, one assumes that the literary is not an effect guaranteed by devices within the text, but rather something experienced and bestowed on the text by a reader, then the translational policy just described will be a mistaken one. Instead one will argue, as we do, that every literary text translated must be translated back into its literariness, that literariness might well be relocated by the process of translation, that the literary might well reside not just in the linguistics of a text, but in its paralinguistics, that is to say, in certain vocal inflections or rhythmic choices, in certain dispositional and/or typographical manoeuvres, wherever the reader's psycho-physiological or kinaesthetic relationship with a text 'deepens' and ramifies. These issues are explored with reference to translations of passages from Virgil's *Aeneid* and Apollinaire's 'Zone' (*Alcools*), and cover the paralinguistic in both its verbal and visual manifestations.

Chapter 8 ('Writing and overwriting the sound of the city'), the concluding chapter, returns to the area of exploration of Chapters 3 and 4, reading and the textual environment, and does so using CRESSON (Centre de recherche sur l'espace sonore et l'environnement urbain), the inheritors of R. Murray Schafer's World Soundscape Project, as its tutelary spirit. It undertakes an examination of Baudelaire's 'À une passante', guided by the proposition that the poem's sound-structure is informed by the different sonic effects at work in the street, and that, indeed, its language generates the urban acoustic within which its action occurs. At the same time, the chapter returns to overwriting as a translational resource (first broached in Chapter 5), and in particular as a translational resource which keeps text in contact with the outside world, in two senses. First, a consideration of Sean Bonney's overwritten translation of Baudelaire (2008) shows how overwriting turns language outwards: it casts language as the flotsam of urban dereliction, and thus prevents the smooth 'inward' text from establishing itself; overwriting seems to be both the debris of a failure and the instrument of a revolution; the typewriter is a significant protagonist in this drama. Second, a superimposition of translations of 'À une passante' reveals how overwriting affects the status of the page and keeps the sheet of paper locked in a dialogue with extratextual reality. The chapter closes with reflections on translation in two intermedial guises: as a homologue of walking, and as an activity comparable to drawing.

The Epilogue ('Portrait of a reader – Malcolm Bowie in search of the critical interworld') refocuses on the book's central preoccupation – literary reading – in an assessment of Malcolm Bowie's critical orientations. Bowie's reading practices are the embodiment of certain readerly/translational features we deem capital: the foregrounding of the dynamics of reading, reading seen as an experience located in a vivid here and now, text as a mobilisation of the kinaesthetics of reading, reading as an awakening of what is multi-sensory and synaesthetic in language. But Bowie remains a critic rather than a translator, or rather, with him, the translational cast of mind inhabits critical perception in such a way that the hermeneutic is informed and multiplied by the constructivist. Bowie uses the languages of the other arts to articulate the experiential intuitions of reading, in what might be called acts of transubstantiation; correspondingly, through recourse to the other arts, the critic is better able to perform the creativity of thought in his/her writing. In his pursuit of the appropriate interlanguage, Bowie looks particularly to psychoanalysis as a potential methodological and linguistic model.

My objection to the current over-preoccupation with translation for those ignorant of the SL, at the expense of intralingual and intermedial translation, and the consequent exclusion of translation from many kinds of literary reading, might lead me to the proposition that literary translation should dissociate itself from translation studies. Intralingual and intermedial translation are bound to assume in their readers knowledge of the SL/ST. And a more thorough theorisation of intralingual and intermedial translation would, I believe, lead to the practices I am anxious to promulgate: expanding and proleptic TTs; multiple translation; multi-sensory translation. Where translation studies has addressed literary translation, it has developed no theory about the literariness of the translational act itself, nor about how translation might re-locate or develop the literariness of the ST; and it has failed in any marked degree to incorporate literary theory into its thinking, in particular textual theory and reader-response theory. By this last, I do not so much mean the extent to which translation might be seen to project or re-project literary paradigms, 'horizons of expectation' (Jauss, 1981), or to anticipate readerly competencies (Iser, 1974, 1978), but rather how translation might engage with exchanges of consciousness (Poulet, 1969–1970) or help us to 'rediscover the movements of... reading within the body itself' (Certeau, 1984, 175). Only in this way will translation be able to create a poetics/eco-poetics of its own, and discover its true and fruitful affinities with life-writing and creative writing.

As this book unfolds, one overriding proposition should constantly be borne in mind: translation is a mode of reading which gives textual substance to reader response; reading is reading-to-translate. This book imagines that every reader should be a translator and that no other translator can translate our reading for us, although other translators may change the way we read. Thus, while the translations which appear in this book do indeed claim to cast new light on their STs, to give them new expressive being, to have validity as free-standing translations, their principal function is to act as models for a translational practice in which all readers of literature are exhorted to indulge.

But my subject in the pages that follow is almost exclusively poetry, and it may seem that the intricacy and extravagance of my translational methods could not easily be applied to prose fiction. I would claim otherwise, for these reasons: translation is a way of discovering how we read, and of enhancing reading, and can be used diagnostically either of a brief, whole text, or of a portion of text, as my treatment of a sentence of Maupassant's 'La Femme de Paul' (see Chapter 3) is meant to demonstrate; any translator of a longer fiction can intermittently, for the space of a sentence, or a paragraph, or a page, turn from 'straight' translation to something more experimental – when translation is intended tirelessly to explore and intensify the reading experience, there is no virtue in consistency of translational approach.

CHAPTER I

Reading and translation

My critical preoccupation in this book is not with the translation of textual meaning, but with the translation of the linguistic experience of text, or, rather, that sequence of sensations activated in the reader by language and linguistic structure, in the process of reading. My underlying stance is thus anti-interpretative; this book looks, instead, to be a contribution to the phenomenology of reading.[1] But what does it mean for us to speak of reading as a phenomenological event? It means that reading constitutes a whole-body experience in which words, and grammar, and syntax, and typographic phenomena such as typeface, margin, punctuation, activate cross-sensory, psycho-physiological responses prior to concept and interpretation, at a stage when essences, thanks to language, 'reposent encore', as Merleau-Ponty puts it, 'sur la vie antéprédicative de la conscience' (2010, 16) [still rest on the pre-predicative life of consciousness]. For Baudelaire, it is one of the virtues of hashish that it endows grammar with a new phenomenological intensity (1975, 431):

La grammaire, l'aride grammaire elle-même, devient quelque chose comme une sorcellerie évocatoire; les mots ressuscitent revêtus de chair et d'os, le substantif, dans sa majesté substantielle, l'adjectif, vêtement transparent qui l'habille et le colore comme un glacis, et le verbe, ange du mouvement, qui donne le branle à la phrase.

[Grammar, arid grammar itself, becomes something like an evocative sorcery; words are restored to life clothed in flesh and bone, the noun, in its full-bodied majesty, the adjective, transparent garment which covers and colours it like a glaze, and the verb, angel of movement, which sets the sentence in motion.]

On a different scale, for Dickens's Joe Gargery, in *Great Expectations* (1860–1861), the word 'rampage', when he first utters it (1953, 7), can only be inhabited by its true spirit, can only work its horror, if it is spelt with a capital R and if 'Ram' and 'page' are separated by a hyphen; it is only by this readerly morphology, and by the false etymology attached to it,[2] that Joe can speak and hear his own psycho-physiological perception of the word, a word whose scope only Pip's formidable sister can do justice to.

Translation, for its part, is, equally, a process of phenomenological rather than interpretative recontextualisation. If translation relocates a text from the there and then in the here and now, the crucial question is: what *is* the here and now, what constitutes it? I guess that the translator usually thinks of an extended, slow-moving present, an ongoing present, a present continuous. And the concomitant topography is therefore a set of well-established cultural practices. There is no lack of work on the difficulties of cultural transfer in translation. But I am looking for a here and now of a relatively instantaneous kind, a here and now of the punctual rather than continuous present, poised around an individual consciousness, a here and now of text coming to itself in an individual voice, in an individual performance. But this here and now cannot entirely stabilise itself, is always in developing metamorphosis. This here and now is a here and now of my body, and translation is about registering the text in my body, and, conversely, inscribing in text my bodily responses. In other words, translation is the process whereby I register the kinaesthetics of reading. By 'kinaesthetics of reading' I mean the dynamic of our organism as it is set in motion by the act of reading, and the sensations associated with that dynamic (for the kinaesthetics of rhythm, see Reynolds (2008)).

This translation of the kinaesthetics of reading is easier to understand when it involves the palpable gestures of the 'reader's' body. I hear a piano-piece. I go about humming it. I give more relief to certain passages, increase rubato, get a few notes wrong for my own convenience. I am practising a kind of kinaesthetic empathy; my body weds and enacts the energies, the impulses, the hesitations let loose in the music, translates the music towards my own viscera.[3] I am reading *and* translating the music as a single, undivided act. I have translated a piano into a vocal organ, into different timbres, different respiratory patterns, different degrees of tonal definition. As I pass the music through my body, I write an arrangement of it. I am not describing or analysing the piece, I am humming it. Translation provides us with the opportunity to insert our reading back into the text, our humming back into the music.

We begin to see that the single face of translation as realisation, or performance, of inner readerly behaviour or readerly response, has in fact another face, is Janus-faced. That other face is about how a text survives in consciousness and across consciousnesses. If works cannot project intentions beyond a certain date, if they lose their way in history and cease to understand themselves, then they must constantly be reimagined, their expressive potentialities re-assessed, their forms re-adapted. In the phenomenological world, readerly behaviour tells us about the modes in which a source text (ST) can best survive; readerly behaviour reveals the evolutionary road travelled by the ST between then and now, there and here.

But two obstacles prevent our doing translational justice to these phenomenological ambitions. The first of these is the concentration of translation studies on interlingual translation, translation between languages, at the expense of intralingual translation (translation of one language into itself) and intermedial translation (translation across media); I prefer 'intermedial' to Jakobson's 'intersemiotic', which is confined to the translation of *verbal* signs into other media. Interlingual translation – which Jakobson calls '*translation proper*' (1992, 145) – has produced a preoccupation with an excessively narrow conception of language, a conception of language which ignores the paralinguistic, that is, considerations of vocal input such as pausing, loudness, tone, intonation, patterns of emphasis, tempo, and ignores, too, the involvement of language with the other senses. Intralingual translation encourages us to experiment with the reformulations of our native language, more boldly incorporating the paralinguistic, that is to say, the performative, while intermedial translation alerts us to the activations of other senses and the slippages between them. Giving intralingual and intermedial translation a full role alongside the interlingual will help us to rethink the forms and functions of translation as a broad transtextual practice, and will draw interlingual translation out of its preoccupation with the narrowly linguistic, with issues of fidelity and equivalence, and out of its suspicion of allied practices such as imitation, pastiche, and adaptation, which are inevitably an integral part of translational thinking.[4]

Fidelity and equivalence are not, of course, simple terms, and have become increasingly relativised. Equivalence, for instance, ramifies into Eugene Nida's functional and dynamic equivalences (1964) and Gideon Toury's relatability to shared relevant features (1980, 37), or, expressed more negatively, Hervey and Higgins's 'not dissimilar in relevant respects' (1992, 24); for Pym, equivalence is a necessary illusion (2010, 37, 165). Even so, while translation remains geared to the monoglot reader, equivalence, in some form, will remain a translational ambition, and even if achieved by transformational means (transposition, amplification, explicitation, etc.), it is a static, juxtapositional view of linguistic relationship. I want a translation which realises language's metamorphic impulses, its solicitation towards the allophonic and the allomorphic. Translation begins in equivalence, but is itself the very process of superseding equivalence, of setting language on the move; in translation, we use words precisely in order to reinflect them towards, or away from, the languages they confront or summon up, indeed *by means of* the languages they confront or summon up.

The second obstacle to phenomenological ambition grows from the first and has already been adverted to: interlingual translation tends to assume that the reader has no interest in the source language (SL), the language of the original. Indeed, one might say that translation gives the reader a warrant to turn his/her back on other languages. But translation should, surely, be designed to increase the circulation of languages, to encourage the reader actively to participate in that circulation.[5] In the world of the phenomenology of reading, familiarity with the ST is indispensable, simply because the significance of translation lies not in the demonstration of a skill of substitution, but in the fruitfulness of the relationship established between the ST and the target text (TT), and what that relationship sets in creative motion. And the circulation of languages thus activated does not necessitate the learning of languages, however desirable that is, but fosters a familiarity with the multiplicity and proliferation of language itself; it also develops the *constructive* capacity of our linguistic awareness, and sharpens linguistic hearing.

The particular investigations of this chapter necessitate a further distinction, which parallels that between interpretation and phenomenology, namely the distinction between 'hermeneutic' reading on the one hand, and 'constructivist' reading on the other, as I adapt it from Jerome McGann (1991).[6] Hermeneutic reading I am bound to disparage; it represents for me the development of linear decoding, of extracting from word sequences what is already presumed to be there in the way of meaning. Even while this mode of reading protests that the text is irreplaceable in its organic wholeness, that it provides us with new insights each time we return to it, it underminingly indulges in the process of translating the text out of itself. This is an image of reading inevitably made crude by the needs of my polemic. Of course, the counter-proposition, the proposition of constructivist reading, is that the reader should translate texts into themselves, paradoxically by processes of variation and ramification.

Constructivist reading begins with a passionate interest in how one negotiates the act of reading itself – something that the hermeneuticist tends to take for granted – an interest in what kind of performance readerly perception requires. Constructivist reading looks to multiply and elaborate reading styles, and this in turn implies the proliferation of different versions and editions of the text. Every version and edition embodies a re-fashioned reader, and in its turn invites further constructions of the text.

The constructivist, of course, assumes that language is always in progress and to that extent we can never control it, never quite catch up with it; but conversely, it also means that language needs to be acted upon, cannot be trusted, might be persuaded in different directions. The text is a living organism, sensitive to, and accommodating of, changing readers and other texts. In order to be this living organism, it always desires to be other, to elasticate its language, to find its possible variants, its potential morphings in sound and structure.

Constructivist texts are based on language, not as a vehicle for meaning, but as a material performing its own body and expressive resourcefulness, encouraging us to savour its generative diversity. The act of translation is the fullest realisation of the reading experience as conceived of here, because translation has a warrant for intervention and diversification. And in order not to become itself an unwitting instrument of closure and textual decision, translation will tend to multiply obstructions to a fluent, linear, recapitulative kind of reading, and pass on its own constructivist persuasions to its readers, by various processes of linguistic provocation.

Before proceeding to the practice of translation, I would like to anticipate the scepticism that my argument may provoke. Can the wily snake of interpretation ever be outwitted, given that any metatextual remark can be identified as interpretative and any intentional act (e.g. the choice of a margin in a translation) be regarded as a creation of meaning? For me, these traps are (merely) an inescapable concomitant of academic writing and translational choice-making. The important thing is not whether the remnants of interpretation continue to haunt my allegedly phenomenological account, but the underlying shift of emphasis from text to reading, from a translation of meaning to a translation of readerly perceptions and sensations. What I ask my reader to assent to is this: that there is a real and significant difference between interpretation as a post-reading recuperation of text, as the analysis of an immobilised body of writing, as the construction of a meaning which will comprehend the text and bring the engagement with it to closure, and phenomenology as an in-reading encounter with text, as the tracing of the psycho-physiological dynamic of the reading consciousness, as the undergoing of a language experience which may end, but does not come to closure. Phenomenology does not ask what a text means but what reading is, as a psycho-sensory response to the mechanics of language. I also want my reader to accept that the translation of the phenomenology of reading requires the development of a new kind of translation, the kind that I practise and describe, that is to say a 'multilingual' and multi-sensory translation, rather than a bilingual and linguistic one. 'Multilingualism' here refers not only to national languages, but to textual languages, the languages of textual presentation and projection: diacritical marks, punctuation, typefaces, layout, all forms of graphism (doodling, sketching, calligraphy, etc.) and all forms of voicing (speaking, murmuring, singing, and, indeed, humming). What prevents the fulfilment of these ambitions is, primarily, a continuing sense of obligation to the monoglot reader, a paralysing influence on translation. Existential involvement with text is what my translations set out to capture. This may not be what some readers understand by 'translation'. It is that prejudice I am trying to find a way out of.

My excursion into constructivist reading, into reading as translation, begins with Edward Thomas's 'Adlestrop' (Longley, 2008, 51):

> Yes. I remember Adlestrop –
> The name, because one afternoon
> Of heat the express-train drew up there
> Unwontedly. It was late June.
>
> The steam hissed. Some one cleared his
> throat.
> No one left and no one came
> On the bare platform. What I saw
> Was Adlestrop – only the name
>
> And willows, willow-herb, and grass,
> And meadowsweet, and haycocks dry,
> No whit less still and lonely fair
> Than the high cloudlets in the sky.
>
> And for that minute a blackbird sang
> Close by, and round him, mistier,
> Farther and farther, all the birds
> Of Oxfordshire and Gloucestershire.

If we address the poem interpretatively, we might say that it speaks of those sudden ruptures in daily existence when we have access to the heart's desire, that the poem belongs to a thematics also to be found in Yeats's 'Lake Isle of Innisfree' or Housman's 'Into my heart an air that kills'. Put another way, it is a poem about an unexpected jolt out of functional, impatient, purposeful time, epitomised by the train, into Bergsonian inner duration, elastic, qualitative, heterogeneous, the time of experience itself. Or we might translate this jolt into the experiential terms of Baudelaire: from a state of perceptual defensiveness, tightness, withdrawnness, the self suddenly expands right to the horizon of consciousness, surrenders itself to phenomena, in a process of self-evaporation; Edna Longley (2008, 165, 177) draws our attention to Thomas's remark in his essay 'England' (*The Last Sheaf*, 1928): 'I believe... that England is a system of vast circumferences circling round the minute neighbouring points of home' (*LS*, 111). Or the poem is about language, about the spells and compulsions of the proper name: Adlestrop contains the poem, Adlestrop contains two counties' worth of flora and fauna; it is the proper noun's purpose not to mean, but to be endowable with meaning; the proper noun lets everyone in, every memory and association.

About this name, I want to make two phenomenological observations: (1) Adlestrop is consonant-heavy. I hear in this something 'farouche', as the French would say, something shy in a hostile or defiant manner. This may have something to do with a false etymology: addle + strop, something muddled and something recalcitrant and awkward. The true etymology is Tætelsthrop (outlying farmstead or hamlet belonging to a man called Tætel) (Mills, 1998, 3). Harvey (1999, 28) lists twenty-two versions of the name between 714 and 1684. Let us not forget that proper names have protean lives of their own, teasing us with mirage and misapprehension; how often is our response to text inflected by false assumptions about etymology, by what we might call a folk etymology, no less authentic than the true. (2) The first draft of the poem (Harvey, 1999, 19–20) makes it clear that Thomas originally thought to rhyme 'Adlestrop' with 'drew up'. Some of the imitations and parodies of the poem rhyme 'Adlestrop' with the more obvious 'stop' (see Harvey, 1999, 24, 68, 80, 100, 108, 111, 112). Why did Thomas resist this move, which also momentarily implied an abab stanza rather than the looser xaxa stanza he turned to? Because the rhyme-word comes to close down the name's sound, and to stake a prior claim to its meaning. 'Adlestrop' needs to be free to cultivate its own field of acoustic association; to my ear, the real rhymes of 'Adlestrop' are those words or collocations which follow its amphimacer (/ x /) pattern, thus: 'afternoon', 'willow-herb', 'meadowsweet', 'haycocks dry', 'lonely fair', 'blackbird sang', 'all the birds', 'Oxfordshire', 'Gloucestershire'. Listening to the poem requires the same vivid attention as listening to the ambient countryside.

Reading is not primarily about interpretation, the digested read, but about reading itself, as a complex dynamic of perception and consciousness of language. Poetry naturally gravitates towards those linguistic categories and structures which aid a perceptual loosening of the world. But unless we inhabit them as psychic or affective states, as organisations of perception and knowledge, we will tend to think of them as stylistic devices or rhetorical tricks. They are more primitive and communal than either style or rhetoric suggest. Poetry has a weakness for certain linguistic features, those that organise the reading metabolism in a certain way: we have already explored the attractions of the proper name, and its ability to supplant the semanticised by the semanticisable. Poetry likes the indefinite, and here Thomas's use of zero articles (nouns without articles) – 'willows', 'willow-herb', 'grass', etc. – must lead us to ask whether the poet actually saw these things (as a definite article might have implied). Did he need to see these things? Are they not, on the contrary, the *inevitable* constituents of this utopia? The use of the zero article is here connected with another of poetry's loves: enumeration, as it occurs briefly in the two lines:

> And willows, willow-herb, and grass,
> And meadowsweet, and haycocks dry

Syntax is often presented as poetry's chiefest enemy. The Italian Futurist F.T. Marinetti attacks syntax because it mediates (or, rather, interferes with) our contact with the world, by operating as a force for anthropomorphisation, as a certain human point of view, as a set of predetermined evaluative criteria (Rainey, 2005, 18–19). Syntax is also the linear time of the train, the punctuation-marks its stops. The stanzas of the train, the first two, are peculiarly clipped, choppy, impatient, unable to recover a fluency, an impetus. This is not only about a thwarted, exasperated train, it is also, as Longley points out (2008, 177), about a throat that cannot yet find its song: 'Someone cleared his throat'; ultimately, with 'And for that minute a blackbird sang', the recitative will discover its aria. The last two stanzas undermine syntax by minimising main-verb presence: the third stanza's main verb ('was') has been evicted from the stanza and placed, in anticipation, in the second stanza. Enumeration, as we find it in the first two lines of the third stanza is naturally anti-syntactic: it has no ostensible organising principle, it does not predict its own ending – when are enough items enough? – and consequently it has no perspectival drive towards a vanishing-point. The space of enumeration is potentially a space that we need never leave. Enumeration belongs to the simultaneous, and here, as in still life, wonderfully denies human agency and eventfulness. Do these items have a function? No, that would be to trespass on their naivety; but they have an availability to experience of any depth or consequence. Here Thomas can get to his final horizon only by installing movement across space in the comparative forms of the final stanza: 'mistier', 'Farther and farther'.

If a text *performs* its meaning, what sense would the question 'What does it mean?' have? Does that question simply indicate that the questioner has failed to read the text as a performance, or does it simply confirm a Western prejudice, that meaning does not occur in the body, that it must be translated to the analytical faculties in order to come into existence? As I read Thomas, it invades my body, in the sounds, rhythms, the variable patterns of respiration, the psycho-physiological impulses and responses which I conspire to supply. It is usual for commentaries on literary translation to concentrate their attention on what are identified as characteristic linguistic difficulties – metaphors, puns, humour, proper nouns – or on formal features; but the truth is that every punctuation mark, every article, every 'but' and 'and' is full of existential import.

In Thomas's 'Adlestrop', the 'and' of the last two stanzas has a rather complex mode of operation. I identified enumeration as a structure of simultaneity. This is not quite the whole story, because coordinating 'and', besides acting inclusively, also acts propulsively, implies sequence as much as encompassment. It is the natural vehicle of narrative in the Bible, as it is in many fairy tales, implying a fluency of purpose, an achievability of things, a certain lack of environmental resistance. We also mentioned that the choice of zero articles, rather than the definite, pushes the flora out of the focus of direct observation and into the hazier realms of memory and imagination. This view, too, needs to be qualified, because Thomas supports his 'ands', a little unusually, with commas, so that sequence is measured, each step marked by a pool of wilful reflection and connecting.

But this enumerative 'and' of 'Adlestrop' has another characteristic. If we again look at the poem's drafts (Harvey, 1999, 19–20), we notice that Thomas uses ampersands, in all instances other than those where 'and' is capitalised. In none of the ampersand instances does a comma appear before the ampersand. Both drafts have commas before the initial 'And' of the third stanza, and the second draft, curiously, has a comma after it. I want to suggest a simple, possibly mistaken, explanation. 'And' has, of course, both a strong form /ænd/ and a weak form /ənd/. Thomas uses the ampersand for weak forms. 'Ands' preceded by commas are strong forms, not stressed, but with a full open /æ/; the others are weak. He seems to want us to vary the vocal pressure we bring to bear on these 'ands'; we have to use the voice on the keyboard of language as a pianist might use touch; rhythm is not about whether a syllable is stressed or not, not a quantitative question about numbers, but rather about the changing quality of consecutive vocal pressures.

My first version of 'Adlestrop' runs as follows:

Adlestrop?
   Yes I,
        remember,, the name.
                          One sun-scorched; afternoon,
          Exceptionally
          The through-train,
                  Drew, up,,.. there
                              It was; late June
The steam hissed.
               Someone cleared his throat.
                         On the bare platform,
                         No, one, left
                         No; one. came.
  Adlestrop was what I saw
                  only
                  the
                name:
      and willowsmeadowsweetwillow
    herbgrassesdocksanddandelionandthistleand
  dryhaycocksjustasstilljustas'lonelyfair'asthehighclouds
        and for that moment
              only
          ablackbird
        sang close by
    and round himmoremistily
furtherandfurtherthe birdsofOxfordshire
        and
          G
          L
          O
          U
          C
          E
          S
          T
          E
          R
          S
          H
          I
          R
          E

Before further comment, I want to emphasise a fundamental assumption: different typographical layouts present and enact different models or images of human consciousness. I have multiplied the margins of the first two stanzas, to increase the dispersiveness of the syntactic fragmentation and exacerbate the reader's sense of disorientation. At the same time, all segments, apart from 'remember', begin with capitals: this is intended to indicate the utterer's repeated attempts to regain control of utterance, to re-establish authority and give the impression that all is intended, even if intention is difficult to rationalise. Equally, I have increased and destabilised punctuation. If punctuation belongs to train-time, to the chronometric and external time of timetables, then it as if the clock is broken, is running riot, can no longer make sense of itself. The stalled train is as if chasing a maddened temporal sequence, even though it is stuck in the station.

In the last two stanzas, I have introduced *scriptio continua*, the absence of spacing between words, not thoroughgoingly, but with sufficient frequency to capitalise on its conventional capacity to express unbroken consciousness and the unbroken stream of the unconscious; after all, these last stanzas occur as much in the unconscious as in consciousness. I have added to the enumeration. I have found no satisfactory translation for 'lonely fair' and have left it directly quoted. I have done away with margins and laid these stanzas out around a medial axis. Margins, as we have said, are a taking possession of utterance: the margin, with its capital letter, is the sign of a consciousness gathering itself, the sign of purpose and authority. The margin testifies to the will to create a verse-line, a metre. The medial axis, on the other hand, is like a sinking of consciousness into the centre of experience, a consciousness shorn of identity, not speaking but being spoken, listening to the lines that the world creates. But these are not lines, since their beginnings and endings are the accidental result of their pivoting around an invisible central spine; they are, rather, verbal radiations and gravitations. This is a structure that expands from the inside, can indeed expand indefinitely with the infinite embedding of new words, new perceptions.[7] The line becomes a display, as if laying out a stall. And because of its symmetrical layout, this medial-axis verse is bound to suggest a calligram, a *carmen figuratum*, or a Rorschach test. Bizarrely, but wonderfully perhaps, the emergent form here has nothing to do with birds; it is a dragonfly. I cannot pretend that this dragonfly is entirely involuntary, but I only opted for it after it had begun to emerge. I like to think that the flowers and birds were what Thomas *thought* had engaged his consciousness, but that what, glimpsed out of the corner of his eye, had darted straight into his soul, had been a dragonfly. I have made other small linguistic changes.

But reading Thomas is reading my own reading and listening. An essential part of constructivist reading is this radial reading (see McGann,

1991, 116–28),[8] reading out into, and incorporating, other acts of reading and reference, ancillary texts and contexts, marginal notes, glosses, intertextual materials, such that the constructing of texts is intimately part of an autobiography of reading and associating, a process without end. Literary criticism is bound to think of texts as isolates, occurring in chronological order; my reading experience tells me that texts exist in ungovernable strings and clumps, and activate all kinds of achronological relationship.

Reading 'Adlestrop', it is impossible for the reader of Proust not to think of that incident when, on his return to Paris from a sanatorium, Marcel's train suddenly stops in the countryside next to a row of trees, to which he responds only with indifference, a confirmation of the desiccation of his artistic soul (1989, 433–4; 1983b, 886). He does not say, or perhaps even know, why the train has stopped. Later, at the final reception at the Princesse de Guermantes's, this episode comes back to him as an involuntary memory, when a servant accidentally knocks a spoon against a plate; and the previous experience of tedium is suddenly infused with the joy of memory, a token of creative self-transformation and re-birth. At the same time, he discovers in himself why the train had stopped: the curing of a fault in a wheel with a hammer-blow (1989, 446–7; 1983b, 900–1).

My second instance of radial reading is entirely different. Revisiting 'Adlestrop' reminded me of my illiteracy in birdsong. The British Library, as if responding to my need, produced simultaneously two CDs, one of recordings of Countryside Birds (NSACD 67, 2009), the other of recordings of Coastal Birds (NSACD 66, 2009). With its usual scrupulousness, the Library had detailed the time and place of each recording, with the names of those responsible. No recordings of countryside birds had been made in Oxfordshire. And there were five from Gloucestershire, out of a total of 65: the goldcrest (May 1972), the swallow (May 1972), the jay (April 1977), the great spotted woodpecker (April 1980) and the wren (May 1990). As I listened, and read the accompanying descriptions, I was again struck by the feebleness of the alphabet's attempts to capture natural sounds, to convert bird-notes and timbres into syllables. But, on the other hand, those Latin names of bird species, often with their curious reduplications – *Troglodytes troglodytes* (wren), *Regulus regulus* (goldcrest), *Pica pica* (magpie), *Carduelis carduelis* (goldfinch) – are a birdsong in themselves, not the song of the birds they identify, but the song of themselves, as names, just as we listen to the song of Adlestrop, only the name.

And so, for my second version of 'Adlestrop' (Fig. 1) I have not only included some allusion to Proust – 'No hammer: was heard', 'in a row of trees' – but also filled the air with birdsong, not only alphabetised bird-calls, but also, and vying with them, the calls of Latin bird-names, the twinnings of bird-name and bird-call being indicated by the use of identical typefaces. Mischievously, I have also introduced the name *Larus marinus* with its associated bird-call 'kau-kau-kau'; this is, in fact, a coastal bird, the great black-backed gull, but I wished to ensure that Thomas's expanding circumferences continue to expand.

It sometimes escapes us that reading aloud is a physical tasting of language, that in articulating words we roll them around in our mouths, engage lips, tongue, teeth, alveolar ridge, palate. And the language of phonetics is a language of the zoo, of classes of vocal animals identifiable by their distinctive calls, with their own peculiar kinships – fricatives, plosives, affricates, approximants. This zoo we keep in our buccal cavities. I want here to turn to a poem by Rilke, no. 13 in Part One of his *Sonette an Orpheus* (1922) (1962, 495):

> Voller Apfel, Birne und Banane,
> Stachelbeere... Alles dieses spricht
> Tod und Leben in den Mund... Ich ahne...
> Lest es einem Kind vom Angesicht,
>
> wenn es sie erschmeckt. Dies kommt von weit.
> Wird euch langsam namenlos im Munde?
> Wo sonst Worte waren, fließen Funde,
> aus dem Fruchtfleisch überrascht befreit.
>
> Wagt zu sagen, was ihr Apfel nennt.
> Diese Süße, die sich erst verdichtet,
> um, im Schmecken leise aufgerichtet,
>
> klar zu werden, wach und transparent,
> doppeldeutig, sonnig, erdig, hiesig – :
> O Erfahrung, Fühlung, Freude –, riesig!

> Full-plumped apple, gooseberry and pear,
> banana... all these speak
> death and life in the mouth... I divine there...
> read it on a child's cheek
>
> who tastes them. This comes from afar. Will it be
> in the mouth something nameless, slow?
> Where words were once, discoveries flow,
> out of the fruit's flesh, surprised and set free,

ADLESTROP

Adlestrop?
    Yes I,
        remember,, the name.
                One sun-scorched; afternoon,
       Exceptionally
       The through-train,
            Drew, up,,.. there
                  It was; late June
No hammer: was heard   The steam hissed.
        Someone cleared his throat.
               On the bare platform,
               No, one, left &
               No; one. came.
Adlestrop was what I saw
            only
            the
           name:
    and willowsmeadowsweetwillow
    herbgrassesdocksanddandelionandthistleand
    dryhaycocksjustasstilljustas'lonelyfair'asthehighclouds
Turdus   and for that moment   merula
Regulus   only   **regulus**
        ablackbird
        sang close by in
        arowoftrees and round him
Cooing **tie** more mistilyfurther&further**chir** the birdsofOxfordshire
        and
        G
Strix aluco **hweet chac chac** jangling   **kee-**
wick **Saxicola torquata**
O
  gurgling **pic pic**   Pink
U
pink   E **Haematopus ostralegus**
S
Dendrocopos major T TUIT TUIT
Erithacus rubecula fluting **NUMENIUS ARQUATA**
    Jeep churring gawking **CARDUELIS**
R
CHLORIS
TSOOEE **COUR-EE** H kau-kau-kau pseep
I
Bubbling Larus marinus   Anthus petrosus
SITTA EUROPAEA Fringilla coelebs wheezing

Figure 1 Translation, with superimposition, of Edward Thomas's 'Adlestrop'

Dare to say what you name Apple. This
sweetness, first condensing, thus
gently created in the taste,

becomes awake, transparent, clear,
ambiguous, sunny, earthy, here –
oh, experience, feeling, joy – how vast!

trans. C.F. MacIntyre (Rilke, 1960, 27; © by the
Regents of the University of California)

The pivot of the poem occurs, not surprisingly, given that it is a sonnet, at the turn or volta, in the first line of the sestet, line 9:

Wagt zu sagen, was ihr Apfel nennt
Dare to say what you name Apple.

This line embodies a standard European Symbolist concern: how are we to re-potentiate a language which has become a devalued currency by dint of daily exchange? How are we to create a language which does not blunt or block perception, but, on the contrary, sharpens it and makes it abundant, or rather, *is* perception itself? Rilke sets authentic saying ('sagen') against facile and shallow naming ('nennen').

Here we begin to see Rilke's ultimate strategy: ostensibly what he is trying to do is actualise in language the eating of an apple, a taste which has life and death in it, an experience we can begin to see enacted in the face of a child, as he/she takes the first bite. This seeing is an act of sympathetic reading. This is a kind of knowledge different from that afforded by the Eden apple; this is a fruit from the tree of life. I say 'ostensibly', because Rilke's real purpose is to express the act of saying as an apple-eating which is indistinguishable from it.

Line 9 sets out the course of action for the sestet, and as it does so, it discreetly draws the /a/ sound from the back of the mouth (/a:/ - 'Wagt zu sagen') to the front (/a/ - 'was...Apfel'). This bringing forward is then again more triumphantly celebrated in line 12:

Klar (/a:/) zu werden, wach (/a/) und transparent (/a/ /a/)

We might fear for a moment that the poem had peaked too early, that the /a/ of 'Apfel' had been too hastily distilled, because it then disappears from view; the only other echo we hear is the back /a:/ in 'Erfahrung'. I do not want to say anything about the a's which occur before line 9, in the octave, as pre-echoes, other than to point out that what makes the word 'langsam' (slowly) suggestive is that it combines both front and back a's, and that 'namenlos', the eviction of the name, has the same back /aː/ as 'sagen', as has 'ahne'.

The a's, then, traverse the mouth from front to back, from back to front, and front /a/ has a little apotheosis in line 12. But line 12 is only the first layer, the outer skin, of this apple-saying. The next layer, line 13, is still adjectival, but the adjectives are now blended by their common -ig suffix. I do not wish to embark on a disquisition on adjectival suffixes, but they are powerful communicators of modality and association, and pose a real problem for translators. The -ig suffix is what our own -y suffix derives from, as -ly derives from the German -lich. MacIntyre's translation is able to stick to etymology with 'sunny' and 'earthy', but 'doppeldeutig', 'hiesig' and 'riesig' escape. One might translate 'riesig' by 'gigantic', simply because the -ic ending sounds as if it should come from -ig, even though its true etymology lies in the Latin -icus; but the -y ending has a buoyancy, an elasticity, a certain fresh vigour and perhaps naivety, that I do not hear at all in -ic. If reading is experience generated by the play of verbal consciousness, then adjectival suffixes are a crucial tonality, no less so than German verb-prefixes: Siegbert Prawer in his brief and penetrating analysis of this poem, reckons that the er- of 'erschmeckt' (l. 5) suggests the exploratory, the 'tracing back to an origin, in which the child unconsciously engages' (1952, 225).

This second layer of adjectives encloses the centre in line 14, wraps it round in a parenthesis. This centre is made up of condensed entities, the apostrophised nouns, but the nouns are abstract and begin to disseminate the energy which is focused in this act of enclosure. And here we discover the alternative story: not the story of a's, front and back, but of another of 'Apfel's' phonemes, appropriately the central one, the labio-dental fricative /f/. What is curious about this /f/ is that, even though a voiceless consonant, that is, not sounded in the throat, it should be called forth just when the voice most wishes to assert itself. This /f/ is, we might say, the very body of the apple ('Fruchtfleisch') and the alternative to words ('fließen Funde'). Its necessary companion is its voiced counterpart /v/. For the English reader, there is some cat-and-mouse here: orthographically, in German, /f/ may be represented by v ('Voller Apfel') and /v/ is represented by w ('Wo sonst Worte waren'; 'Wagt zu sagen'). The voice weaves in and out of voicelessness, because this is the dialogue between the quiet insinuations of the fruit, with its low phonations, its juicy breathings, and language in its throatfulness, in its daring speakingness. Eating an apple is daring to speak, but before the voice can do so, in order to do so, it must replenish itself in the voicelessness at the apple's heart, in the voicelessness of the sensations it releases.

In this poem, as in others, Rilke enjoins upon us an essential receptiveness. But receptiveness is not, as a purely passive state, fruitful; it requires a concomitant and corresponding capacity for 'Einfühlung' (empathy). In his analysis of our apple sonnet, Prawer quotes from a letter of Rilke's of October 1918:

Our eyes need only become a trifle more seeing, our ear more receptive, we would only have to allow the taste of fruit to enter more deeply into us . . . to derive immediately from our most common experiences, consolation more convincing, weighty and true than all the sufferings which may shake us. (1952, 227)

What we are exploring are the senses in which reading can be an exercise of this empathy and translation its true expression. And that involves our also asking to what degree that empathy should become an offering of our own experience, response, wishes.

In my first version of Rilke's sonnet, my designs are all too clear:

> Juicesome aPPle, P:EAR, Banana
> GooseBerry . . . All this sPEAks
> Death and LiFe into the mouth . . . I sense . . .
> REAd it from a child's face
>
> After the first Bite. It comes from far.
> Is there something **nameless**
>   **happening**
>   **slowly**
>   in your mouth?
> Where words were once, finds flow
> Set loose, surprised, from fruit's flesh
>
> Be Bold to Voice what you call aPPle
> This juiciness which first condenses
> So as, set smoothly up in taste,
>
> To grow Pellucid Pin-sharp and transParent
> Two-sensed and sunny, EARthy, **here**ly –
> ex
> PPerience PPass PPress
> ion, P
> LEAsure - i**mm**ense

While Rilke's voiceless /f/ survives in the second stanza, I have taken the voiceless bilabial plosive /p/ of 'apple' as my point of departure and activated where possible its voiced counterpart /b/. This has provided the opportunity to link the voiceless with the musical notation for *piano* and *pianissimo*. At the same time, I have undone 'pear', to allow the 'ear' to emerge as the organ that captures the *piano* and the voiceless; but the presence of the ear is subject to erosion, and it only fully returns in 'earthy' amidst the final apotheosis of double p's. I also wanted to keep the many shades of sense – sense as meaning, sense as intuition, sense as perceptual organ – alive in the string 'sense – condenses – two-sensed – immense'. Finally, I have tried to make rhythm itself an instrument of metamorphosis. Rilke's poem is in trochaic pentameter, with alternating feminine and masculine rhymes. I have paid no heed to rhyme, and have allowed my metre to shift from trochaic (up to line 6), to iambic (ll. 7–13), before drifting out towards the concrete, or to sound poetry, in line 14. And I have introduced 'PPress', primarily to insert, fragmented, the word 'expression', in both its senses, of 'utterance' and of 'squeezing the juice out of', which, in this poem, are the same thing. But I have also used it to increase the doubling of consonants, which here has three functions: (i) to enact the notion of condensation; (ii) to underline the shift from *piano* to *pianissimo* and the linguistic diffusion of the double pp of 'apple'; (iii) to reinforce 'doppeldeutig' ('two-sensed', 'double-meaninged'): this may be seen to refer to the dualities already in the poem – death and life, sunny and earthy – but we need to experience this doubleness not just as pairs of meanings, but as a permeation of the verbal texture, as constituting the acoustic taste of the apple, but silently, since it is only one /p/ that we hear.

My second version of this sonnet (Fig. 2) embroiders my first version with inky doodling. One might wonder what useful function this serves. For me there are two immediate purposes: the first is the involvement of the hand, as an equivalent of the voice: a graphic style is the gestural equivalent of the physiology of the voice. Like the voice, graphic style is both genetic and cultural, both about the innate quality of a hand in its characteristic motions, a graphological key, and also about what hand-motions can achieve in terms of a shared expressivity. Doodling relates to automatic writing, to the somnambulistic line, the liberation *from* the written; and, in this poem, doodling is to the written what voicelessness is to the voiced. As writing wanders into pure graphism, loses its legibility, we might wonder what it is that is speaking, what kind of speaking writing has become; the hand, by not following a uniform code of communication, seems to become the involuntary home of new energies, choreographies, whose language we do not yet understand. Reading invites us to draw on

Juicesome aPPle, P:EAR, Banana
GooseBerry ... All this sPEAks ₀
Death and LiFe into the mouth ... I sense ...
REAd it from a child's face

After the first Bite. It comes from far.
Is there something **nameless**
happening
slowly ❙
in your mouth?
Where words were once, finds flow
Set loose, surprised, from fruit's flesh

Be Bold to Voice what you call aPPle
This juiciness which first condenses
So as, set smoothly up in taste,

To grow Pellucid Pin-sharp and transParent
Two-sensed and sunny, EARthy, **here**ly –
ex
PPerience PPass PPress
ion, P
LEAsure – **im**mense

Figure 2 Translation, with doodling, of Rilke's 'Voller Apfel, Birne und Banane'

other dimensions of ourselves, other psychic impulses. Doodling becomes one of the alternative languages offered by translation.

And this is indeed the second of my purposes: to argue, as I have already argued, that, in order to do justice to a phenomenology of reading, translation needs to multiply its resources, the languages it puts at its disposal; it needs to draw not only on a multilingualism of foreign languages, but also on a multilingualism of textual languages – punctuation, diacritical marks, typefaces, paginal dispositions, *scriptio continua* and variously spaced scripts, graphisms of all kinds (doodling, crossing out, overwriting, sketching), colour work – to capture the individual reading metabolism in all its intricacy, and the perceptually dynamic, multisensory experience we so easily forget that reading is.

It is print which has established the notion of textual exactitude, of every word and every comma being in its allotted and immemorial place. It is this fact which then makes a virtue of verbatim memory; learning by heart has no point unless textual exactitude is maintained. It is the notion of the exact text which creates all the problems for translation, all the soul-searching about fidelity, about translating word-for-word or sense-for-sense. The nature of transmission in oral cultures, on the other hand, is approximate rather than exact, generative rather than genetic (self-replicating). Different performers emphasise different episodes, make additions or omissions, respond differently to external pressures (Goody, 2000, 35–40).

The words we use here – 'approximate' and, by implication, 'inexact' – are dangerous inasmuch as they imply a *failure* of memory, where, in fact, the memory we are speaking of is a *creative* memory: 'Oral memory is, of course, simply experience reworked' (Goody, 2000, 40). To speak of memory in relation to the act of translation may, of course be objected to: translation is a transcription from print to print, rather than a memory from print to mind. But my whole point is that translation is not a transcription of another text, but a transcription of the sensations and memories of a reader of that text. Indeed, one might argue that the very existence of print, of the *permanent recoverability* of the ST, gives us the licence to take our distances from it, to indulge in the creative memory of oral culture. Literary scholarship should perhaps concentrate less on the castigation of the inexact and more on its preservation and exploration.

CHAPTER 2

Reading: voice and rhythm

In this chapter, I want to continue to pursue, against the notion of the hermeneutic or interpretative reading of a text already there, the project of a constructivist reading, a reading which imagines text into existence even as it reads. Constructivist reading moves out of the pre-set into the optional and textually possible. The field of the textually possible is part-generated by the input of the paralinguistic, both verbal and visual. The verbal paralinguistic includes all elements of vocal input into a text: intonation, tempo, loudness, pausing, tone, degrees of stress. The visual paralinguistic, which will come increasingly into its own as this book proceeds, refers to all those visual cues and triggers – typeface, layout, letter shape, margins, the graphisms of calligraphy, space, elements of book design, paratext, the posture and gestures of a performer – which inflect our perception and/or reading of a text. What we are confronting is a simple question: how do you translate the paralinguistic into a text? We can make this question clearer by asking: how would you translate not a play, but the performance of a play? Contrary to popular belief, the text has no voice, other than as a convenient metaphor. But before we plunge into this constructivist infiltration of text by performance, we need to make some underlying distinctions, distinctions which lie at the heart of the verbal paralinguistic and threaten to divide it against itself.

We have long laboured with an inability to incorporate into critical discourse the physiology of particular voices, the organic accidents of an individual's vocal apparatus (see Laver, 1980). Size of tongue, of velum, of pharynx and jaw, length of vocal tract, the volume of nasal cavity, dental configuration, all these factors contribute to a voice's range and timbre. But, even though, in everyday interaction, we treat the voice as a vital vehicle of social, psychological and physical information about the speaker, in the world of literature we treat these voice-qualities as accidentals, irrelevant to the analysis of text. It is easy enough to understand why. We have no vocabulary adequate to the idiosyncrasies of an individual voice, although we have plenty of *generical* adjectives (thick, soft, husky, velvety, shrill). We have an alphabet, and an International Phonetic Alphabet, which average out sounds. We have a phonetics which is interested only in language sounds and not in other vocal emissions. We have a voice-setting, an accepted vocal style, for the reading of verse, which draws even the most recalcitrant regional accent and eccentric voice towards received pronunciation. Besides, it is commonly held that it is not the purpose of poetry to individuate the speaker; voices may change, but the printed text affirms its constancy to itself. But my argument has been, and continues to be, that the function of translation is to individuate, in the here and now, the translator as reader, and to feed that individuation, that individual voice, back into the ST. Hitherto, critical investigation has focused its attention on *shared* systems of voice-use, for communicative and expressive purposes: we learn to maximise the resourcefulness of our voices, so that they can be put to strategic, communicative uses. It is not a question of what kind of voice you have, your physiological voice, but what you can do with it, your expressive voice. But, even so of course, print makes the paralinguistic features of language invisible.

This rough distinction between the physiological voice and the expressive voice is doubled by another distinction which ascribes to each a different relationship with the body. In his comparison of the voices of two singers, Charles Panzéra and Dietrich Fischer-Dieskau, in his 1972 essay 'Le grain de la voix' [The Grain of the Voice], Roland Barthes argues that Panzéra's cultivation of the grain of the voice means that his voice emerges directly from his body, 'du fond des cavernes, des muscles, des muqueuses, des cartilages' (1982a, 238) [from deep down in the cavities, the muscles, the membranes, the cartilages], that it is principally located in the throat and is concerned with the diction, that is, the pronunciation, of the language. Pronunciation is about the phonetic production of language, about acoustic quality in the voice. Fischer-Dieskau's singing, on the other hand, concentrates on expressivity, subjectivity; it privileges the lungs and breathing, and is concerned with articulation, that is to say, with clarity of projected meaning, with the coded ways of communicating feeling, with the rhetoric of the voice. The world of the expressive voice is a world not of the individual body, but of 'une culture *moyenne*' (1982a, 241) [an *average* culture]. It is this version of voice which is paramount in the training of actors; it is the voice which is 'the voice of success'.[1]

But that is not all. The voice remains a peculiarly schizophrenic instrument, both inside our bodies and issuing from our bodies, in what sound like two distinct manifestations. The voice inside our heads, which no one else can hear, is almost the only version of our voice that we ourselves hear; it is made resonant by the vibrations conducted by bones in the head, in a way that the external voice is not, and has, for me, a particular capacity for fictions, fantasies, precisely because it is heard only by us, as if in a private inner room. The outer voice, by contrast, might belong to someone else, since we can only hear it recorded, since, usually, we can only hear it in the past. And we may well be disappointed by this outer voice; it has always struck me as less modulated, less versatile than its inner counterpart. When it comes to performance, given this division of voices, we might wonder whom exactly we are performing for; whether in fact two different performances are not taking place simultaneously.[2]

There is another sense in which this division of inner and outer voices has significance for my present argument. On the one hand, I am asking how, through translation, we might fully possess our own (inner) voices on paper; but I am also asking how we might represent vocal effects which do not belong to us, which have to do with the so-called acousmatic, with our separation from our own voices. This separation from our own voices has to do, among other things, with the advent of vocal telephony, vocal recording and vocal synthesis (see Bök, 2009).

Some time ago, I embarked on a piece of research into speech indicators, those verbs or verb phrases which accompany dialogue in fiction and which reveal either *qualities* of voice ('he growled'), or *kinds of speech act* ('she insisted'), or the *interactive engineering* that dialogue involves ('he interpolated'). My principal subject was a comparison of such speech indicators in French romances (the *roman rose*) and crime fiction (the *roman noir*). The system of classification I adopted was fourfold: under *qualities of voice*, I chose two subdivisions – (1) enunciation ('he muttered', 'she blurted', 'he mumbled' – I give my examples in English) and (2) expressivity ('she lamented', 'he shrieked', 'she howled'). *Speech acts* were the third category, with verbs such as 'she protested', 'he conceded', 'she conjectured'. And the fourth category, *dialogue engineering*, included verbs such as 'he rejoined', 'she interrupted', 'he added'. 'Said' is a kind of zero position, but can of course be qualified by an adverb or adverbial phrase which does assign it to a category: e.g. 'he said hoarsely' (enunciation), 'he said, his voice full of invitation' (speech act). This classification must remain tentative, both because certain verbs hang ambiguously between categories – is 'she sighed' about enunciation or expressivity, is 'he lamented' about expressivity or speech act? – and because when verbs are combined with adverbs or adverbial phrases, they can equally combine different categories: 'he assented bitterly', 'she continued in a strangled voice'. One should also remember that, frequently, no explicit speech indicator is provided; instead, speech colourings are, as it were, projected by the narrative accompaniment, which, through gesture, or look, that is, through visual paralanguage, reveals the psychological state of the speaker, e.g.

'Even so, I did want to see him.'
She removed a brooch from her dress.

He pushed his cigarette case to the table's edge.
'I could do with a change of air.'

Here we begin to see the purely visual construction of an acoustic, what we might call the seeing ear or the hearing eye.[3]

In my investigation into the romance and thriller, besides statistical comparisons of categories, I was concerned with vocal stereotyping – both of gender and of social and sexual relationship – and with the associated ranges of tone and timbre. In the thriller, for example, I found, not surprisingly, that timbres are grittier and tones more uneven, as is consonant with a language of sustained exasperation and poorly controlled dissatisfaction. The voice of the police officer, or detective, seems to be made up of a nasal ground, with vowels moving from the dark recesses of the mouth forward; reverberation is often provided by frequentative morphology ('marmonner', 'marmotter', 'ronchonner', 'grommeler', 'maugréer' – all verbs of mumbling, muttering, grumbling, grousing).

We associate speech indicators with those genres that have a particularly melodramatic view of voice, a view of voice as the source of self, as the reactive mirror of the action, as a gauge of narrative temperature, as the intensifier of participation. These genres belong to popular fiction, not only the romance and thriller, but the western and the adventure novel. And there is a historical factor too; even though romances and thrillers still thrive, the habit of speech indication seems to belong to an older generation. Lydia Davis, in her recent translation of Proust's *Du côté de chez Swann* (2003), observes that her translation is plainer, less dressy, than Scott Moncrieff's 1922 translation: 'For instance', she writes, 'each time Proust uses the word *disait*, I have translated it simply as "said", whereas Moncrieff often introduces a variety not in the original by choosing instead: "remarked", "began", "murmured", "assured them", etc.' (2003, xxxiii). We may suppose that this cultivation of speech indicators is an attempt to animate the inertia of the printed word, to restore the paralinguistic information that print silently erases, to re-establish the voice, rather than its words, as the agent of social interaction and self-affirmation. But modern writing in general fights shy of this vocal exhibitionism, presumably because of its associations with gung-ho adventure, and because it intrudes too pre-emptively on the reader's own pursuit of an appropriate voice or voices, excludes the reader as a protagonist in the work's unfolding. Voice is never manifest in a work (in print); the reader's search for a voice is a search for the work's deeper energies.

The fortunes of voice in poetry have been remarkably disappointing, despite poetry's oft-professed belief in the indispensability of voice to its completeness. It is the invariant in a poem (i.e. the linguistic) that is treated as *the* poem; the paralinguistic, the variable, is contingent and accidental. By this definition, it sounds as if oral traditions have no poems. Metre is the primary form of acoustic patterning in regular verse, but it does not need to be realised by voice to be perceived. Furthermore, analysis implies that words not only have a stress-pattern independent of voice, but also a music of their own. The music of words resides not in the unfolding line of speech-flow, but in isolated phonemes or phonemic clusters, gathered after reading; the instrument that best plays this music is therefore not a particular voice, but the perfectly tuned International Phonetic Alphabet, not a voice but a table of average sounds. I would mention just two further pernicious prejudices: (i) it is often claimed that the voice should allow texts to speak for themselves (but, we might again object, the text has no voice; it is elicited by voice into voice); (ii) it is also often claimed that the voice has the disadvantage of disambiguating texts, of making decisions about meaning (but are there not subtleties of tone and intonation that can sustain these ambiguities?).

These are the unjust prices that the voice must pay to a poetry ever more embedded in its writtenness. Why should phonemes, for example, be allowed to monopolise our attention in a text, and in the crudest of repeated patterns (assonance, alliteration, rhyme), just because they are all that is readily visible, or all that criticism feels can be reliably reported on? Why not give due attention to tempo, or loudness, or intonation – or indeed to acoustic patterns based on difference or modulation? And since a text is made in performance – unless by layout and typographical device, it is already a performance *on the page* – let us not erroneously continue to insist that a text is greater than its performance. We remember Yeats's words: 'There is no poem so great that a fine speaker cannot make it greater or that a bad ear cannot make it nothing' (1962, 212). To suppose that scripts might be matrices, might be syntheses, of all possible performances of them, is to delude ourselves and to endow chronological priority with a power it does not merit. If we instead imagined the printed text to be a notation of a performance, *after the event*, a transcription, rather than a matrix, then we would think it profoundly inadequate and incomplete, just as anthropologists have been cruelly disappointed by attempts to transcribe, to linguistify, the richly physical performances that belong to oral peoples. In land art, all texts – journals, photos, maps, commentaries – are post-performative; they are documents which bear only partial testimony to an event that cannot be recovered; to be creative texts in their own right, they have to renounce all claim to being necessary to the performative event that land art is.

The task, then, seems to me to fall into three parts: (1) how to reinstate the voice; (2) how to extend the voice, the vocal repertoire; (3) how, by prosthetic devices, to explore the realms of the infravocal and the ultravocal – we must remember that electronics and digitalisation have taken us into the world of the post-human.[4] The necessary strategies seem to be: (1) to give proper status to vocal paralanguage, particularly in our habits of scansion and notation, and in translation; (2) to extend vocal ambition by relating it to newly versatile kinds of listening; (3) to take the vocal beyond the vocal by exploiting visual paralanguage.

We have argued that, ironically, metrical analysis, as presently practised, evicts voice from text; rhythm, on the other hand, we might argue, is the presence in text of voice and of the paralinguistic. The relationship between rhythm and metre has long been a contested one. For Timothy Steele (1999), the relationship is harmonious and reciprocally fruitful: 'Metre is *organized rhythm*' (3); rhythm is the performance of metre's potential for modulation and counterpoint: 'The metrical pattern gives the personal voice a resistant grace and solidity, while the voice infuses the pattern, in itself merely an abstract schema, with vigor and suppleness' (3). My view is the reverse: metre and rhythm belong to radically opposed principles and pull hard against each other. Metre ensures that the conditions of reception coincide with the conditions of production, which in turn ensures that the reader is schooled to listen, rather than being free to speak. Metre is anterior to text and the agent of chronometric time, time quantified, spatialised, homogeneous. Metre is a uniform consciousness, already formed, not a coming to consciousness, in all its unevenness. Rhythm, on the other hand, is text-immanent and indivisible from the time of reading, and from the reading consciousness; there is no ready-made repertoire of rhythms; it serves the inner duration of the individual reader, time as quality, as continuous, heterogeneous experience, engaging both the conscious and the unconscious self. Rhythm is opportunistic and wayward and improvised, and thus there is little chance that the rhythms of the reader will coincide with those of the writer. The rhythmicisation of a text allows us to inhabit text, to feed text through our organism, like a staining fluid which will reveal to us our psycho-affective condition in the here and now. I should emphasise that, in my argumentative need to polarise metre and rhythm, I turn metre into an insensitive scoundrel. The metrical is a fluid and relative position, which I push to an extreme.

I want to trace, with unseemly brevity, a path from metre to rhythm, using translations of Yeats's 'Leda and the Swan' (1965, 241) as my text:

> A sudden blow: the great wings beating still
> Above the staggering girl, her thighs caressed
> By the dark webs, her nape caught in his bill,
> He holds her helpless breast upon his breast.
>
> How can those terrified vague fingers push
> The feathered glory from her loosening thighs?
> And how can body, laid in that white rush,
> But feel the strange heart beating where it lies?
>
> A shudder in the loins engenders there
> The broken wall, the burning roof and tower
> And Agamemnon dead.
>   Being so caught up,
>
> So mastered by the brute blood of the air,
> Did she put on his knowledge with his power
> Before the indifferent beak could let her drop?

In a first translational move, I have let myself settle into Yeats's iambic world, changing elements of syntax and lexicon, but maintaining the underlying point of view:

> A sudden blow: great wings beat ... beat
> Down a stumbling girl, these dark
> Webs caress her thighs, her neck
> Caught quick by his bill, her breast helpless on his.
>
> Could her vague fingers, terrified, have pushed away
> That self-insinuating feathered flow?

How could she not, in that white rush,
Have felt the heart-beats that she did not know?

A shudder in the loins: Troy razed
And, awaiting the return,
Clytemnestra.   Being so caught up,

So beaten down by shock-waves in the air,
Did she . . . did *his* knowledge come to her,
Before, indifferently, the beak let her fall back?

The first stanza is metrically more turbulent, as in Yeats, but this turbulence occurs within a pattern of preset expectations, as an express disruption of a certain order. The swan is the force that generates this metrical disturbance quite literally, with the syncopation of beating wings, of treading webs, and of the jerking bill, before the commentator-poet reinstalls the steadied metrics of observation and meditation. I often think of metre as a perspectival and Euclidian arrangement, as a landscape stilled and stabilised and framed. Perspective is as much a conventionalised listening as it is a conventionalised seeing, a seeing/listening that is measured, that holds things in place, an immobilising overview. Metre seeks to be transfixative. Let us listen to Merleau-Ponty on perspective:

[The painter] sees the tree nearby, then he directs his gaze further into the distance, to the road, before finally looking to the horizon; the apparent dimensions of the other objects change each time he stares at a different point. On the canvas, [however], he arranges things such that what he represents is no more than a compromise between these various different visual impressions: he strives to find a common denominator to all these perceptions by rendering each object not with the size, colours and aspect it presents when the painter fixes it in his gaze but rather with the conventional size and aspect that it would present in a gaze directed at a particular vanishing point on the horizon. (2004, 40)

The metrical poem, then, does have a point of view, but an expressly manufactured one, which has little to do with actual processes of perception. In my second version:

Wing-walls in the air
The girl sprawls
                backwards
And the swan's upon her
                the dark webs

                                    treading
                                    the bill
Like a tight-sprung peg
Compressing her neck
                    plumage plumped on her evasive breasts
                                              is this the time
For disquisitions on divine brutality
                    there's nothing she can do

. . . Leda, bared
Under the blizzard of the swan

I watch as voyeur and
                    historian . . . *these nymphs*
I want to perpetuate them
. . . and pictured Leda as she lay
Under the white swan's wings

These versions, Argus of language
Looking out
          on her slow motions of defence
          numbed fingers against the
                                    snowstorm
          legs clamped against
          the burrowing   white
                              I don't suppose
          that pulse which she could feel
          was any warmer
          than the sly tide of darkness

I watched the shuddering
Consummation   but had no idea
                    what he was subject to

Troy passed away
In one high   funeral
                              gleam
The cuckold   heaped upon
                    the cuckolded

                              the knowledge that
                              he had
                              was never his

And   even if hers
                    but little consolation   as
Locked in her lap

He felt a feather grow on every feather
and became
entirely swan

I move into a landscape without a vanishing point, without that reference point which re-arranges vision; I move into the landscape of rhythm. Rhythm tries to recover the sequence of free visual impressions and changing points of view in real time. Rhythm is the record of the actual audio-visual perception of a world, not already there but in the process of emerging, a world which the body of the speaker is progressively inhabiting.

Some of the changing points of view here are intertextual memories, picked out in italics. '*Leda bared / Under the blizzard of the swan*' and '*and pictured Leda as she lay / Under the white swan's wings*' are two translations, one by Ted Hughes (1997, 179), the other by A.D. Melville (1986, 124), of the brief reference to Leda in Ovid's *Metamorphoses*. '*These nymphs, I want to perpetuate them*' is a translation of the first ten syllables of Mallarmé's 'L'Après-midi d'un faune'. '*Troy passed away in one high funeral gleam*' is a line from Yeats's own 'The Rose of the World' (*The Rose*, 1893). And the final lines – '*Locked in her lap . . . entirely swan*' – are an amalgamation of the final lines of two translations of Rilke's 'Leda' (*Neue Gedichte*, 1907–1908), one by J.B. Leishman (1964, 167) and the other by Stephen Cohn (1992, 145). As my version comes to its close, from 'I watched the shuddering / Consummation', so iambic becomes a more insistent presence; but this iambic is not a metrical iambic, but a rhythmic iambic, designed not to create lines of verse, but to act as a bedding medium for its intertextual memories, to embody a certain rhythm of attention, a certain way of engaging the voice. Listening to iambic rhythmically is a very different experience from listening to it metrically, and this rhythmicisation of iambic is much to do with the added contrapuntal activity of differential spacing and line-breaks. Rhythm is the dynamic of perception and cognition, where the cognitive is not to be put asunder from the performative.[5] Rhythm is knowing and perceiving in the very activity of enunciation, and this is why questions which metre never asks, about grouping, phrasing, differential highlighting, the *quality* of acoustic phenomena, are crucial to rhythm.

Metrical scansion can, thus, in free verse, act misleadingly, even in the attribution of stress values. Consider the first stanza notated instead, very crudely, as a set of shifting numerical intensities 1–4 (I might have chosen 1–8 for a more nuanced differentiation):

```
4   2   1   1 3
Wing-walls in the air
  1   2   3
The girl sprawls
                4   1
                backwards
1   1   3   1 4   1
And the swan's upon her
              1   3   4
              the dark webs
                        2   1
                        treading
                        1 4
                        the bill
1   1 3     2   4
Like a tight-sprung peg
  1   3 1   1 3
Compressing her neck
          3 1     4     1   1  1 3 1   2
          plumage plumped on her evasive breasts
                                    1   3   1 2
                                    is this the time
1   2   13 1   1   1 2     1 3 11
For disquisitions on divine brutality
                  1   3   1     2 1   2
                  there's nothing she can do
```

Even this rough notation, as opposed to a weak/strong, or non-stress/stress, system, helps me do better justice to rhythmic values: (i) there is no pressure on me to reduce the complex relativities of stress, the variations in vocal touch, to a binary opposition; (ii) I am not embarrassed by stress-clustering because I do not have to deem stresses equal (the problematic case of the spondee); (iii) I do not have to produce a 'plausible' continuity of utterance, based on the balancing out of uneven acoustic asperities; (iv) the system positively encourages me to explore varying intensities and to hear the acoustics of syllables; and (v), in conjunction with the layout, it encourages me to develop phrasing, where phrases have different tempi, and beget different relations between pause and impetus.

This refashioning of stress in the direction of syllabic acousticity and the writing of perceptual sensation already occurs in Gerard Manley Hopkins's sprung rhythm, and coincides with the emergence of Impressionism in France. In the early twentieth century, Ford Madox Ford became something of an official champion of literary impressionism in both the novel and in poetry, and we find him writing about free verse in terms that align it with impressionism: he declares, for example, that 'every one has his own rhythm which is his own personality' (notes for a lecture given in New York in the 1920s) (MacShane, 1964, 160).[6] Ford had a mind, in 1921, to claim that he himself was 'the doyen of living writ- ers of *Vers Libre* in English' (1966, 198), but, in terms of its 'invention', he was prepared to yield precedence to a collection of poems published in 1888, and written between 1873 and 1875, W.E. Henley's *In Hospital* (1966, 198).

In his youth, Henley contracted tuberculosis of the bones in his hands and feet. Some years after the amputation of his left leg, he was admitted, in 1873, to the Royal Infirmary in Edinburgh, to be treated by Joseph Lister as a test-case for antiseptic surgery, and survived two testing but successful operations on his right foot (see Cohen, 2000, 227, for this material). *In Hospital* is a sequence of twenty-nine poems (including the 1888 'Envoy'), five of which (including the 'Envoy') are written in unrhymed free verse, the others in regular verse-forms.

One should say immediately that Henley's shift towards free verse is impelled by the wish to find a medium that will allow a dynamic and unmediated response to real events. He presents his hospital experience not as emotion recollected in tranquillity, but as the anxious, vulnerable, spontaneous reactions to the ongoing life of the ward. These are what Hen- ley calls his 'impressions', as he explains that, to use rhyme, would have been an obstacle to what he sought: he refers to his poems as 'those unrhyming rhythms in which I had tried to quintessentialize, as (I believe) one scarce can do in rhyme, my impressions of the Old Edinburgh Infirmary' (1904, vii). In his article 'The Decadent Movement in Poetry' (1893), Arthur Symons commended *In Hospital* as an artistic experiment and suggested that Verlaine's 'theory of poetical writing – "sincerity, and the impression of the moment followed to the letter" – might well be adapted as a definition of Mr Henley's theory or practice' (867); he was of the view that: 'The poetry of Impressionism can go no further, in one direction, than that series of rhymes and rhythms named *In Hospital*' (867). We have then an image of free verse as a medium which mediates between the pressures of an external world, to whose every shift it is able to adapt itself, and the inward life of the poet, which is itself unlike any other life, with a rhythm all of its own. And this will remind us of the Impressionist painter who records every subtle nuance and change in atmospheric conditions, but who, in the very rhythm of brush-strokes, the gestures of the hand on the canvas, the coloration, expresses a perceiving consciousness, and a set of optical associations indelibly peculiar to it. And this recording of sensation takes place in real time, in the midst of event.

I take a stanza from the seventh poem of Henley's cycle, 'Vigil' (1904, 10–12), the second, in which the poet lies awake, in discomfort, irked by a variety of sensory intrusions, unable to sleep:

> Shoulders and loins
> Ache – – – !
> Ache, and the mattress,
> Run into boulders and hummocks,
> Glows like a kiln, while the bedclothes –
> Tumbling, importunate, daft –
> Ramble and roll, and the gas,
> Screwed to its lowermost,
> An inevitable atom of light,
> Haunts, and a stertorous sleeper
> Snores me to hate and despair.

At first glance, we might agree with Ford's judgement that Henley's 'rhythms were almost always ready made. It was less the personal cadence of his mind that he gave us than unrhymed echoes of former metricists' (1966, 209); Yeats is of the same opinion: he acknowledges that the *vers libre* of *In Hospital* is innovative, but declares that Henley 'did not permit a poem to arise out of its own rhythm as do Turner and Pound at their best' (1936, viii); and, indeed, if we through-read these lines, we will find ourselves drawn to the lulling chant of dactyls. But that is to make Henley easier than he deserves.

I let the text have a new beginning, simply by presenting it first as prose:

Shoulders and loins ache, ache, and the mattress, run into boulders and hummocks, glows like a kiln, while the bedclothes, tumbling, importunate, daft, ramble and roll, and the gas, screwed to its lowermost, an inevitable atom of light, haunts, and a stertorous sleeper snores me to hate and despair.

In this form, I can explore it relatively without prejudice, rationalise my reading by an act of writing, read my way into rewriting it, into its construction as a translation. My first version is relatively conservative, mapped out, to begin with, with both a metrical and numerical notation of rhythm and degrees of stress:

```
 3   1 1   3        4    4
shoulders and loins . . . . . . ache..ache                / x x /    / /
1   1   3 1
and the mattress                                          x x / x
                            3  1 1  4   1
                            run into boulders             / x x / x
                                   1    4   2
                                   and hummocks           x / x
 4    1   1  3
glows like a kiln                                         / x x /
   2   1  3   2
while the bedclothes                                      x x / x
                                    3    1
                                    tumbling              / x
                                    1   3 1 2
                                    importunate           x / x x
                                     3
                                    daft                  /
 4     1 1   3
ramble and roll                                           / x x /
1    1   3
and the gas                                               x x /
                          4     1 1   3  1   2
                          screwed to its lowermost        / x x / x x
              1  1 3  11  (1)
              an inevitable                               x x / x x (x)
              3 1   1   3
              atom of light                               / x x /
    4
haunts                                                    /
              1   1   4 1 1    3  1
              and a stertorous sleeper                    x x / x x / x
    4     1 1 3
snores me to hate                                         / x x /
                          1     1 3
                          and despair                     x x /
```

If we listen searchingly, probingly, we hear beneath a potentially metrical surface the bubbling anarchy of varied rhythmic impulses, which intermittently find focus in the third paeon (x x / x), the choriamb (/ x x /) and the anapaest (x x /).

Next I 'ornament' this text with handwritten indications about performance (Fig. 3). What we are sketching out here is a policy which picks up the Roman practice of *praelectio*, the preparation of a text by reading it

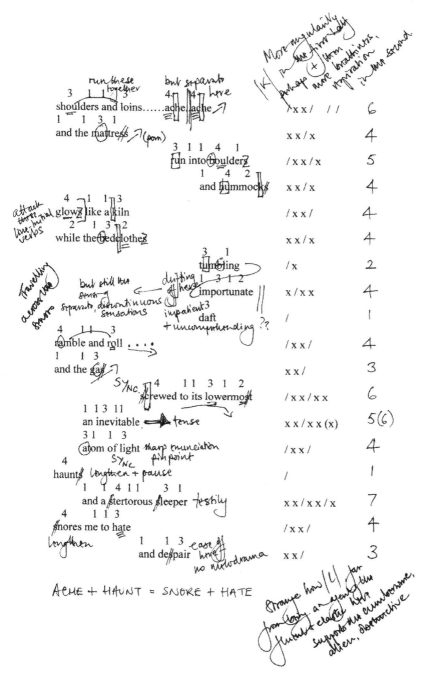

Figure 3 Translation, with handwritten notations, of the second stanza of Henley's 'Vigil'

to others, in which marks were introduced by teachers and/or pupils into *scriptio continua* – the language-string without division between words – to indicate pauses, phrasal segmentation, long vowels, and so on, to help towards the most effective oral delivery of the text. For us, it is a process which involves experimentation with speed of delivery, phrasing, pausing, quality of accentuation, intonation and so on. It is an attempt to ensure that, hereafter, I do not read the text as something already written, but rather the reverse, that the text looks like an inadequate transcription of what I am speaking or have already spoken. This is also to propose a kind of translation we do not hear much about: a kind of pre-textual translation, an anticipatory translation which does not allow the ST to settle into its writtenness, and which makes the ST a poor reflection of, a consequence of, the TT.

The translator is thus no executant, but a composing performer. There is textual material, but as yet no version of text; it is a play of possibilities and probabilities. As with a musical cover, there may be a tune and lyrics, but at each performance it must become a song again, invested with the vocal personality, the instrumentation, the singing and playing style of singer, group or band.

A crucial element of this compositional performance, that which acts as a guarantor of its improvised and spontaneous nature, is handwriting. Handwriting here helps to give the text a dynamic, to present it as a centre of developing energies, to endow it with an urgent time-boundness, to plant it firmly in the here and now. Handwriting is the present of the gesturing body; it makes the text mobile and polymorphous, by making indistinguishable the pre-textual, the textual and the post-textual. Handwriting is a visual paralanguage of the verbal paralanguage of a voice; it gestures the voice, it physically traces words, rather than representing them, and projects meaning in its calligraphic tracings as much as through the words it delineates.[7] And within handwriting and in handwriting's extensions, are other expressive resources, notably crossing out and doodling. In a new world, in which one can float seamlessly between visual and verbal paralanguages, handwriting and crossing out and doodling hold out the promise of access to the intricate physiology of the writer's or speaker's voice. I am thus further arguing that handwriting, crossing out and doodling should be harnessed, along with typography, in all its manifestations, to the act of translation, should become standard translational resources.

In the act of crossing out, we are, paradoxically, unconcealing an eradicated word. Crossing out is an attempted cancellation, a retraction, a change of mind, a non-selected option, a sound turned to silence, dramatised in the movement of a hand. And crossing out is an expressively diverse act, out of which may grow other languages. One is reminded of Rabindranath Tagore, and of his habit, as he moved towards painting in the latter part of his life, of graphically elaborating his manuscript deletions until they became decorative figurations or images (see Subramanyan, 1986). Tagore worked both with the metamorphic potentialities of graphism, the mark of deletion that comes to enhance the text, and with graphism's rhythmic-ity, as an accompaniment of text: crossing out, itself a rhythmic gesture, naturally begets the more reflective rhythmicity of doodling.

What is doodling? As Barthes observes (1995, 821), it hardly has a name: it relates to colouring, to graffiti and, however crudely physiological it is, it also draws to some extent upon articulatory values, upon the culture's stock of calligraphic and painterly resources. Reading invites us to draw on other dimensions of ourselves, other psychic impulses. Doodling becomes one of the alternative languages offered by translation. If we are to judge by Barthes's words, doodling is an essential liberation from the deviousness and compulsions of language. As Barthes puts it, doodling is 'le soulagement (le repos) de pouvoir créer quelque chose qui ne soit pas directement dans le piège du langage, dans la responsabilité fatalement attachée à toute phrase: une sorte d'innocence, en somme, dont l'écriture m'exclut' (1995, 821) [the relief (the restfulness) of being able to create something which is not directly caught in the trap of language, in the web of reponsibility inevitably attached to any sentence: a sort of innocence, in short, from which writing excludes me]. Elsewhere (1995, 239–40), Barthes describes the doodle as 'La graphie pour rien ou le signifiant sans signifié' [The graphic sign for nothing or the signifier without a signified].

Crossing-out and doodling both belong to the arts of illegibility,[8] in which processes of recognition begin to waver until we find ourselves in the world of pure graphism; the hand, by not following a uniform code of communication, seems to become the involuntary home of new energies, choreographies, whose language we do not understand. These lines and squiggles seem to be freely at play, making spontaneous decisions about how they will move, occupy space, what they might visually suggest. What kind of noises does the illegible make audible: explosions, rubbings, creaks, vocal timbres and wordless mouthings? Illegibilities, pure graphic movements, are perhaps the alphabets of another world, beyond the reach of full consciousness. At all events, the illegible can be seen as the refusal of writing to surrender to a functional role, to the production of alphabetised communication; instead it reclaims handwriting for its pure gesturality, for the truth it tells about a hand, and about the metabolism and vocal physiology made visible by the hand.

In this way, the calligraphic and the graphic allow the linguistic not only to incorporate the paralinguistic, but also to cross media boundaries. Different typefaces, too, may endow letters with different expressive values, values which belong particularly to urban technology, to the overtones of architectural and design styles, and those of commercial relationship – I think of typefaces like Algerian, Bauhaus, Britannic, Broadway. But with typefaces, letter-shapes do not wander, nor, consequently, do the sounds they make.[9] Even so, we must remember Apollinaire's words of 1918: 'Les artifices typographiques poussés très loin avec une grande audace ont l'avantage de faire naître un lyrisme visuel qui était presque inconnu avant notre époque. Ces artifices peuvent aller très loin encore et consommer la synthèse des arts, de la musique, de la peinture et de la littérature' (1991, 944) [Typographic artifices pushed to extremes with great boldness have the advantage of begetting a visual lyricism which was almost unknown up till now. These artifices can be pushed further still and accomplish the synthesis of the arts, of music, painting and literature].[10] If, then, one finds the traditional notation of verse inadequate, two options seem to offer themselves to the scansionalist and translator: (1) to increase and diversify the notational language in order that the voice has better instructions, is more challenged to be its complex self;[11] here I present a crude vision of what typefaces and punctuation might achieve in the way of perceptual and acoustic versatility, in relation to the first line of Baudelaire's 'Recueillement':

SORROW (CASTELLAR)
Sorrow (Wide Latin)
Sorrow (Bauhaus 93)
Sorrow (Lucida Sans Typewriter)
SORROW (ALGERIAN)
Sorrow (Impact)
Sorrow (Old English Text MT)

Sois sage, ô ma Douleur, et tiens-toi plus tranquille.
SORROW, my own, be good and quieten down
Sorrow, my own – be good . . . and quieten down
SORROW my own: be good and quieten down
Sorrow, my own! Be good! And quieten down
Sorrow,,,,,,, my own//be good; and. Qui:ETEn down
S+orr:ow***MY**o*wnnnn*|be gooD :- and **Qui:ETEn.>.>** down

or (2) to develop the equivalent of *musikalische Graphik* [musical graphics], notational constructs whose relation to performance is almost completely aleatory, or which are best performed as purely mental projections (see, e.g., Cage, 1969; Sauer, 2009). Such a strategy may, paradoxically, serve the interests of a much enlarged, multi-sensory perceptual experience. As I feed more decisions, information, desiderata into my pre-reading of Henley, I see that I am beginning to take the written notation beyond what the voice can audibly or perceptibly realise (Fig. 4). Perhaps I am trying to develop an intermediate phase, a notation which both encourages a performance *of* the text and yet constitutes a performance *in* the text, which no physical act can do proper justice to. In this sense, this pre-reading text is a prerequisite for the audience of all performances *of* the text, since it supplements and completes performance, but in the mind of the individual listener. This creates a particularly powerful collaborative relationship between speaker and listener.

This supplementation of the voice by the written and by graphism, or the imagination of a new, purely conceptual vocality in the written, is necessitated by the shortcomings of our ears and voices. Our relative inability to describe voices in an individuating fashion is perhaps symptomatic of our inattentiveness to their complex physiologies, or, as we have said, of a language which is profoundly unresourceful when it comes to voice. If the inadequacy lies with our hearing, then we might suggest several reasons for it:

(1) the need to listen for sense as the priority of listening;
(2) long-inculcated habits of listening for a very limited number of acoustic effects (rhyme, alliteration, assonance);
(3) the assumption that the written translates directly into the spoken and vice versa, with the concomitant assumption that the voice is bare of all effects other than those that can be represented by the written word;
(4) a failure to acquire the new habits of listening, to inhabit the new soundworlds, that modern music, among other things, has made available to us (see, e.g., Perloff, 2009).

We need a new image of voice, an image other than the printed word, if we are going to hear voice. If, for example, multiple margins were an image of vocal fluctuations of various kinds, then we might be able to listen to margins better and thus better produce them vocally. At the moment, vocally, we tend to do nothing with them. In any case, we need to re-invent written and/or printed resources – handwriting, diacritics, typefaces, margins, etc. – as a diagnostic and prosthetics of voice. Given that the written word is so frequently indicted for omitting paralinguistic

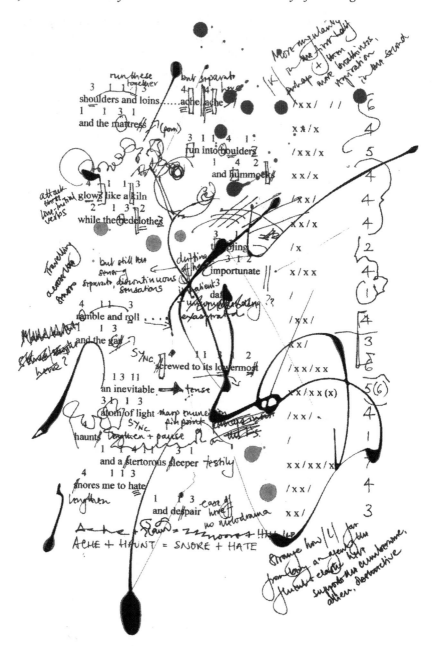

Figure 4 Fig. 3, with further decoration

and prosodic features, this would indeed be an ironic turnaround. Strategies are already available which might liberate this other voice: we might achieve our ends by increasing the materiality of language, so that the materiality of the voice is both acted out and solicited; or by interrupting and frustrating articulacy; or by projecting alternative forms of linguistic disposition. These solutions act together in the tabular text.

Here I start out from Philip Cranston's translation (2008, 169) of a short poem by Jules Supervielle, 'L'Errant' (*Les Amis inconnus*, 1934, 101):

> J'ai tant de fois, hélas, changé de ciel,
> Changé d'horreur et changé de visage,
> Que je ne comprends plus mon propre cœur
> Toujours réduit à son même carnage.
> (© Éditions Gallimard)

> I have, alas, so often changed my skies,
> Changed horrors and changed faces,
> That I no longer understand my heart,
> Which its same carnage every day debases.
> (trans. Philip Cranston)

I provide a pronunciatory, tabular, re-writing of it, this time a post-textual translation of a translation (Fig. 5), which removes all the ways in which Cranston's rendering might be said to correspond to Supervielle's text, that is, his iambic pentameter, answering Supervielle's classic French decasyllable, but in a syllabic pattern of 10, 7, 10, 11; his alternating masculine and feminine rhymes, in an xaxa scheme, answering the same pattern as in the original. By this re-disposition, I have hoped to transform reading from an act of utterance, or articulation, to one of vocal palpation, or pronunciation; from harnessing a medium for expression, to finding one's way back into a medium which has become obstructive, alien even; from converting a medium's materiality into concept, to encouraging a medium not to compromise its materiality, but to demand an answering, effortful, vocal physicality from the reader. By varying typefaces, I have tried to suggest not only different kinds and degrees of vocality, but also the foregrounding of different kinds of vocal and audible feature.

I have elsewhere argued for tabular text as the true type of the translational text (2009) and as translation's true perceptual mode. I do not here wish to stop over the changes in textual time produced by the tabular, nor over the way in which it turns the perspectival into the planar. Instead, I want to pause briefly over the way in which it deprives us of knowledge, in particular the knowledge of how to read and to write.

THE
WAND
ER
ERR ANT

I
HAV
E
ALA
S SO

ofte
n
tʃa
ng(j
e)e
d
my
s(k)
iel(s
)

TʃANG
ED
HORR
ORS
AND
TʃANG
ED
FACES

THAT I
NO
LONGE

R U
NDER
STAND

MY HE
ART

e ry
day
deb
ases

Whi
tʃ
its
sam
e
car
nag
e e y

Figure 5 Tabular re-arrangement of Philip Cranston's translation of
Supervielle's 'L'Errant'

My first point is a simple one: that were we, as our first move, to translate this text back into horizontal linear verse, we would be nullifying the text. Its whole point is that it is a translation out of the continuous linear into a language called 'tabular English'. This we must *learn* to read; this is a translation of our own language towards the foreign, not so much towards the original French, as towards a foreign language in our own language. This is a language we do not speak, a language we do not know, but upon which we involuntarily draw in moments of linguistic fantasy or verbal inventiveness. The tabular here begins to throw into doubt ingrained habits of pronunciation and accentuation in our own language, to teach us to hear language as an acoustic multitude, full of phonetic possibility, where, normally, this anarchy is peremptorily subdued by lexical and syntactical imperatives.[12]

There is neither a history nor an anthropology of uttering and listening, but in our own time we may feel that metre and the articulate lyric voice are on the edge of archaism; that, faced with a poem like this, we need to expand the spectrum of uttering and listening to a wider range of frequencies and decibels, that we need to find ways of expressing the infra-sonic (below sixteen cycles per second) and the ultra-sonic (above 20,000 cycles per second). (So this is what white paper expresses – the teeming world of unheard sounds, the vast tracts of auditory experience where human acoustic territory ends and on to which it abuts.) Accordingly, we would need to acknowledge this shift in what we listen to – our auditory tolerances – and what we listen for – what we treat as acoustically significant – with a new vocabulary. It is already apparent that, in the performance of verse, audiences are much more likely to be struck by paralinguistic features such as loudness, changes of tempo, pausing, than by standard metrico-rhythmic features of stress and non-stress.

We need to develop different auditory habits, along two lines: (1) we need to think of verse language as a larger soundscape, composed not of the leavings of words, not of phonemes, morphemes, syllables, but of 'sound objects' which constitute events of a re-configured sound-flow. A tabular text, like the one we have before us, might indeed persuade us that we are engaged in a process not of reading off what is there (i.e. hermeneutic), but of reading something into (another) existence, by cutting and splicing (i.e. constructivist); (2) we need to think of verse language not as the manifestation of a set of binary options (strong/weak), or of a principle of recurrence; we need to hear relations of difference, based on a much broader, qualitative range of phenomena (timbre, duration, loudness, pitch, speed). We need also to remember that a reading of a text is not a question of *reproducing* a soundscape that is already there, ever consistent with itself. Just as we might, in listening to music, adjust and re-adjust the loudness, the treble and bass settings, the tone, so, as translators, we can make selections with our uttering and listening mechanisms, and endlessly re-improvise the text. How to expand soundscape will become a central preoccupation of Chapter 4; first, in Chapter 3, we must look at the ways in which the text and the world can enter into fruitful dialogue.

Translating the textual environment (1)

I look at Botticelli's *Birth of Venus*, in its frame. I take some steps away from the image and find myself looking through another frame, a window frame, out over the roofs of Florence: the sun is just going in, a flock of birds scatter across the sky. This new frame suddenly restores me to my physical presence, to myself on a particular afternoon. The Botticelli ceases to be a mythological event and becomes a picture on the wall.

I stand gazing at a sloth in its cage, making its patient way along a branch. I am working to construct in my mind a habitat, a space in which the sloth feels at home, can re-occupy its own privacy. Suddenly, the spell is broken; a handful of loudly chirping sparrows flies into the cage, before re-dispersing through the rafters of the tropical mammal house. The sloth is unable to enter the fiction I wish to make for it. How can it make its peace with the sparrows?

The septet by Proust's composer Vinteuil is first performed at a soiree at Mme Verdurin's. As she listens, Mme Verdurin adopts a characteristic posture, her face buried in her hands:

voulait-elle comme certaines personnes à l'église dérober aux regards indiscrets, soit par pudeur leur ferveur supposée, soit par respect humain leur distraction coupable ou un sommeil invincible? Cette dernière hypothèse fut celle qu'un bruit régulier qui n'était pas musical me fit croire un instant être la vraie, mais je m'aperçus ensuite qu'il était produit par les ronflements, non de Mme Verdurin, mais de sa chienne. (1988, 756)

[Did she wish, as some people do in church, to hide from prying eyes, out of modesty or shame, their presumed fervour or their culpable inattention or an irresistible urge to sleep? A regular noise which was not musical gave me momentarily to think that this last hypothesis was the correct one, but I realised later that it was produced by the snores, not of Mme Verdurin, but of her dog. (1983b, 253)]

In standard recording conditions, the dog's snoring would be edited out of Vinteuil's septet. But avant-garde music, or performance art, might, on the contrary, wish to leave the dog-snores as they are, or indeed to edit in further dog-snores, and other coughs and wheezes.

But there are moments when this separation of the inside world of an imagined work and the outside everyday world are not so clear. In reading, it is the very body of the reader that holds him/her suspended between the worlds of the text and of the everyday, and that body is active in both these worlds. For literary criticism, the assumption is that the reader, in a featureless, evacuated environment, reads the book with a uniform critical attention, at a uniform speed. And one can understand why. Otherwise, there would be no end to anecdotalism; literary criticism is not sociological study; we have no system for translating the circumstances of reading into a cognitive or evaluative code. And yet the circumstances of reading are inextricably linked with the reading experience, with reading as an essential part of our autobiography.[1] So we move from the ergological dynamics of reading (its physiology, its kinaesthetics) to a socio-ecological dimension (see Perec, 2003, 108).

In 'Sur la lecture' [On Reading], the preface to his translation (1906), with Marie Nordlinger, of Ruskin's *Sesame and Lilies* (1987b, 99–129), Proust describes the strategies required to keep the world out of his reading space. But so nostalgically rich are his descriptions of the dining-room, his bedroom, the park, that we see them as clearly integral to his reading experience. Memory of the book is memory of the venues of its reading and vice versa.

And whatever misgivings Proust may have had about Ruskin's own approach to reading, he marvelled at his architectural accounts and found his manner of approaching his objective, church or cathedral, highly instructive. In the age of the photographic reproduction, we too easily forget that the point of visiting a work of art is not merely to see the thing as it is, but to envelop the thing as it is with the circumstances of the visit. And this is what the sketches made during the course of the visit perpetuate. Proust writes that: 'Ruskin ne séparait pas la beauté des cathédrales du charme de ces pays d'où elles surgirent, et que chacun de ceux qui les visite goûte encore dans la poésie particulière du pays et le souvenir brumeux ou doré de l'après-midi qu'il y a passé' (1916, 68) [Ruskin did not separate the beauty of cathedrals from the charm of the regions from which they sprang, and which everyone who visits them still enjoys in the particular poetry of the region and in the remembrance of the misty or golden afternoon he spent there (1987b, 42)]. And integral to this pleasure, this encapsulation of object and ambience, is a gradualism of approach towards the object, through 'zones d'harmonie graduée' (1916, 68) [zones of graduated harmony (1987b, 43)], afforded by walking or by car journeys, but not by 'ces bottes de sept lieues que sont les grands express' (1916, 68) [these seven-league boots that express trains are (1987b, 43)]. This kind of approach is both a mental preparation and a gathering up of the environment into the object.

For Virginia Woolf, reading is not a teachable skill but a vital process of self-discovery and self-definition: 'The only advice, indeed, that one person can give another about reading is to take no advice, to follow your own instincts, to use your own reason, to come to your own conclusions' (1966, 1). But in her writings about reading, Woolf does promote her own ideal ambience for reading. A library – public, or part of a country house – seems to be her space of choice; to be surrounded by texts, from Homer to the present, is to invest the text in one's hands with a multifarious chorus of other voices, waiting to chip in with their pennyworth. Reading brings into being and animates this wonderfully rich literary backdrop, where Pope stands behind Keats and memoirs jostle with poems. But if this seems to draw Woolf deeper into the world of the self-regardingly literary, a counter-pull encourages her to assimilate into her book and into her reading experience the world outside the library window:

I liked to read there. One drew the pale armchair to the window, and so the light fell over the shoulder upon the page. The shadow of the gardener mowing the lawn sometimes crossed it, as he led his pony in rubber shoes up and down, the machine giving a little creak, which seemed the very voice of summer. (1966, 12)

In translating Woolf, might we then write that 'little creak' into the text? The world outside the window becomes the atmospheric envelope of the reading experience, and, in return, is as if transformed and absorbed by the book –

But, as I say, even the gardener leading his pony was part of the book, and, straying from the actual page, the eye rested upon his face, as if one reached it through a great depth of time. That accounted for the soft swarthy tint of the cheeks, and the lines of his body, scarcely disguised by the coarse brown stuff of his coat, might have belonged to any labouring man in any age . . . The man took his place naturally by the side of those dead poets. (1966, 13)

It is reading's power to absorb the reader, it is images of people letting the world go hang in the name of their engrossment, that make our hearts soften. But Woolf tells us of another experience, that moment when our eyes stray from the page and reconnect with the world. Why is this moment so rarely described or depicted?

I wish briefly to explore this thematics of looking up from the page. My concern here is not with *unwelcome* interruptions of reading, interruptions which are short hiccoughs before reading is resumed and which are often represented by the finger held in the text at the point the interruption occurs. Nor do I wish to dwell overlong upon that carriage of the book into the environment, by the face of the reader, who still has, imprinted on his/her features, the experience that the book is. Rilke's poem 'Der Leser' [The Reader] (1962, 392–3), from the second part of his *Neue Gedichte* (1908) explores this phenomenon:

Wer kennt ihn, diesen, welcher sein Gesicht
wegsenkte aus dem Sein zu einem zweiten,
das nur das schnelle Wenden voller Seiten
manchmal gewaltsam unterbricht?

Selbst seine Mutter wäre nicht gewiβ,
ob *er* es ist, der da mit seinem Schatten
Getränktes liest. Und wir, die Stunden hatten,
was wissen wir, wieviel ihm hinschwand, bis

er mühsam aufsah: alles auf sich hebend,
was unten in dem Buche sich verhielt,
mit Augen, welche, statt zu nehmen, gebend
anstieβen an die fertig-volle Welt:
wie stille Kinder, die allein gespielt,
auf einmal das Vorhandene erfahren;
doch seine Züge, die geordnet waren,
blieben für immer umgestellt.

Who knows him, he who's let his face descend
to where a new existency engages,
only the rapid turn of crowded pages
will sometimes violently suspend?

Even his mother could not feel quite sure
it's he, there reading something saturated
with his own shadow. And, clock-regulated,
can we know how much ebbed from him before

he labouringly uplooked: thereby upheaving
all the book's deepness to the light of day,
with eyes which, now outgiving, not receiving,
impinged upon a filled environment:
as quiet children, after lonely play,
will suddenly perceive the situation;
his features, though, in full co-ordination,
remained forever different.

(trans. J.B. Leishman, 1964, 287)

The reader, sinking into his book, sinks into a second existence; the book is another, private life, in which it is impossible to know what the reader gets up to. In reading on his own, the son is weaned from the mother; a child being read to by its mother, on the other hand, is still drinking at the breast.[2] When at last the reader looks up, the book's effect still radiates from his look, and the changes he has undergone will never leave his face. Will we ever know what our reading has done to us? Our translations of the texts of our reading are portraits of this ever-renewed face. Words that Rilke uses to describe the world we turn to after reading or, as children, after solitary play – 'die fertig-volle Welt', 'das Vorhandene' – might be thought to have affiliations with Yves Bonnefoy's notions of Being and Presence. At all events, it is as a supplement to reading that I wish to address the ambient.

Bonnefoy's essay 'Lever les yeux de son livre' (1988) [Looking up from One's Book] expresses a dissatisfaction with the exhaustive textual analysis by which he finds himself surrounded, because its language is a meta-language, constantly drifting off towards the conceptual and the abstract, preoccupied with what is in the work rather than with what the work cannot say. And the work cannot say Bonnefoy's mantra: the Presence, or Being, of the world to itself. For Bonnefoy, textual criticism thus makes imperceptible what is essential in poetry, that falling short, that gap, that intuited something, which bids us turn away from the poem. These moments of turning away, of interruption of reading, are the moments when the poem escapes from textual signification into real meaning, into time, contingency, finitude: 'C'est bien parce que le lecteur est prêt à quitter le texte qu'il peut en accepter et revivre la proposition fondamentale, qui est qu'il y a eu à son origine, ou plus tard dans sa formation, un affleurement de présence' (1992, 231) [It is because the reader is ready to leave the text that he can accept and relive its fundamental proposition, which is that there was, at its conception, or later in its composition, a trace of presence]. Thus poetry might well be read fragmentarily, sometimes against its own textual grain, since it is primarily an opportunity given to the reader to pursue his/her own search for presence, to consult his/her own lived experience, to recover existential origins.

Bonnefoy's account of reading enjoins upon the reader a weighty responsibility. He has little sympathy with those for whom the text is made of the play of the signifier, guileful in its deferrals of meaning, in its ability to detain the reader in the textual web. For him, Mallarmé is a founding architect of this web of purely intraverbal relationship, homogenising verbal material in its reciprocal self-sufficiency, when, in his view, looking up from the text requires a heterogeneity of text.[3] Nor will

Bonnefoy condone Roland Barthes's programme of reading, deriving from his *S/Z* (1970), in which looking up from the text is motivated by the associative, digressive thinking of the reader, what we, after Jerome McGann, are calling 'radial reading'.[4] For Bonnefoy, this associationism fails to escape from verbal representation into authentic being. For Barthes, on the other hand, this associative mode is a necessary guarantee of the reader's liberation from author-fixation. Barthes (1984, 34–5) sets against this authorial control, and the channelling of text towards a specific meaning, a dissemination of text by the reader, an associative dispersal of text. And as we have been arguing all along, it is translation's business to enlarge text, to inject text with readerly individuation, to let text proliferate, to thrust text into its ramifying futures. Reading, for Barthes, is a process of supplementation of text, of expansion and addition, a writing: 'Qu'est-ce donc que *S/Z*? Simplement un texte, ce texte que nous écrivons dans notre tête quand nous la levons' (1984, 34) [What then is *S/Z*? Simply a text which we write in our head when we lift our head [from the page]].

We might then identify two kinds of 'reading-into-the-environment': the re-infusion of the reading experience with the pressures or urgency of existence, that kind of reading which seems to provoke an appeal from the outside world, that kind of reading that lets the outside world infiltrate the text's texture, or renews our return to the world (Bonnefoy); and, on the other hand, that day-dreaming, digressive reading which generates an inner fertility, which triggers images and associations and memories, and the desire to write, all of which, as a consequence of writing (translation), flows back into the text (Barthes).

As an example of this latter, 'Barthesian' mode, I want to consider the translation of Apollinaire's poem 'Marizibill' (*Alcools*, 1913) (1965, 77):

> Dans la Haute-Rue à Cologne
> Elle allait et venait le soir
> Offerte à tous en tout mignonne
> Puis buvait lasse des trottoirs
> Très tard dans les brasseries borgnes
>
> Elle se mettait sur la paille
> Pour un maquereau roux et rose
> C'était un juif il sentait l'ail
> Et l'avait venant de Formose
> Tirée d'un bordel de Changaï

Je connais gens de toutes sortes
Ils n'égalent pas leurs destins
Indécis comme feuilles mortes
Leurs yeux sont des feux mal éteints
Leurs cœurs bougent comme leurs portes

First, as a 'control', we should absorb Oliver Bernard's admirable translation (2004, 67):

In the High Street of Cologne
Evenings she came and went
Pretty enough for anyone
Then drank tired of that pavement
Late in one-eyed bars alone

Never put a farthing by
Had a redhaired rosy ponce
Jew smelt of garlic caught his eye
Coming from Formosa once
In a brothel in Shanghai

I know all kinds none are quite
Equal to their fates but doubt
Shakes them like dead leaves their bright
Eyes are fires not quite out
Hearts bang like their doors all night

I begin my own translation with linguistic doodling in French and German:

MARIZIBILL

in the Hohe-Straße

in Köln (ô de, Öde)

pé

ripat   enne   ellefaisait

étici   le trottoir

EAch

Evening   not one to say no

a real poppet

and when shE'd had enough

of her bEAt

shE'd drink –

a night owl

in sEEdy bars

she clEAned herself out

A garlic-scented Jew

for a pimp
pink-faced
ginger-haired
who'd

shanghaied her   from a brothel in Shanghai

starboard home

from

Formosa

I know types of every ilk
Who can't quite match
What they might be
Shiftless, unfixed, like dead leaves
Their eyes are dying embers
Not quite out, their hearts
As restive as their unclosed doors

In the bracketed '(ô de, Öde)', for example, there are allusions to Lancôme adverts, and to Eliot's *Waste Land* (his quotation from Wagner's *Tristan and Isolde*, III, 24: 'Öd' und leer das Meer'); and the terms 'péripatéticienne' and 'faire le trottoir' are what might be found in the titles of photographs by Brassaï. As I proceed, other photographic images – some that I would expect to visit me, others more mysteriously motivated – come to mind. The reverse is also true: seeing these photographs unavoidably conjures up 'Marizibill'. This latter point is worth underlining: reading is as much a post-reading act of memory as a present, textual activity, but, as a phenomenon of memory, it is activated by the process of *being reminded*, by triggers whose exactness may, paradoxically, increase the inexactitude of the remembered source text (ST); the reminder may be as sharp as a photograph, but the textual memory it begets may set the text afloat, in mixings and indeterminacies and sudden, disproportionate highlights. In the previous chapter, we looked at translation as a pre-textual activity; we have, inevitably, looked at translation as a post-textual activity. But here we consider it as a post-post-textual activity occurring long after the event of reading. Translation can thus also be an account of a text after a lapse of time, a remembered reading and an enactment of the process of memory. In these circumstances, it might be translation's task to capture the creative, existentially fruitful aspirations of these inexactitudes of memory.

The photographic images activated as I undertake the translation become a corpus, a corpus of translational resource:

Richard Avedon, *Renée, Place de la Concorde, Paris*, 1947
Erwin Blumenfeld, *Maroua Motherwell, New York*, 1942
Brassaï, *Introduction at Suzy's*, 1932
Manuel Alvarez Bravo, *Nude*, 1936–1980
Walker Evans, *Steps of an Old Residence on State Street*, 1950
Robert Frank, *City of London*, 1951
Nan Goldin, *Empty Bed, Priory Hospital*, 2003
Aino Kannisto, *Untitled (Room 310)*, 2007
Peter Lindbergh, *Modèles de Christian Lacroix et Thierry Mugler*, 1991
Charles Marville, *Rue de la Parcheminerie*, 1865–1869
Willy Ronis, *Nu*, 1949
August Stauda, *Escalier de la porte du ciel, Vienne*, c. 1900
Shoji Ueda, *Quatre Filles*, 1939
Albert Watson, *H. Stern Project, Lost Diary*, 1997

As I sort through these images, I realise that only two of them – the Charles Marville and the August Stauda – predate Apollinaire's poem. The others cover the period up to 2007 and range geographically from Japan to Mexico. In other words, these images belong to the poem as part of its projection of itself into new futures, and belong to me as a reader whose available image-bank spontaneously and unavoidably re-inflects, or re-metabolises, the poem, inserting it into new intertexts and other fields of reference.

But what is the appropriate mode of incorporation of these photographs? How do I transform them into protagonists within the text? How do I make them textually active, themselves text? I must change the kind of language they are; they must surrender their self-sufficiency as images and become part of ongoing utterance by the devices of overlapping, insetting, cutting and cropping, and by the creative dynamics of their disposition. What I am looking to generate is something of the erotics of the street – glimpses, glances, transitory contact, momentary flirtation – but also the variable atmospheres and social colourings of the prostitute's life.

These acts of cutting and disposing will, like my typographic design of the text, reflect another mechanism, that of memory itself. As I make aesthetic decisions about 'plotting' and 'textual thickening', I also trace and dramatise, with these 'doctored' photographs, the activity of memory, its different tempi, its slidings, its fixations, its effort to reconstruct and stabilise. The mind reads text and remembers images; the mind sees images and remembers text; the tabular layout enacts this unsteady dialectic.

But then I turn in another direction. If my first photographic version is to be about the involuntary eruption of images from text and text from images, such that the poem expands outwards in space, far from Cologne, and forward in time, well beyond 1913, then my second version (Fig. 6) is my own photographic adventure: to take photographs (in Norwich and Bristol) and to find 'Marizibill' in them, sometimes in their main subject, sometimes in some inconspicuous detail. In my photo-collage, I have tried to introduce a perceptual approach which is more interrogative and speculative. The photographic eye looks for answers, for identities, at the same time as it recognises the dangers of coming to conclusions. If the headless mannequins of the opening images are the prostitutes of shop-window commerce, should we attribute any face to Marizibill? Or is it, precisely, a particular face which explodes the imaginative licence/licentiousness of shop-window display, and of literature? At the same time, photographs are convenient targets, pulling into singleness and focus objects of potential anger, desire, contempt, prurience. This mute vulnerability of the photograph to the viewer is here countered by the photograph's multiplication or fragmentation. The photograph becomes elusive, its elements redouble, or refuse to coalesce. The poem's condescensions, however compassionate they may be, are outmanoeuvred by the images, which also make possible, make visible, other narratives. Put another way, the 'Indécis comme feuilles mortes' which, it is implied, is a reason why the likes of Marizibill are not equal to their destinies, becomes, in the photographic account, a positive capacity always to decamp, or dismantle the situation, or drift into another story.

This particular version ends with a photographic cliché: the playing out, through the figure of windows, of the changing temperaments of the human eye. The half-open 'œil-de-bœuf', which belongs with the plush and animated restaurant images of the previous page (contradicting Apollinaire's 'seedy bars'), is intended to convey an inquisitive, searching, animated, two-way communicative eye, while the rectangular panes

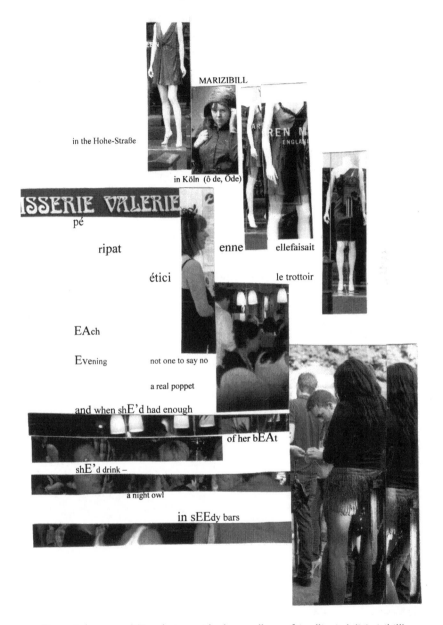

Figure 6 (two pages) Translation, with photo-collage, of Apollinaire's 'Marizibill'

she clEAned herself out

for a pimp

pink-faced

ginger-haired

A garlic-scented Jew   who'd

shanghaied her   from a brothel in Shanghai

starboard home

 from

Formosa

I know types of every ilk

Who can't quite match

What they might be

Shiftless, unfixed, like dead leaves

Their eyes are dying embers

Not quite out, their hearts

As restive as their unclosed doors

Figure 6 *(cont.)*

of the suburban bay-windows are reflective or net-curtained surfaces out of which no sight comes and which nothing penetrates, eyes that are 'dying embers / Not quite out'. While in the text, in Apollinaire's five-line stanza, the 'answer' of the b-rhymes is repeatedly stifled by the relentless, paralysing return of the a-rhymes, the photographs provide an alternative vision, in which a deadening condition is refused, in which something inextinguishable survives, thanks to an indefatigable opportunism, thanks to reality's narrative resourcefulness, thanks to the very inventiveness of uncertainty.

Translation allows me to gather together all this associative activity, and to provide visual escape-routes from the destiny mapped out by the printed text, as a constructive input into the very fabric of the poem, not just as a record of a reading, but as part of a renewed creative-critical project. These elements of my other, extratextual life, which, in a literary-critical context, would be ruled out of court as anecdotal or impressionistic, unless I could demonstrate some specific intertextual intention on Apollinaire's part, achieve a status beyond personal caprice, by being incorporated not only into textual being, but into the text's aesthetic purpose. What is autobiographical in reading becomes compositional. It is only translation that permits this transformation, which permits this integration of personal response into text as an integral part of the text's tireless capacity to re-imagine itself.

As we now turn from the reading of readerly digression and association to the infiltrations and intrusions of the outside world into the world of the text, I first wish briefly to consider another case of collage. In this instance, it is the text of Shakespeare's Sonnet 71, 'No longer mourn for me when I am dead' (2005, 112), in which words in five of the lines have been replaced by glued-in pieces of newsprint and magazine-print (Fig. 7). This might look like the most minimal of translations, but its consequences are considerable. The collaged words are like found words, words bodily uprooted from another world – *The Guardian*, *The Radio Times* – of which they still bear the imprint. They seem to plaster over gaps in the text, where the Shakespearean text was suddenly at a loss and had to wait some 410 years for completion. Is this a work of remedial textual archaeology, or is it that 2012 has the power to utter certain things not available to Shakespeare? Or is it, on the other hand, a case of mischievous substitution, subversive re-writing, Situationist *détournement* or misappropriation or piracy?

These verbal plasters are interventions by the contemporary world, the here and now – just as the collages of Synthetic Cubism are – whereby a

No longer mourn for me when I am dead

Than YOU shall hear the surly sullen bell

Give warning to the **World** that I am fled

From this vile world with vilest worms to dwell.

Nay, if you read this line, remember not

The hand that Writ it, for I love you so

That I in your sweet thoughts would be forgot

If thinking on me then should make you woe.

O, if, I say, you LOOK upon this verse,

When I, perhaps, compounded am with clay,

Do not so much as my poor name rehearse,

But let **YOUR**   love even with my life decay;

Lest the wise world should look into your moan,

And mock you with me after I am gone.

Figure 7 Translation, with collage, of Shakespeare's Sonnet 71

game of illusions is created, a double vision which will not quite resolve itself: are they pieces of Shakespearean text or random fragments of newsprint? But, in fact, their effect is even more significant. Our view of the Shakespearean text is that it can be printed at any time on any paper and remain the same text; the nature of its physical support may inflect or colour our reading of the text, but it does not change the text. The paper is dispensable. But to collage other paper on to the text's paper brings the text's paper into existence, *into question* one might say, historicises it, makes it subject to temporal change. The paper which we might have felt was of no account, invisible, suddenly obtrudes as the locus of a vulnerability. Instead of being the poem's support, it is treacherous ground, without defence against textual trespassing. It compels the text to share its own precariousness. The old equation – neutrality of paper = timelessness of text – turns into a new one, namely: historicity of paper = mutability of text. If collage introduces the impatience of time, it begins, too, to entail the specificities of context, in particular the immediate context of a typeface, the multiplicity of possible or probable sources.

This scrappy piece of collage alerts us to the imminent invasiveness of the here and now; this is no more than the tip of an iceberg. Collage is an unprincipled mechanism, which knows nothing of tickets of entry. It is as if environment has decided to gate-crash an unguarded textual party, threatening to introduce any element it chooses. And since consistency of typeface speaks for consistency of voice, collage imports the chatter of the universe, in strange acousmatic arrangements, is an incipient *poème-conversation* [conversation poem], heteroglossic, without our knowing to whom any of the competing voices belong. Do we have any idea how to concoct a reading of 'No longer mourn for me . . . ' which would do justice to these collaged scraps of voice?[5]

My second foray into the outer world focuses on onomatopoeia, the verbal imitation of ambient sounds. Our starting-point must be the obvious one: the more ambient sound is absorbed into language, the less accurately imitative it is likely to be. As Dickens puts it in *A Tale of Two Cities* (1859) (1949, 120), as night settles over the château of the St. Evrémondes: 'the owl made a noise with very little resemblance in it to the noise conventionally assigned to the owl by men-poets. But it is the obstinate custom of such creatures hardly ever to say what is set down for them'. There are three stages by which ambient sound is absorbed into language: (1) the raw sound is alphabetised; phonetic data are translated into the phonological system; (2) the word thus created becomes a part of speech, is grammaticalised, and can thus be assimilated into syntactic operations; (3) the word becomes conventionalised or genericised; even though owls have a rich vocal range, in language they only hoot. My immediate subject is the BD (*bande dessinée*) or graphic novel, a kind of writing in rebellion against linguistic orthodoxy in the treatment of onomatopoeia. This is not always so, let it be said: a comparison of onomatopoeia in the original and revised versions of the Tintin adventures shows that Hergé reduced and standardised the onomatopoeic element, and that this standardisation often compels particular onomatopoeias to do double and triple acoustic duty, to cover a wide range of sounds with different origins. But, in this respect, Tintin is the exception rather than the rule.

Sounds in their eruptive vulgarity are linguistically anarchic, stretching language to its limits, deforming it, and as if forcing the reader into direct contact with them. Consider a page from *The Walking Dead VIII: Made to Suffer* (Kirkman, Adlard and Rathburn, 2008, n. p.) (Fig. 8). What are the characteristics of this rough, ideophonic language?

(1) Most important of all, it occurs outside the speech balloon. Ambient sounds and noises, to our ears, as they occur, are without a grammar or syntax, are always an intrusion, an interruption, or accompaniment, insertable at any point in the continuum of sound. They stand outside our own linguistic order.

(2) It often breaks the border of the vignette, flying out of the narrative into our space and time, creating an acoustic third dimension. It cannot be contained by the fiction it ostensibly inhabits.

(3) It favours consonants over vowels, that is, it favours noises over sounds, in the ratio of 4:1 (Fresnault-Deruelle, 1971, 85) and is generally mono-syllabic.

(4) It often contains reduplications of phonemes and operates permuta-tionally in order to make discriminations between closely allied sounds. In *The Walking Dead VIII*, five consecutive images show individuals being struck by gunfire, with the sound-sequence: PLAKK! SPAKK! SPUKK! PLOKK! SPLUDD! Outside the horror genre, we would probably have heard only the gunfire itself: PKOW! or BLAM!. Comic strips are instrumental in the lifting of perceptual taboos. And in *The Walking Dead V: The Best Defense* (Kirkman, Adlard and Rathburn, 2005, n. p.), I note, on a single page, the following variations in human cries of pain and distress: UNGH! UGHN! UGGH! UGH! UFF! AAHH!! AAAAHHH!!!! YEEAGH!! EEAAGGHH! EAAGGHHOH!! Not surprisingly, with these predominantly open-throated utterances, vowels are in greater evidence.

If we describe this exploitation of the onomatopoeic in the comic strip as a rebellion against an acoustic orthodoxy, then that orthodoxy is what cuts us off, what positively alienates us, from our own ambient sound-world. And we should ask ourselves what we need to do in our written works for that state to be reversed. How can we use translation in such a way as to turn writing into an eco-writing? Before we decide, we might briefly look in another direction. If comic strip is the popular medium of the subversive liberation of onomatopoeia, then the art movement which perhaps most concerned itself with this issue was Futurism.

Figure 8 Page from Kirkman, Adlard and Rathburn's *The Walking Dead VIII: Made to Suffer*

Marinetti's 'words-in-freedom', acousmatic products of the 'wireless imagination', connect to each other telegraphically rather than syntactically. We have previously explored his hostility to syntax. Words act on each other through their lines of force, the energies of sound and sense that they let loose. Of syntax Marinetti writes: 'We must suppress this intermediary so that literature can directly enter into the universe and become one body with it' (Rainey, 2005, 19). With Futurism, art dedicates itself to the immediacy of the present, of the circumambient, to the ephemerality of the lived environment. To this aesthetic agenda, onomatopoeia is central: 'Whence the bold introduction of onomatopoeic harmonies to render all the sounds and noises of modern life, even the most cacophonous', as Marinetti puts it (Rainey, 2005, 32).

About onomatopoeia in a Futurist context, we need to say four things. First, onomatopoeia parallels in language Luigi Russolo's art of noises in music ('The Art of Noises: A Futurist Manifesto', 1913); Russolo proposes the creation of an acoustic art derived from, but not passively imitative of, the noises of city and countryside, an anti-music, just as one might say that onomatopoeia is an anti-language. Just as one might ask where noises fit into a certain system of tonality, into a pattern of intervals and durations, into a musical metre, so one might ask what part of speech an onomatopoeia is. It is classified as an interjection. We hear the interjections of the world around us; and some are mightily prolonged. The grammar-book tells us that interjections do not 'enter into syntactic relations' (Quirk, Greenbaum, Leech and Svartvik, 1985, 853), are 'grammatically peripheral', 'peripheral to the language system itself', using sounds which do not otherwise occur in the language. This 'expressive vocalizing' (Quirk, Greenbaum, Leech and Svartvik, 1985, 74), whether of humanity, nature, or machine, is also 'associated with nonsystematic features such as extra lengthening and wide pitch range' (853). These latter phenomena – extra lengthening and wide pitch range – are what Marinetti treats under the heading 'free expressive orthography': 'Further, our lyrical intoxication must be free to deform and reshape words, cutting them, lengthening them, reinforcing their centers or their extremities, increasing or diminishing the number of vowels and consonants... This instinctive deformation of words corresponds to our natural tendency to use onomatopoeia' (Rainey, 2005, 34). One should just add that, for the Futurists, speed, too, is an important agent of acoustic distortion.

My second point is that the promotion of onomatopoeia is a symptom of the Futurists' cultivation of intuitive empathies with organic and inorganic matter: 'To capture the breath, the sensibility, and the instincts of metals, stones, woods and so on, through the medium of free objects and capricious motors. To substitute for human psychology now exhausted, **the lyrical obsession with matter**' (Rainey, 2005, 18; bold in original). This movement towards the inner life of matter entails, as Marinetti here indicates, the dissolution or multiplication of human identity.

My third observation is that onomatopoeia, intuitive relationships with organic and inorganic matter, all point in the direction of the multi-sensory and the synaesthetic. And Futurist dynamism itself becomes one of the agents of the blending of materials and their sensory manifestations. In his argument for a painting of sounds, noises and smells, Carlo Carrà argues that, to get sounds, noises and smells into painting, we need, among other things, to increase the dynamic and vibratory features of colour, which Carrà represents onomatopoeically:

THE PAINTING OF SOUNDS, NOISES AND SMELLS DESIRES:
1. Reds, rrrrreds, the rrrrrreddest rrrrrrreds that shouuuuuuut.
2. Greens, that can never be greener, greeeeeeeeeeeens, that screeeeeeeam, yellows, as violent as can be; polenta yellows, saffron yellows, brass yellows. (Apollonio, 1973, 112)

If we are to translate towards the environment, then this quotation from Carrà immediately suggests two further moves for the translator. We should seek to translate the non-onomatopoeic into the onomatopoeic, or, put another way, to project the non-onomatopoeic as onomatopoeic. And, relatedly, we need to develop an onomatopoeia of the other senses. This might grow out of kinds of onomatopoeia experimented with by Marinetti, in particular what he calls indirect, complex and analogical onomatopoeia (syntheses of a whole range of sense-data) or abstract onomatopoeia ('noisy, unconscious expression of the most complex and mysterious motions of our sensibility') (Apollonio, 1973, 158). Alternatively, one might typographically manipulate non-onomatopoeic words, in order to achieve a maximal, more inclusive sensory vividness. If I write, for example:

TTt àᴨᴨ~bb~L (ə

what might one conclude about the table's physical condition, its style, size, stability and so on? About its smell and colour and sound when struck? Or about the family that sits round it? Or about the dishes that have been served on it? In a world of free expressive orthography, how should one write or print words in order to get the most out of them? The synaesthetic experience that words are full of will perhaps only emerge if coaxed out by typographic versatility.

My fourth and final point is one addressed in the previous chapter, albeit in relation to different materials. What kind of performance, what style of voice, would be appropriate to the Futurist vision of words in freedom, permeated by onomatopoeic intrusions? Fortunately, Marinetti has left us an answer, in his manifesto on 'Dynamic and Synoptic Declamation' of March, 1916. Here Marinetti continues to insist on the sinking of the lyric 'I', the speaker's identity, in the energies of the words-in-freedom themselves, so that, not surprisingly, two of the guidelines for declamation read: 'Completely dehumanize [the] voice, systematically doing away with every modulation and nuance'; and 'Metallize, liquefy, vegetalize, petrify, and electrify [the] voice, grounding it in the vibrations of matter itself as expressed by words-in-freedom' (Flint, 1972, 144). The declaimer will be able to accompany himself on all manner of 'elementary' instruments (hammers, saws, bells, horns, etc.) to help with the production of ono-matopoeias and should concentrate his gestures on geometrical shapes, to create the right kind of lines-of-force dynamic: 'Gesticulate geometrically, thereby giving [the] arms the sharp rigidity of semaphore signals and light-house rays, to indicate the direction of forces, or of pistons and wheels, to express the dynamism of words-in-freedom' (Flint, 1972, 144).

To reformulate translation as an eco-activity, to translate towards the environmental, we need also to think anthropologically and ethnographi-cally. In her exploration of the linguistic habits of the Runa, from the upper Amazonian region of Ecuador, Janis Nuckolls (2004, 65–85) singles out their use of onomatopoeia, or ideophones, that is, the expression of sensory alignment with the natural world through performative utterances; ideophones 'provide Runa with a linguistic medium for modelling and con-structing nonlinguistic natural processes' (65–6). Is our own language still capable of being driven by these kinds of animistic impulse? As Nuckolls points out (84), within our own social structure, there are already different ideophonic ranges for different cultural areas – for children, for example, or for the comic strips we have already explored – and these we perhaps ought to extend and diversify. It is not, however, just a question of finding the language, but also of entering the space of the sound to be made and becoming as it were the source of that sound.[6] The Runa achieve this en-vironmental immersion by exploiting the enunciatory flexibility of words, that is, by adopting affective forms of intonation, or by vocally sculpting the word (by elongation, segmentation, varying loudness), in the manner of Marinetti's 'free expressive orthography'. In this way, they can capture not only sounds, but other environmental sensations, including patterns of movement.

In her discussion of Runa ideophones, Nuckolls uses the example of a jaguar licking itself: 'Licking his whole body *illung illung illung* he sits there calmly.' As Nuckolls points out, the repeated *illung* is non-syntactic and semantically redundant. But it is only seemingly redundant, because its function is not in fact semantic, but what Nuckolls calls 'semiotic' (2004, 73). I would much prefer to call it 'phenomenological', for while, in truth, for the Runa, it may belong to a *coded system* of ideophones, I want to imagine an ideophonic usage which is less answerable to shared codes than to a perceptual contact which, each time, must find its own way to expression, by bodily empathy (gesture, facial expression, vocal shaping). And if the semantic is doubled by the phenomenological, might the phenomenological not come to displace the semantic?

Here I must passingly broach an issue which is crucial, but which I have no space to do justice to, namely: what is the relationship between language as an object of perception, and language as an instrument of perception? Onomatopoeia holds out the promise of language as the instrument of perception, of language as a direct corridor to an experience of ambience. But much of our previous argument and analysis – our exploration of enumeration and 'and' in 'Adlestrop', for example, or our investigation of phonemic interactivity in Rilke's 'Voller Apfel' – has been connected with the perceptual richness of linguistic experience itself, and our proposal has been that this adventure in psycho-physiological perception is more rewarding for reading, is more productive for language, than semantics and the processes of interpretation. Lying behind this question of divided perceptual loyalty, or of perceptual bifocalism, is the bifocalism of writing itself: writing as a transcriptive medium – but able to transcribe non-human sounds and noises, as well as human speech – and writing as a matrix, as a matricial medium, able to generate neologism and new sensory experience out of its own materials. The transcriptive brings the world into language, while the matricial takes language into the world. And for the linguistic idealist – and, after all, it must be emphasised that, for us, translation is primarily translation towards a linguistic utopia – the interaction of the two faces of language, transcriptive and matricial, is essential to language's ecological wholeness, its ability to both contribute, and do justice, to the world.

In trying to imagine a translational model which might do justice to our thoughts about onomatopoeia, about the relocation of the onomatopoeic in the non-onomatopoeic, about a multi-sensory onomatopoeia, about onomatopoeia as an exercise in sound alignment with the environment, about onomatopoeia as an agent of relationships with the non-human, and in trying to find a layout which would capture not only the simultaneity of multiplied perception, and of multiple planes of experience, but also the dynamism which is the instrument of ramification and fusion, I have chosen what Marinetti describes as 'multilineal lyricism': 'On several parallel lines, a poet will launch several chains of colors, sounds, odors, noises, weights, densities, analogies. One line, for example, might be olfactory, another musical, another pictorial' (Rainey, 2005, 33). I have translated a sentence from Guy de Maupassant's story 'La Femme de Paul' (1881), which describes the behaviour of the male frequenters of the celebrated riverside *guinguette*, or open-air dance-café, 'La Grenouillère' (Fig. 9). Marinetti suggests that the multilineal lyricist should use the lines as a descending scale of conspicuousness, and that correspondingly the different degrees of foregrounding should be reflected in typefaces of different boldness and size. My own practice is only relatively true to Marinetti's precepts. And I have introduced two features which do not figure in Marinetti's plans. The first is a purely calligraphic line (the third line) which is traced by the reader as he/she speaks the text. It captures the movement of the men in the movement of reading itself; or, more accurately put perhaps, it tracks the reader's kinaesthetic relationship with the unfolding text, which corresponds to the muscular movements of the men depicted by the text. This doodling is the calligraphic vocalisation of a sequence of psycho-physiological events produced by the readerly 'in-bodying' of text.

I have also introduced two lines of phoneme patterning from the two texts, ST and TT, in the fifth and seventh lines. The purpose of this tactic is twofold. First, I want to maintain the bifocalism of which we have just spoken: whereas other lines attempt to generate a sensory ambience beyond language, as if we might become, like spectators of film, participants in an ongoing action, despite the past tense of the verb, these two lines are a here and now of apprehension of text, a here and now of the mouth and ear which do not just read the text, but re-improvise it, or hear into it, or hear with differential focusing. And one of the things that is heard is the inarticulacy at the heart of languages, an inarticulacy which lets loose a certain drunkenness, a certain 'need for noise natural to brutes'. This recovery of pure vocalisation, this resurgence of preverbal drives, the nonsense of sense, reminds us that speaking can be a pretext, or cover, for the exercise of more primal, psycho-phonetic kinds of orality.

Second, I wish to come back to that sense, encountered in Rilke, that where two languages share the same alphabet, translation allows sounds to drift from one language into another, although not in the same doses and

Les hommes, le chapeau en arrière, la face rougie, avec des yeux
The men, their hats tipped back on their heads, faces flushed, with

crimsonbluecrimsongreycrimsoncrimsonbrownbloodshotbrown

l - - - ----- l-- a-- -- a-- la fa --- aV-- --

sweatpomadebeercolognewinecigarette smokedustcolognedust

—-_e- - Ha t t- _ ba —__ - He_f- fl - -
CRRUNSPISSPIOUUUGHWHUMPWHUDDDCRUNNSKII

luisants d'ivrognes, s'agitaient en vociférant par un besoin de
the glassy eyes of drunks, barged about shouting, with that need

crimsongreyblue brown   bloodshot   ruddy

l i ----iV ___ --------a - - -------V f _----a ____ -------- --

breathbeerbeerbreath(carnation)   perspiration   garlic wine

__ - l/a:/ _—- - - b/a:/ b/au/-_/au/t - -_ — t n
TRIFDGSTXHOWOWKWNNEELEAAGHGHGHUFFFOSOL

tapage naturel aux brutes.
for noise natural to brutes.

florid rubescent   fauve

--a_a__--a /y/   /y/

aniseed   sweat   cologne

f-- n _ -_n t —t _b_t
YTDFLJDHJSGGGAAA

Figure 9 'Multilineal' translation of a sentence from Maupassant's 'La Femme de Paul'

combinations. This is, of course, the basis of homophonic (or perhaps, better, allophonic) translation, the translation of the sounds of the source language into closely related sounds in the target language. We might thus maintain that translation reconstructs the acoustic material of language, the material of the language of the ST. Translation, as we have already intimated in our second chapter, vocally engages with Barthes's 'grain of the voice', the pronunciatory function of raw bodily engagement, as much as with the articulatory function which gives expressivity to meanings already arrived at. As I shift from French to English, I in effect change bodies. As the reader shifts from French to English, he/she in effect moves from one manifestation of his/her voice's physiology and temperament, of its habits and variations, to another, a task both eased and complicated by those phonetic elements common to both languages.

The ambience I try to capture through this multilineal translation is, strictly speaking, the ambience within the fiction. But because of the manner of its presentation, it could easily have its source in the real world; the techniques of collage, fragment, juxtaposition, facilitate this oscillation between the real and fictional. The presence of the ambient in text has less to do with its representation than with its incorporation; the ambient is not the subject of the text, but interjections, fragments, interruptions within the text. The ambient, inextricably bound up with the devices of collage and montage, becomes part of the writerly or textual medium itself. One writes with one's environment locked into one's writerly practice.

CHAPTER 4

Translating the textual environment (2)

In assessing the relationship between text and environment, or text and ambience, this far, we have concerned ourselves primarily with the infiltration of text by elements of ambience, elements which, to use our comic-strip example, resonate with a world beyond the frame of the text, elements which attempt to install some kind of direct trace of external reality. This gives us three broad tasks to complete in this chapter: (i) to examine the exfiltration of literary works into the environment; (ii) to re-consider the relationship between the written and the spoken; and (iii) to draw some threads together by distinguishing between transmissional translation and survival translation.

Before taking the step forward into what I am calling exfiltration, we need to take a step back. In treating the infiltration of ambience into text, we have considered collage and onomatopoeia or ideophonic writing, but we have not imagined what this might mean for the status of the original text. I therefore re-present Shakespeare's 'No longer mourn for me...', first in its full, uninvaded form:

> No longer mourn for me when I am dead
> Than you shall hear the surly sullen bell
> Give warning to the world that I am fled
> From this vile world with vilest worms to dwell.
> Nay, if you read this line, remember not
> The hand that writ it, for I love you so
> That I in your sweet thoughts would be forgot
> If thinking on me then should make you woe.
> O, if, I say, you look upon this verse,
> When I, perhaps, compounded am with clay,
> Do not so much as my poor name rehearse,
> But let your love even with my life decay;
>   Lest the wise world should look into your moan,
>   And mock you with me after I am gone.

and then just its first eight lines, after they have undergone exposure to an environment:

> No longer mourn Oh, did you? I am dead
> Than you aha per tum per tum per tum
> Don't push me to the world . . . compassion . . . fled
> (Scre(cre-creakk)ech) with Toby! worms (cough) dwell
> Nay, if you bbffbaashovffel remember whud
> The hand tippa(phut)tippa(phut)tippa I love With cream?
> So lumpy . . . your sweet thoughts RONSEAL LOCTITE
> If thinking on me krra krra chak-chak woe

This kind of skeletalised or eroded text is one that translation can peculiarly produce, first because translation, in the translational ethos of this book, only comes to sense in coexistence with its original; it never replaces that original – that only happens in those instances of interlingual translation designed for readers ignorant of the source language (SL); and secondly because translation, as presented here, is translation into a vivid here and now. So I have moved a Shakespearean sonnet, a late sixteenth-century example of fixed-form writing, into an environment in which it is always intruded upon. But these intrusions do not destroy the text; they radically re-orientate it.

It is not usual for us to think of the text as vulnerable to time. Locked safely in an object, the book, infinitely reprintable, we look upon the text as a refuge from time and its pressures. But, as we have already observed, both reading and translation bring the text into time, and not only into time, but into space, too, the space of reading and of translating. The here and now that translation thus constructs delivers the text to the instantaneous and potentially simultaneous. Translation becomes a snapshot, a sliver of time, captured, however, in the potential totality of space. The sliver of time radiates out to infinity and gathers that infinity back into itself, even if we see only the smallest portion. Where did these interjected words, phrases and sounds come from? Perhaps one was from Vancouver, another from a pub in Castle Rising, and a third from a bus-stop in Aberdeen? In order to give the text more opportunity to live out its spatial simultaneities and instantaneous textual re-orientations, I need to give it a tabular disposition (Fig. 10).

So the Shakespearean text operates as a kind of spider's web for incoming sensory information. In this sense, it acts to integrate the world, even at the expense of its own text. The incoming matter is sometimes language direct from the environment (conversation, product names), sometimes acoustic

No   n   I am
long   *Oh,*   dead
er   *did*
mour   *you?*

Than you *aha* **per tum per tum**

per tum

                                              Toby!
                                              worms
Don't push   **(Scr**   **(cough)**
me to the   **e**(cre-
world...   **creakk)e**   dwell
compassion   **ch)**
... fled   *with*

Nay, if you   **vff**l remember
ebbffbaasho   whud

                        *So lumpy...*your sweet
    The hand   thoughts **RONSEAL**
tippa(**phut**)tippa(**ph
ut**)tippa I love *With*

                                    LOCTITE

                cream?
    If   chak-chak
thinking on   woe
me **krra krra**

Figure 10 Translation, with environmental noise, of Shakespeare's Sonnet 71

material translated by the writer into imitative language. The structure of Sonnet 71 is, then, an orchestration of ambience, and at the same time a text trying to survive against an overwhelming tide of invasive noise. The failure of the Shakespearean text to establish itself as the primary text turns it, equally, into snippets of overheard speech; it shares the same status as its interruptions. In this sense, the whole text is somewhere else.

But this leaves us with two searching questions. Why is this sound-scape necessary to this Shakespearean text? Because translation is not a transmission of texts as they are, but a tireless interrogation of their textual complacency, a determination constantly to reintegrate them into a reading environment understood more ecologically than culturally. Sound-scapes position the reader, heighten our sense of readerly consciousness and perception, and dramatise the process of listening.

The second question is: but is this not simply a standard literary text, with alphabetised sounds absorbed into it and with the Shakespearean original used citationally, to produce piquant and playful juxtapositions: 'So lumpy . . . your sweet thoughts RONSEAL LOCTITE', 'I love with cream?', 'Thinking on me' associated with bird-calls? These juxtapositions may raise a momentary smirk, but the effect is soon played out. It is true that I am a victim of my lack of time and resource: I should have recorded a reading of the sonnet and then, over that, ambient noises and snippets of conversation. The only way, for the moment, that I can draw away from the literarisation of materials is by calling once again upon collage to underline the importedness and the dissociatedness of the ambient noise (Fig. 11). I do not want this text to be interpreted, to be reduced to a sequence of jokey meanings. I want it to be infected with the sensory and experiential, as irrepressible elements in, as integral constituents of, the ongoingness of the text.

As we move from infiltration of environment into text, to exfiltration of text into environment, we move from performance in the text to performance of the text. The kind of performance we envisage is an extension of performed poetry as we already know it. A 'text' is projected into a *group of people*, not, I hasten to emphasise, an *audience* and all that that implies of concerted attention with a shared objective, but a group of people, random elements of the sociosphere. The 'text' is also projected into an acoustic, and into a sound field. What such a performance is attempting to do is break down those performance conventions in which recital of script, in conditions of minimal sound and movement, projects a psychologically unified speaking persona or ego and/or the interpretation of the text's meaning. The minimisation of sound and movement in such recitals is designed to

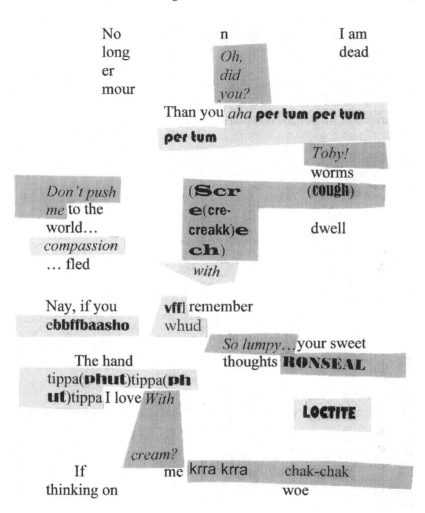

Figure 11 Fig. 10, with collage

produce a concentration and sacralisation of listening, a listening called 'rapt', which naturally edits out all material which interferes with auditory absorption of the words of the reciter. Our view of listening, on the other hand, is one that edits in; a listening which multiplies its attentions and in so doing improvises with auditory phenomena, constructs the text within an acoustic envelope, with ever-changing patterns of foregrounding and spatial distribution. Performance of a text is not just a projection of a text into an environment, but also an elicitation of what lies in the environment beyond the text.[1] This implies that environments for performance might be more actively prepared, with much more attention paid to ambient input and its potential expressive effects, than has been usual hitherto.

As an earlier example of this kind of performance, we might cite Antonin Artaud's *Pour en finir avec le jugement de dieu* [To Have Done with the Judgement of God] (2003). This piece, or collection of pieces, was designed for radio broadcast by four voices, two male and two female (Roger Blin, Artaud, Maria Casarès and Paule Thévenin), accompanied by various sound effects: cries, chants, recorded sounds, percussion, including xylophone. The radio, as in the hands of Marinetti, offers particular expressive opportunities: the voice can be detached from a vocal source, from a specific utterer, so that it can become *the* human voice, or an infinitely transferable resource; furthermore, voice thus de-psychologised, de-subjectivised, can become a purely physiological instrument, organic energy, that is to say, its meaning will lie less in the sense of its discourse than in its value as interjection, vociferation, expostulation, remonstration, emission, ejaculation – the vocal counterpart of the secretions, excretions and emanations of the body. But, actually, this translation into performance, of texts dictated by Artaud for the purpose, a performance due for broadcast on 2 February 1948, but blocked at the last minute by the Managing Director of Radiodiffusion française, Wladimir Porché, might have been better served by a performance of the preparatory sketches which Artaud made for this broadcast, the provisionally finished, the half-finished, and the half-started. In these preparatory sketches, Artaud more consistently resorts to glossolalia, which we might call 'phonetic doodling' (2003, 118):

> **agnagna**
> **rabuda**
> **kabadia**
> **abah**
> **agnagna**
> **rabudia**
> **kobadia**
> **krrrrrebufa**
> **krrrrrrebadia**
> **abah**
> **krrrrramagna**
> **krrrrremufe**
> **agnagna**
> **rabuda**
> **abadia**

and to that dialect he calls 'le langage auvergnat' [Auvergne patois] or 'le langage charabia' [Double Dutch] (2003, 125):

> Fu fe tou fais, outo, quand tou fais ça,
> tu enlèves les zesprits d'oun l'air,
> alors t'es pas ancore gari, tou crois encou aux zesprits.
>
> Jou vous dit que lo vie est malade,
> lo vi est très malade.

I say this because such a performance would chime better both with what performance means for us and what theatre means for Artaud, to wit: the capturing of that 'impulsion psychique secrète qui est la Parole d'avant les mots' (1964, 91) [secret psychic impulse which is the Word prior to words], the revelation of the repressed, the escape from the expressly devised script into the drives of the actorly body (which 'agit' [acts] rather than 'joue' [play-acts]), the translation of text into renewable textual materials. And, as in all Artaud's practice, we must recall another underlying preoccupation: to encourage words to expand beyond themselves, not only into pronunciation and intonation as forces acting dissociatively on the spectator's sensibility, but also into the visual: 'C'est ici qu'intervient, en dehors du langage auditif des sons, le langage visuel des objets, des mouvements, des attitudes, des gestes, mais à condition qu'on prolonge leur sens, leur physionomie, leurs assemblages jusqu'aux signes, en faisant de ces signes une manière d'alphabet' (1964, 138) [What intervenes here, beyond the auditory language of sounds, is the visual language of objects, movements, attitudes, gestures, but on condition that one extends their meaning, their physiognomy, their combinations into signs, making these signs into a kind of alphabet].

The important protagonists in the performance are not the voice simply – as if the voice were some unproblematic, unified instrument – but the voice's timbre, its enunciatory clarity, its respiration, and beyond that the speaker's body, gestures, positions, attitudes, and the props, and the space, and the ambient acoustic. In his account of the international festival of *Phonetische Poesie*, held in Vienna (4–6 February 1983), Bernard Heidsieck feels bound to provide performance portraits, descriptions of the poets in action, their behavioural idiosyncrasies, which he calls the 'plus factor' of performance (2001, 259–71); he prefaces these portraits with this justification:

Mon propos se voudrait de tenter donc, de montrer ici, ce que fut sur scène, pour chacun d'eux, ce '+ ça' venu se coller à leurs textes ou leur travail, cette part, en somme, physique ou visuelle, qui, au-delà de ces derniers, ou de ce dernier, fournit à chacun son label ou sa marque de fabrique. C'est ce '+' précisément, qui permet au Poème, extrait, arraché à la page, ou à la bande, de se tenir debout, à la verticale, face au public, qui dans l'instant, le colore, l'anime et le fait vivre. (2001, 259)

[My intention, then, would be to try to show, here, what, for each of them on the stage, that 'plus factor' was, which attached itself to their texts or to their work, that factor, in short, physical or visual, which, in addition to the texts or to the work, provided each with his label or trademark. It is this 'plus factor' precisely, which allows the Poem, extracted, torn from the page, or from the tape, to stand upright, vertical, facing the public, which, in that moment, colours it, animates it and brings it to life.]

It might seem that the kinds of thing I speak of here are already well embedded, in the performances of adepts of sound poetry or concrete poetry, in poetry slams, and other happenings;[2] and that would be true. But there are important elements missing. One element, as we have already intimated, is the cultivation of a new kind of listening. Just as we distinguished, in the opening chapters, between two broad currents of reading, the hermeneutic and the constructivist, so we might apply this same distinction to listening. Hermeneutic listening is a listening that is directed and purposeful, its objectives recognition and decipherment. It is neither participatory nor interactive. Constructivist listening, however, is. Constructivist listening is improvisatory, dispersed, volatile, permutational. It does not listen for meaning, but rather for the processes of meaning-making; it listens not for signifieds, but for the dynamics of signifiers. Just as in avant-garde music, music is made, composed, not beforehand, in a score, on paper, but in the listening ear, so too with text. The ear hears not just rhythm and intonation and tempo, but also timbre, acoustic proximities and distances, accompanying noise and the resonances of space; the ear disposes sounds, segments them, groups them. The ear also listens the visual – movement, gesture and so on – into the acoustic.

A second element that needs to be added concerns critical consequence. A text projected in the way imagined here is, at present, no part of translation studies and no part of literary criticism, though it is part of performance studies. This may look like a call to abandon literary criticism and encourage readers to become stage-directors and impresarios instead. In a sense it is. All students of literature should have a training in practical drama, for perhaps three reasons: first, in order to understand clearly the symbiotic relationship between the linguistic and the somatic – the theatre is where utterance issues from everything, including the mouth, as Artaud might put it; second, in order to master the arts of improvisation, so necessary to constructivist reading, constructivist listening and constructivist performance; third, and most important of all, to understand the gulf that exists between the written text (the script) and the performed/oral text (the dict). We might itemise some of the more evident differences:

(i) In oral contexts, sounds inevitably have more materiality, since the body is more thoroughly involved in their production.

(ii) In oral contexts, there is inevitable vocal distortion (Fónagy, 1971), such that the perceived semantics of a word is more fully produced by the enunciation of the word than by its dictionary definition.

(iii) Because of the temporality of the oral text, sounds come into existence and evanesce, and are thus not as structurally significant as they are in the printed text, where they can more easily be plotted. In the oral rendering, memory and anticipation are more important.

(iv) Sound's relation to rhythm changes. When one identifies rhythm in relation to printed text, syllables make their contribution to rhythm by virtue of being either weak or strong, not by virtue of the sound they make. In the oral world, the gamut of rhythmic elements is increased by paralinguistic input (intonation, tempo, pausing, degree of stress), so that sounds are involved in a correspondingly wider range of sound-effects and thus in a wider range of connotative operations.

(v) In oral production, acoustic elements are the vehicles of the qualities of the performing voice. About the relationship between a poem and the particular physiological qualities of a performing voice, criticism has nothing to say. But for a live audience, this relationship is certainly significant, and it very well may be that the text is, as it were, invested with, informed by, the psychic drives and temperamental features reckoned by the listener to characterise the performing voice.

My final foray into the field of exfiltration is rather more speculative and projective, and moves out of the performance venue and into the wide world. Here I wish to consider two methods of implanting text in environment. Both continue the acoustic theme, but in the second, acousticity has a more metaphorical application.

To introduce the first method, I want to focus briefly on the Vancouver-based World Soundscape Project of the 1970s,[3] led by R. Murray Schafer, which gathered urban and rural soundscapes and devised different methods of measuring, collecting and enjoying ambient sound (see, e.g., 1977b). This project was also referred to as 'soundscape ecology', 'acoustic ecology' and 'acoustic design'. The project's interest in 'macro-cultural composition, of which man and nature are the composer/performers' (1977a, 102) had, as a spin-off, the keeping of sound-diaries, e.g. from Peter Huse's diary, [13 March] 1975:

Sounds heard at Jung's house in Bollingen: traffic on highway, 70 meters above on hillside – gentle ripple of Zürich lake from passing rumble of a barge – coots and other birds – swish, screech of electric train passing beside the highway – roar across lake from an industrial village. Trying to imagine the relative quiet of the place when Jung began to build his house here in the 20's. (1977a, 24)

Another spin-off was the devising of soundwalks, walks 'composed' with a view to maximising encounters with interesting and varied sounds. The Louvre soundwalk (Schafer 1977a, 86–91) asks walkers to listen to paintings. The hour-long Stuttgart soundwalk (1977a, 95–9) operates with the following thematic categories: human, ambience and reverberation, electroacoustic, doors and transitions, and, finally, imagination (e.g. '*Schillerplatz*. Stand at the base of the poet's statue and imagine the sounds Schiller himself may have heard here at the beginning of the 19th century' (1977a, 96)). The Vienna soundwalk (1977a, 83–5) contains invitations such as:

10. Main Post Office, 19 Fleischmarkt.
(a) Enjoy the squeaky doors as people come and go.
(b) Two more great grates, before these doors. Scrape them to compare their tone colours. (1977a, 84)

My second contributory factor is Henri Lefebvre's writings on 'rhythmanalysis' (2004), that analysis of everyday life through the rhythms it generates, not just the rhythms of objects, movements, activities themselves, but also the rhythms set up between them. At the origin of the apprehension of circumambient rhythms is the polyrhythmia of the human body itself. Although one might attempt to capture the rhythms of a place (street, square, town) or of a time (the media day, periods of history), rhythms themselves are born of the interactions of time and space. Lefebvre's ambitions are as exciting as they are unmanageable; he develops classificatory coordinates – linear, cyclical and 'appropriated' time; mechanical v. organic rhythms; eurhythmia, polyrhythmia, arrhythmia, isorhythmia – but the difficulty of systematising their application, of coping with differences of scale (macrocosmic, microcosmic) seems almost insurmountable. Rhythmanalysis works better perhaps as the instrument of highly localised investigations, rather than as a principle that might encompass and organise social totalities.

But our present concern is with ways of expanding the experience of reading by reconnecting the activity of textual assimilation with an environment, through the practice of translation. When we think of reading in the light of Lefebvre and Murray Schafer, we have to think about it as something that asks us where we are (in time and space), what our position is, and how the rhythms and sounds of reading might relate and contribute to the rhythms and sounds of the reading milieu, and beyond. And it might be translation's task to record and embody that particular position within time and space, and within the rhythmic network that generates and locates that position.

For example, Thomas Nashe's 'Song/In Time of Pestilence' (Quiller-Couch, 1927, 202–3), from *Summer's Last Will and Testament* (1600), might be taken for outings, to re-establish its place in the rhythms of the sociosphere, the *Umwelt*:

> Adieu, farewell earth's bliss!
> This world uncertain is:
> Fond are life's lustful joys,
> Death proves them all but toys.
> None from his darts can fly;
> I am sick, I must die –
> > *Lord, have mercy on us!*
>
> Rich men, trust not in wealth,
> Gold cannot buy you health;
> Physic himself must fade;
> All things to end are made;
> The plague full swift goes by;
> I am sick, I must die –
> > *Lord, have mercy on us!*
>
> Beauty is but a flower
> Which wrinkles will devour;
> Brightness falls from the air;
> Queens have died young and fair;
> Dust hath closed Helen's eye;
> I am sick, I must die –
> > *Lord, have mercy on us!*
>
> Strength stoops unto the grave,
> Worms feed on Hector brave;
> Swords may not fight with fate;
> Earth still holds ope her gate;
> *Come, come!* the bells do cry;
> I am sick, I must die –
> > *Lord, have mercy on us!*
>
> Wit with his wantonness
> Tasteth death's bitterness;
> Hell's executioner
> Hath no ears for to hear

What vain art can reply;
I am sick, I must die –
Lord, have mercy on us!

Haste therefore each degree
To welcome destiny;
Heaven is our heritage,
Earth but a player's stage.
Mount we unto the sky;
I am sick, I must die –
Lord, have mercy on us!

The poem's own rhythms shift, predominantly between juxtaposed amphimacers (/ x / / x /), when the line has a medial caesura ('I am sick, I must die', 'Queens have died young and fair', 'Hath no ears for to hear'), and dactyl + amphimacer (/ x x / x /) when it does not ('None from his darts can fly', 'Gold cannot buy you wealth', 'Swords may not fight with fate'); but in the fourth stanza we begin to feel the need to stress the first two syllables of the line, then to shift into a double iamb (/ / x / x /):

Strength stoops unto the grave;
Worms feed on Hector brave;
...
Earth still holds ope her gate;
Come, come! the bells do cry.

The refrain is trochaic.

I turn to Nashe not altogether innocently. I have often wondered whether I should keep my own sound-journal of Nashe in different urban settings. Then, thinking of its pressing but syncopated rhythms, and the return of the refrain, thinking, too, of Auden's 'Night Mail' and its relation to rap, I pondered two further possibilities: that, just as one sets poems to music, one might set poems to cars, to trains, to water dripping into a bucket, to wind swirling through the branches; and that I might make a sound-journal of Nashe on different trains – Nashe on the 2.25 from Norwich to Yarmouth, Nashe on the 16.14 from Durham to Edinburgh; Nashe on the 20.42 freight train from Ely to March. I then thought that I might make use of a translation of Nashe which would imagine his text with a very different set of rhythmic variables, not syllables, but letters, graphemes, and therefore very different principles of environmental embedding. I turned to George MacBeth's LDMN analysis of the poem in his collection *The Night of Stones* (1968, 72–3):

D, LL   L,
LD NN   ,
ND   L LLL   ,
D   M LL   ,
NN M   D N L,
M   , M D:
        LD   M N .

MN,   N N L,
LD NN   L,
ML M D.
LL N, ND MD,
L LL   ,
M   , M D :
        LD   M N .

L,
NL LL D,
N LL M   ,
N   DD N, ND ,
D   LD   LN .
M   , M   D :
        LD   M N .

N   N ,
M D N   ,
D M N   ,
LL LD   .
M, M, LL D .
M   , M D :
        LD   M N .

NN ,
D N :
L N,
N
N N L.
M   ,   M D:
        LD   M N .

D,
LM   DN :
N   ,
L ,
MN   N .
M   ,   M D:
        LD   M N .

Many have expressed opinions about the expressive or pictographic values of letter-shapes. One of the classic expressions of graphemic sensitivity is to be found in a letter written by Victor Hugo on 24 September 1839 as he travelled from Geneva to Aix-les-Bains (1971, 715–16). He provides interpretations of all the letters of the alphabet, except for the non-French characters K and W. L is the leg and foot; D is the back; M is a mountain or a camp, two adjoining tents; N is a closed door with a bar running diagonally across it. Hugo has large cultural-historical ambitions for letter-shapes: all human activities, disciplines, institutions, are encapsulated in the alphabet: war, justice, geometry, astronomy, the animal kingdom, and so on. The alphabet is the book of human existence. Hugo's account of Nashe's letters will do very well as visual fragments of pestilential times and remind us again what influence upon the acoustic realisation of a poem visual paralanguage may have. Nashe's third stanza, on beauty queens and Helen, also brings to mind Vitezslav Nezval's *Abeceda* (1926) (typography by Karel Teige), in which a female dancer strikes different poses which 'sympathise' with the letter shapes, or Erté's 'feminised' alphabet of 1976.

But I needed another translation, I needed to escape from the graphic back to the phonetic, from the static back to the rhythmic, and that entails abandoning capitals in favour of lower case:

```
æd,  I            I!
      ld   n    n :
nd   I   I I    ,
d          m   I .
n n  m  d  æn  I;
  æm  ,   m  d –
      I d, æ m n !


m n    n  n      I,
ld  æn           I ;
      m   I m     d;
I      nd    m d ;
  I   I              ;
æm  ,     m  d –
      I d, æ m n !


                    I
      I    I     d ;
  n  I   m        ;
  n  æ  d d    ænd ;
d   æ   I  d   I n  ;
```

æm , m   d –
    I d, æ m n !

          n,
m   d   n   ;
d   m n   ;
  I   Id   ;
m, m ! I d ;
æm ,   m   d –
    I d, æ m n !

        n   nn
    d   n ;
I   n
æ n
    n   æn I;
æm ,   m d –
    I d, æ m n !

      d
I   m d   n ;
n   ,
    I   .
m n   n   ;
æm ,   m   d –
    I d, æ m n !

Accordingly I must sacrifice the meanings of letter-shapes, which are bestowed on capitals alone. But I can recover some of that semantic loss by adopting a new typeface, Broadway, which, like the images of Nezval and Erté, insinuates productive anachronism into the text, speaks another language and gives Helen and her ilk another kind of chance. In producing this new translation, I can also remove those graphemic n's whose phonetics is not /n/ but /ŋ/, remove double consonants where there is only one sound, and correct the odd, small errors in MacBeth's text.[4] And I can shift from MacBeth's low-key punctuation – a punctuation borrowed from Ronald McKerrow's authoritative 1904–1905 edition (1958, 282–4), but substituting commas for McKerrow's semi-colons in the first two stanzas, and adding commas in the fifth stanza – to the more heart-on-sleeve, more intrusive, more vocal, Victorian mode of punctuation in my 1927 edition of *The Oxford Book of English Verse* (ed. Arthur Quiller-Couch), where the semi-colon becomes an almost standard stop, at the expense of commas and full-stops alike. But above all I want, in moving to lower case, to avoid certain other overtones of capital letters. I present in brief tabular form what I take to be the principal differences of orientation and intention as between capitals and lower case:

CAPITAL	lower case
VISION	voice
/di:/	/də/
ORTHOGRAPHIC (N, O SPELLS NO)	phonetic
ALPHABET (GRAPHEME)	word (phonolexeme)
CRYPTOMETAPHYSICAL MEANING (SYMBOL)	contingent meaning (referent)
INITIAL (LINE OR SENTENCE)	non-initial
PROPER	common
PRIMORDIALITY	functional embedding
IDEOGRAM (ILLUMINATED CAPITAL, ERTÉ)	constitutive element

And I want to add a vowel (/æ/), too, to give some sense of the possible making of syllables, of continuities of speaking, which lower case pronunciation permits: I assume that /di:/ *spells* a capital D, while /də/ *pronounces* a lower-case d in its connection with other phonemes. This, then, is the version that I will test, in the industrial sociosphere, first, perhaps, against the dynamics of the Paris Eurostar.

Performance, whether in the text, or of the text, transforms a two-dimensional object, a text, into a three-dimensional event. How would this transformation take place as part of a land-art project? How would a literary work resculpt itself, or three-dimensionalise its textual space? It might transform itself into a cross-country configuration of readings or of scattered textual fragments. Lines 1, 7 and 10 of a sonnet by Gerard Manley Hopkins, say, might be the epigraph to a grass field; lines 2, 9 and 14 might be the graffiti on a wayside telephone box; lines 3, 8 and 11 might adorn the hides of grazing livestock; and so on. In this sense, the text would not exist within space, but would form space, a spatial envelope, dynamically conceived. Thus the text becomes a location, in a broader landscape perhaps, but setting the coordinates for its own eco-system, its own configuration of habitats, as if the Hopkinsian text were not only a set of ancestral traces, the still animating marks of itineraries and dwellings, part of the landscape's memory, but also the inhabitation of landscape by reading, reading as the restoration of language to a sensory eco-activity, reading and landscape reverberant with each other. When considered in the light of graffiti, or Ian Hamilton Finlay's garden of Little Sparta, in Lanarkshire, none of this is so fanciful.

My second mode of implantation of text in environment is a motivated and tendentious insertion, where the need for the recontextualisation of the text is the excuse for the insertion. This is to imagine soundscape or rhythmanalysis not simply as a multi-layered and interwoven dynamic, but as a network of repercussions consequent on the intrusion of the alien body. This is to suggest two things. First, not only does the introduction of any new element inevitably compel a reorganisation of the rhythms of the status quo, but the new element also needs the rhythms of the status quo to manifest itself as the force it wishes to be. The text that moves out into the environment offers itself new dimensions through the very process of its integration. R. Murray Schafer expresses it thus: 'Without the cooperation of the trees the wind would be helpless to rustle. Without the assistance of the pebbles, the brooks would not bubble . . . In other words [sounds of the past] depended on environmental feedback to give them their precise tone and character' (1974, 69). In fact, this principle applies equally to performance: recited or spoken, words discover new resonances for themselves either because of the amplifying equipment or the acoustic, or both; or perhaps, as one carries texts in one's head, or mumbles or whispers them to oneself, they set up critically interactive relationships with traffic, clocks, pneumatic drills, shoes on gratings, snippets of conversation.

Second, while it is possible to translate tendentiously or politically, whenever the translator is ideologically driven, we have in view not a tendentious translation, but a translation which looks to unsettle a status quo merely by the place or manner of its insertion. I need only briefly exemplify the action I have in mind. The poetry of Arthur Rimbaud has been inserted into the modern cultural scene by, among other things, popular music; Wallace Fowlie has written on Rimbaud in the music of Jim Morrison (1993); one might equally turn to Bob Dylan or to Patti Smith. Writers of the Beat Generation, Jack Kerouac and Kenneth Rexroth, provide another manner of Rimbaldian implantation. In my own work, I experimented with something more specific (2006, 196–202). I first made a translation of Rimbaud's fairy-tale prose-poem 'Royauté' [Royalty]:

> One fine morning, among a peace-loving people, a man
> and a woman, poised, self-assured, beautiful, loudly
> proclaimed in the public square:
> > 'Friends, I

> want

her to be queen!'

'I *want* to be queen!'
She laughed
and trembled

He told his friends of a revelation,
of an ordeal finally at an end

                                        Every now
and then
                    they fell weakly
                    against each other

And, indeed, they *were* king and queen
for a whole morning, when
                        the carmine-coloured drapes were
            hoisted on the house fronts, and throughout the
            afternoon, too,
            when
            their progress
            took them towards
                                        the
            gardens
                                of
            palms.

I then inserted it as a *fait divers* or a news-item-in-brief, into *The Sun* and the *Daily Mail* of Monday 23 July 2001. In *The Sun* (Fig. 12), the translation appears alongside a story about a girl injured in a hit-and-run incident while showing off her bridesmaid's dress and tiara, and below two stories about police officers involved in car crashes. Looked at against this accompaniment, Rimbaud's story of a temporary coronation among a peace-loving people, where individuals are allowed to enjoy their moment of sartorial splendour and popular admiration without incurring the wrath of a jealous destiny, seems as innocuous as it is pointed. And, as a prose poem, it is in excess of the news, resists all incorporation into agendas of pity, indignation, contempt, anger. What would the news be like if, like the prose poem, it failed to identify places and times and people, if it had nothing to do with motivation, implication, consequence, if its signifiers exceeded any signified and were without referents, if it were a shaggy dog story?

After this excursion into exfiltration, our next task is a reconsideration of the relationship between the written and the spoken, or 'the structural and perceptual relation between visual and auditory signs' (Jakobson, 1987,

Figure 12 Page from *The Sun* (23 July 2001), with a translation of Rimbaud's 'Royauté'

466). If we were to write a very short history of the relation between the written and the spoken, then we might pick out just two significant steps: first, of course, the invention of the printing press and all that that entailed for epistemology, cognition, the changed status of handwriting, the development of silent reading and the analysis and standardisation of language.[5] The second step, to which we have been intermittently and implicitly referring throughout these chapters, is the typographical revolution. This revolution dates from the later nineteenth century and grows out of the exploitation of expressive typography in journalism, commercial catalogues, posters and other forms of advertising, and its gradual incorporation into literary texts (Mallarmé, *Un coup de dés*, 1897). For us, the significance of this revolution lies in the ways in which the new typography can either embody verbal paralanguage, as a new notation, or produce a visual paralanguage homologous with the verbal. An ornate grapheme is as much in expressive excess of its orthographic function as the acoustic foregrounding of a phoneme is in expressive excess of its strictly phonological function.

In an essay on 'Typography' of 1932, Raoul Hausmann noted, in relation to the poetry of Dada,

Not without reason the purely phonetic was discovered which was optically supported by a novel Typography . . . It was already recognized then that the increasing need of the age for the image – thus the doubling of a text through optical illustration – was not to be solved through simple juxtaposition, but rather only through an optical construction referring back to linguistic-conceptual foundations. (quoted in Morley, 2003, 67)

The typographical revolution attempts to push vocal awareness beyond its present narrow tolerances, to mobilise the visual as a vocal prosthetics, and to relate the vocal to what the ear is capable of hearing. And it is important that we should repeat the lesson of avant-garde music in this respect, namely that composing takes place in the ear of the listener rather than on the score. The devices of collage and tabular writing, of free expressive orthography and diacritical notation, provide the reader not so much with a text as with textual materials, which the reader must listen *into* a text, must, as it were, auditorily sculpt into a text. If we remember the senses in which modern painting, Impressionism first of all, is a problematisation of looking, a problematisation of the physiology and neurology of looking, then we might better understand the senses in which modern literary texts are problematisations of reading, of seeing text and hearing text.

Just as it is not sufficiently usual to suggest that the literary may lie in qualities of vocal delivery,[6] so, equally, it is still not sufficiently usual to say that the literariness of a literary text lies in its typography. It is still not sufficiently usual to suggest that transforming a text into a new typography is a significant translational act, that typographical translation should constitute a significant branch of translation studies. Typefaces have always been signals of attitudes, mind-sets, ideologies, communicative intentions, with Times New Roman now as the default or neutral position.[7] With an expanded typographical palette, complex psychotypes and affective states can be depicted on the page, and complex psychodramas can be played out. Paradoxically, it is only when it becomes independent of the voice, a creative medium in its own right, that print can contribute afresh not only to the re-imagining of the voice, but also to the visual recording of the motions of human inwardness, and to those motions in their outward manifestations of facial expression and gesture. Marinetti had already imagined that his 'free expressive orthography' would perform this function: '7. *Free expressive orthography and typography also serve to express the facial mimicry and the gesticulation of the narrator*' ('Geometric and Mechanical Splendour and the Numerical Sensibility' (1914), in Apollonio, 1973, 157).

The exploitation of visual paralanguage within performance might indeed be pursued to the exclusion of language, so that speech becomes purely the gesture of the face. One thinks of Isidore Isou's 1959 introduction, into the programme of the Lettrists, of 'aphonisme', or 'aphonie', the silent performance of literary/musical works: '*Grosso modo* – et en attendant la publication du manifeste détaillé – *l'aphonisme* consiste dans une récitation sans émission de sons, muette' ('Le Néo-lettrisme III', Curtay, 1974, 121) [Roughly speaking – and in anticipation of the publication of the detailed manifesto – aphonism consists of a recitation without the uttering of sounds, a mute recitation]. Or one thinks of Ernst Jandl's 'Lippengedichte' [lip-poems]: 'das visuelle lippengedicht ist die umkehrung des visuellen papiergedichtes. der rezitator ist das papier des visuellen lippengedichtes. das visuelle lippengedicht wird ohne tonbildung gesprochen. es wird mit den lippen in die luft geschrieben' (1985, 10) [the visual lippoem is the reversal of the visual paper-poem. the reciter is the paper of the visual lip-poem. the visual lip-poem is not spoken aloud. it is written in the air with the lips].

Our principal concern is with the relationship between the visual and the acoustic. But we should not forget that another of our underlying preoccupations is with the multi-sensory experience that language potentially affords. We may wonder how to capture the vocal or acoustic difference between two typefaces, or between italics and bold roman, but it may be that the differentiation of smell, or of palpability, or of savour is more, or just as, relevant. And the very difficulty of making that decision should draw us to the conclusion that synaesthetic responses are the right ones. It is part of the phenomenological enterprise, after all, to rid us of 'sense atomism' (Ihde, 1976, 43–4), the isolation of the senses from each other. A text is a putting together of an integrated and total sentience; or, rather, it is translation's business to draw out of texts, make manifest, the total sentience, the total sensory gamut, which lies dormant within them, and which reading activates. To produce this overlap or mingling of the senses, translation needs to produce a field state, that is to say, a state in which focus, fringe and horizon of perception (see Ihde, 1976, 36–7) begin to blur into each other, so that perceptual experience dilates and becomes all-embracing, so that consciousness is more dispersed and receptive (see also Ma, 2009, 261–9); in a field-state text, the reader's attention is discouraged from settling on a particular spot, or from following a particular optical itinerary. One can achieve this perceptual field state by recourse to tabular text; but one can equally create it, and, at the same time, a simultaneity of sensory effect, not only by multilineal lyricism, which we have already visited, but by superimposition. By way of illustration, I come back to the text with which we started, a translation of Edward Thomas's 'Adlestrop'. For this version (Fig. 13), I have laid a sheet of calligraphic dance figures, somewhat in the manner of Henri Michaux's drawings for 'Mouvements' (1950–1951), on to music paper, and then overprinted the poem. These dance figures are both a choreography for the poem and a sequence of movements and postures which might be adopted by someone performing the poem. I have then added to the staves what is intended as a reminiscence of medieval musical notation, in changing colours. Translation is necessarily anachronistic, but it is so, usually, in one direction, that of updating and modernisation. I want to propose an anachronism in the other direction, an anachronism of archaism, which pre-dates the text. This is, by the way, no comment on the spirit of Thomas's poem, but rather is intended to capture the wonderful historical inclusiveness of our associative mechanisms.

By way of conclusion to this chapter, and working out from the observations of Walter Benjamin, I would like to identify two underlying models of translation: that of transmission and that of survival ('Überleben').[8] The translation of transmission is interested in communicating the source text (ST) just as it is, without judgement about its possible futures, pursuing a policy of fidelity, living by the criterion of reliability. If, as I wish, the

Figure 13 Translation on to music paper, with notation and superimposed calligraphic dance figures, of Fig. 1

translator can assume that the ST is already known to the reader and under-stood, then the transmissional model loses its point. The survival model is interested in transforming the ST, in an effort to capture its changing states, and to project it forward; it assumes that everything that happens to a text, as it passes through time, becomes an integral part of the text; and the translator can freely insert himself/herself into this ongoing progress of the text. The survival translation has nothing to do with reliability, and all to do with possibility, with giving the ST new options on ways of being. Its task is to make what we might have thought we knew into something unknown, linguistically disestablished, which must therefore be re-assimilated, re-acculturated, in some form or other. Survival translation thus also displaces, or re-locates, the literariness of the ST. Literariness, as an aesthetic rather than a generical value, does not inhere in the literary text, as of right; it is attributed by the reader, on the basis of the richness activated by the text in his/her own world of the imaginary, and that rich-ness may be activated by paralinguistic and typographical features as much as by linguistic ones.[9]

For me, the survival mechanism is naturally attended by other trans-formations: translation moves the linguistic of the ST towards the par-alinguistic, the silently read towards the performed; it moves the linear of the ST towards the tabular; it moves the potentially self-reflexive and atemporal of the ST towards the ambient and the instantaneous here and now; it moves the single ST towards multiple texts. To achieve these par-ticular aims, we have to multiply and extend the languages of translation: by incorporating doodling with pen and brush, the illegible, crossing out, multilineal presentation, typographical experimentation of all kinds. All this may also occur in one's own language, as intralingual translation. But even this may *feel* interlingual, either because one treats one's own language as linguistically problematic, as ripe for the release of the languages within it; or because this translation often makes desirable the crossover to other languages and the languages of other media. We must let our reading expe-rience circulate freely among languages, without feeling inhibited about proliferation.

One way of understanding this circulation among languages is provided by Seamus Heaney. Faced with the invitation to translate *Beowulf*, he temporised. He needed to find a reconciliation with the text, a way in which he could speak not only Old English and Modern English, but also Ulster English and 'Scullion' (the language of relatives of his father). It was not a question of getting from one language to another, but of finding a way 'into some unpartitioned linguistic country, a region where one's language would not be simply a badge of ethnicity or a matter of cultural preference or an official imposition, but an entry into further language' (1999, xxv). Translation is not the second best of an original language, but rather a re-orientation of language; it is not designed to be a *substitute* for a ST, for those ignorant of the SL, but the opening-up of new linguistic territory, a territory of linguistic cohabitation, for those who know the SL.[10]

I suppose that what I am trying to envisage, what I am trying to propose, is an education devoted to the establishment of a new kind of literary-critical practice. It is not a practice which can in any way do without the knowledge that literary studies has so painstakingly accumulated over the years. Without such knowledge, there is no constructivist reading, no radial reading. But that knowledge has a rather different role to play: it is no longer that by which we explain or interpret text, but rather that by which, through translation, we release text into its other lives, and into the lives of other readers.

This new practice thus gravitates towards life-studies, but, equally, it gravitates towards eco-studies. By deepening readerly response, particularly the reader's vocal and auditory capacity, through verbal and visual paralanguage, we not only extend the range of readerly consciousness, but also open up new channels of communication between the text and the world outside. Eco-criticism (see, e.g., Garrard, 2004) currently directs its attention only to texts which explicitly engage with the environment and its multiple plights. But what *we* have in mind is the ecologisation of all literature. It is by developing new ways of reading and listening and translating, that literature becomes an agent of interactive relationship with the environment.[11] Reading animates our bodies, and, with these animated bodies, we constantly re-read our way into the world.

CHAPTER 5

Translating the acousticity of voice

In Chapter 2, we considered the critical injustices done to voice, particularly by our inability, or unwillingness, to assimilate it properly into the processes of reading and performance. The printed text has produced a valorisation of the linguistic at the expense of the paralinguistic, and the exclusion of the paralinguistic, of the voice's input into the text, has, as its necessary concomitant, the exclusion of readerly autobiography and of the manifold ways in which a voice can in-body text, can construct text, can relate text to environment. A principal line of enquiry has been to assess how far other forms of writing/printing – handwriting, doodling, crossing out, typefaces, fonts, diacritical marks – might be called upon both to dramatise the presence of voice in text/reading (handwriting, for example, as the manual trace of vocal physiology), and to provide indications and guidelines for vocal performance of text. In this chapter, I wish to pursue that enquiry further, concentrating on the translation of a particular poem, Baudelaire's 'Causerie'. What vision of voice do we find in Baudelaire and how should we, through translation, set about oralising his poems?

Helen Abbott remarks on the way in which, during the course of the nineteenth century, rhetoric cedes its place to music as an organising principle in the compositional process (2009, 31, 34 and *passim*). This shift is of crucial significance since, with it, attention moves from the disposition of tropic structures, and the exercise of discursive power, to the scattered, translinear activity of acoustic collocations and networks, in which discourse is an 'innocent' partner of language's own deeper designs and orchestrations. And whereas rhetoric and composition might thrive on boundaries, whereby the ear circumscribes and measures repetitions, antitheses, appositions, enumerations and so on, musical composition tends to loosen and flexibilise verse-lines, so that they become strings of interactive phonemes and syllables rather than figure-bearing structures. Mallarmé gladly envisages the death of that central verse-boundary, the caesura, and the composition by hemistich that goes with it: 'Les fidèles à l'alexandrin, notre hexamètre, desserrent intérieurement ce mécanisme rigide et puéril de sa mesure; l'oreille, affranchie d'un compteur factice, connaît une jouissance à discerner, seule, toutes les combinaisons possibles, entre eux, de douze timbres' (2003, 206). [Those who are still faithful to the alexandrine, our hexameter, have, from within, loosened this rigid, childish metrical mechanism from its measure; the ear, released from an artificial metronome, experiences pleasure in perceiving, on its own, all possible combinations and interrelationships of twelve tonal values] (we note that Mallarmé's actual word for 'tonal values' is 'timbres', a particularly significant choice in relation to modern musical development). If this looks like a move from the paralinguistic to the linguistic, from the language-informing oratorical voice to language-immanent melody, from the art of the rhetorical period to the art of the keyboard, then we must remember that the paralinguistic is recuperated in the late nineteenth century, by poets such as Baudelaire, Verlaine, Laforgue, Mallarmé, particularly through tone, that highly labile modalisation of language. Tone is to be thought of as pianistic touch, as something which might modulate from note to note, something always responded to but always in doubt, not a vocal position or stance, but a play of insinuation.

In the light of these observations, accounts of the voices of Baudelaire and Mallarmé are what one might expect them to be (Abbott, 2009, 59–63): Baudelaire still favouring a more declamatory or oratorical way of speaking ('solennelle et sentencieuse, appuyant sur chaque terme'; 'onctueuse'; 'psalmodiait ses vers d'une voix monotone, mais impérieuse') [solemn and sententious, emphasising each term; thick and rich; chanted his lines in a monotonous, but imperious voice] and Mallarmé reading more quietly and introspectively ('d'une voix basse, égale, sans le moindre "effet", presque à soi-même') [in a low, even voice, without the least striving for effect, almost to himself]. But one might also argue that Baudelaire was on the cusp of a change, since the voice we have had described to us – portentous, mannered in its elevation – is undercut by other, more intimate and variable tones ('belle voix charmeresse'; 'précieuse, douce, flûtée, onctueuse, et cependant mordante') [beautiful, engaging voice; self-conscious, soft, piping, creamy, and yet biting]. It is the dividedness of the Baudelairean voice, in its various aspects, which is the subject of this chapter.

If one takes a sample of performances of Henri Duparc's setting of 'L'Invitation au voyage', one may be surprised by the variety of renderings of the second line of the refrain:

Luxe, calme et volupté.

This heptasyllable allows 'prose' readings of: (1) 1+2+4, (2) 2′+1+4 (where the apostrophe indicates a *coupe lyrique* (vocal juncture after the mute e)), or possibly (3) 3+4, if one feels that 'volupté' is not the third element in an expanding itemisation, as in (1), but a consequence of the fusion of the first two nouns. Bearing in mind that Duparc's score does not allow for version (3), we note that version (2) is opted for by Elly Ameling (San Francisco Symphony Orchestra, Edo de Waart, 1981) and by Felicity Lott (with Graham Johnson, 1987). More surprisingly, the *coupe lyrique* at 'Luxe/' is repeated at 'calme/' by Charles Panzéra ('an orchestra', Piero Coppola, 1933), by Victoria de los Angeles (with Gerald Moore, 1957) and by Janet Baker (London Symphony Orchestra, André Previn, 1977), producing the octosyllable 2′+2′+4, the hiatus at 'calme/ et' buffered by a pause. And just as surprisingly, in his 1934 version, with Madeleine Panzéra-Baillot at the piano, Panzéra sings the hexasyllable 1+1+4. These findings take us to the heart of a debate between text and voice, the linguistic and the paralinguistic, which has never been brought to a satisfactory conclusion, since, however piously the necessity of their cohabitation is canvassed, they seem mutually to exclude each other.

In his survey of metrical analysis, Benoît de Cornulier (1982, 121–31) identifies some twenty possible scansional methods, all of which fall within 'conventional' approaches to the line of verse. The crucial questions which attach to the practice of metrical analysis are these: How does one decide what is metrical (metrically pertinent) and what is not? How determining is the metre identified in any particular poem – for example, an alexandrine metrically has twelve syllables, but might the reader, in realising any particular line, exercise some freedom in the treatment of mute e's, synaeresis and diaeresis, and finish up with a line somewhere between, say, ten and fourteen syllables?[1] Is metrical analysis concerned with the pre-interpretative or the post-interpretative, that is, is metre inscribed in writing in a latent or an actualised state? At what point does metrical possibility become so multiple that metre can no longer be said meaningfully to exist?

From a metrical point of view, the voice is a distraction, because the paralinguistic merely masks the linguistic, and metre properly belongs to the linguistic being of the text. The only admissible voice, therefore, is the ideal voice, the voice which does maximal justice to the linguistic givens of the text. This view is justified by the proposition that metre, as a deep structure, predates rhythm which belongs to voice, to paralinguistic ornamentation, and thus to surface structure.

These two arguments are clearly inadequate. The ideal voice is the voice of the International Phonetic Alphabet, of isolated purified sounds existing in a milieu without an acoustic, without resonance and without a body. Analysts convert the absence of voice in the text into 'verbal music', as if language without a voice had a describable acousticity; but only the voice can make language sound. Against the second argument we have already put the case, in Chapter 2, that metre and rhythm are antagonistic principles, that metre is no matrix of rhythms, but a cultural construct which 'postdates' rhythm, and averages out its psycho-physiological and temperamental drives.

The danger incurred by those who push towards a single understanding of metre is the lure of 'le vers-en-soi', a platonic vision of the line as being either outside time or in absolute conformity with the author's conception of it. To arrive at metrical agreement, one must necessarily adopt a minimalist approach, must identify those lowest common denominators about which there will be little dispute. And those common denominators will be the features that any line shares with all other lines in its verse-context. A maximalist approach, on the other hand, might want to be able to demonstrate in what ways, *despite* their common denominators, all lines can be different from each other, in their movement, tonality, phrasing, pitch-pattern, acousticity. A minimalist metrics is what has already been said by the text, even before we read it, what can only be recited. A maximalist metrics, or, rather, a metrico-rhythmics, is what is being said, singularly and uniquely, in the process of speaking it. The real question is not how to speak the written, to recite the written, but how to introduce the spoken into the written, how to oralise the written. If it is the business of verse to maximise both the materiality of language and the capacity of words to act as shifters, to lend themselves to appropriation, then what matters is the psycho-physiological imprint one finds in language and the way in which language carries vocality, vocal potentiality.

But if we manage to reintroduce voice into the assessment of poetry's metrico-rhythmic being, we still need to ask 'which voice?' This is the issue which concerned us in Chapter 2. In the face of its inability to incorporate into critical discourse the physiology of particular voices, the organic accidents of an individual's vocal apparatus,[2] – what we have also called the 'pronunciatory' voice – the critical world has focussed its attention on shared systems of voice-use (for communicative and expressive purposes) – what we have called the 'articulatory' voice. But this ought to be expressed more strongly: paralinguistic features of the voice (speed, loudness, tone, intonation, enunciation, etc.) have two faces, one turned towards the innate physiology of the voice, its timbre, the other towards expressive resourcefulness, towards strategic uses of voice, towards delivery;

in criticism, we have ceased to acknowledge the former face (or nearly); put another way, the latter face exists at the expense of the former; put another way, voice is superseded by its own powers of expression.

But there are writers in whose work the physiological/pronunciatory voice, and more particularly the psycho-physiological voice, has been given its critical credit. The two faces of voice might, for example, be related to Julia Kristeva's distinction between the geno-text, that pre-systemic process which includes psychic drives finding their way to utterance, and the pheno-text, the text which has achieved system, which obeys the rules of communication, which presupposes a subject of enunciation and an addressee (1974, 83–6). And if the geno-text is the semiotic in the symbolic, then we might ascribe to voice the power to activate, or dredge up, those semiotic presences: 'Si on peut l'imaginer dans le cri, les vocalises ou les gestes de l'enfant, le sémiotique fonctionne en fait dans le discours adulte comme rythme, prosodie, jeu de mots, non-sens du sens, rire' (1977, 14) [If one can imagine it in the cry, the *vocalises* or the gestures of the child, the semiotic functions in fact in adult discourse as rhythm, prosody, word-play, the non-sense of sense, laughter].

In the paragraphs which follow, I do not wish to plunge very far into the psycho-phonetic concerns of commentators like Kristeva and Ivan Fónagy, but we do need to take seriously Fónagy's stern reminder:

Le style vocal est omniprésent. Le phonème, unité abstraite, ne peut apparaître dans le discours sous sa forme pure. Il doit être réalisé, actualisé à l'aide des organes de la parole, la glotte, le pharynx, la langue, les lèvres. Or, il est impossible de faire fonctionner ces organes sans qu'ils puissent s'exprimer à leur tour, en ajoutant au message linguistique des informations d'une nature différente. Ceci peut être en rapport avec le fait que les organes 'de la parole' n'étaient pas destinés initiale-ment à véhiculer des messages linguistiques, mais à remplir certaines fonctions biologiques. (1991, 23)

[Vocal style is omnipresent. The phoneme, an abstract unit, cannot appear in discourse in its pure form. It has to be realised, actualised with the help of the organs of speech, the glottis, the pharynx, the tongue, the lips. Now, it is impossible to get these organs to function without their having their own input, adding to the linguistic message information of a different kind. This may be connected with the fact that the organs 'of speech' were not initially called upon to project linguistic messages, but [rather] to fulfil certain biological functions.]

I want to indicate the way in which Baudelaire's 'Causerie' invites the voice into the poem and reaches for a negotiation between the physio-logical voice and the communicative voice, between pronunciation and articulation, between timbre and delivery, and to consider how this particular negotiation might be captured and expanded upon in a translation.

'Causerie' presents itself as an apt candidate for translation, partly because of its relative neglect, critically and translationally, but more especially because it promises relaxed and intimate discourse within a structure – the sonnet – which implies a high degree of management and lyrical rhetoricity. The facts are quickly rehearsed: this sonnet, on seven rhymes (a maximum for the form) is part of the Marie Daubrun cycle; it brings a curious mixture of *tutoiement* and *vouvoiement*, which most commentators agree, not surprisingly, is to do with changes of emotional and psychological proximity (see Baudelaire, 1975, 56, 933):

1.	Vous êtes un beau ciel d'automne, clair et rose!	2+4+2+4/2+4+3'+3
2.	Mais la tristesse en moi monte comme la mer,	4+2+1+5
3.	Et laisse, en refluant, sur ma lèvre morose	2+4+3+3/3'+4+3+3!
4.	Le souvenir cuisant de son limon amer.	4+2+4+2
5.	– Ta main se glisse en vain sur mon sein qui se pâme;	2+4+3+3/4+2+3+3
6.	Ce qu'elle cherche, amie, est un lieu saccagé	4+2+3+3/5'+2+3+3!
7.	Par la griffe et la dent féroce de la femme.	3+3+2+4
8.	Ne cherchez plus mon cœur; les bêtes l'ont mangé.	4+2+2+4
9.	Mon cœur est un palais flétri par la cohue;	2+4+2+4
10.	On s'y soûle, on s'y tue, on s'y prend aux cheveux!	3+3+3+3/4'+3+3+3!
11.	– Un parfum nage autour de votre gorge nue!...	3+3+4+2/4+2+4+2
12.	Ô Beauté, dur fléau des âmes, tu le veux!	3+3+2+4/3+3+3'+3
13.	Avec tes yeux de feu, brillants comme des fêtes,	4+2+2+4
14.	Calcine ces lambeaux qu'ont épargnés les bêtes!	2+4+4+2

[Note: An apostrophe attached to a measure (e.g. 3' in line 1) in the syllabic tabulation indicates that the e at the end of the measure is read as a *coupe lyrique* rather than a *coupe enjambante*, that is, it is grouped retrospectively (d'automne,/clair et rose), creating a juncture, rather than projectively (d'auto(m)/ne, clair et rose), creating a liaison. To read with a *coupe enjambante* might be reckoned the more usual readerly behaviour. The exclamation mark indicates an unorthodox alternative reading of the line: not only with a *coupe lyrique*, but also with an unelided e before a following vowel – elision of the e is called for by prosodic rule – thus creating an awkward hiatus, and a line of thirteen syllables rather than the correct twelve.]

What the voice does as it finds its way through this text is at once to shape respiration, pausing, pitch, and so on, but without stability, as vocal experimentation, as a testing of parameters, as a path not towards optimal expressiveness, but towards its own timbre, or towards a verse tuned to the voice's own sound. As the voice gains articulation, takes possession of the text in a variety of guises, so it also, equally and oppositely, yields articulation to pronunciation. By that I mean quite simply that the voice releases and scatters the acoustics of the text, or, contrarily, concentrates it in moments of repetitious insistence; and this is a process which, by the very speaking of the text, cannot be prevented: the voice of the reader accedes, as it were, to the extraction by the text of his/her own orality. I do not lend my voice to this text, as a polite visitor, as might anyone else just as well, in order that its textuality may be actualised. I use this text as an instrument to perform my own voice, in a way that releases in it not only its known physiological features, but also its unknown psycho-physiological capabilities.

My analysis of this poem will be unsystematic and selective, but it will give some sense, I hope, of the concerns that I feel a translation should address. The first line identifies a recurrent problem: the case of the *coupe lyrique*. Does one say 2+4+2+4 and give voice to two matching movements of syllabic expansion, the one confirming the other, which shared phonemes only serve to endorse? Such a move helps me pick out, too, the worm already in the rose: the line's central 'hemistich' – '-/es un beau ciel d'auto/mne' – establishes the imminence of the other 4+2's in the poem, in which an adjective, or noun complement, has a peremptory and damning effect, or in which the paired measures dissociate themselves from each other:

> Le souvenir cuisant de son limon amer
> Ce qu'elle cherche, amie,
> Ne cherchez plus mon cœur
> de votre gorge nue
> Avec tes yeux de feu

There are other senses in which this line is the beginning of the poem's undoing. /ɛ/ will become the note of despair and aggression that undermines 'êtes' and 'clair' ('tristesse', 'mer', 'lèvre', 'amer', 'chercher', 'bêtes'). And the /o/ of 'beau' and 'rose' finds very different values in the final stanza ('Beauté', 'fléau', 'lambeaux'). These diverted trajectories of phonemes look like part of a rhetorical strategy – 'fléau' and 'lambeaux', for instance, appear at the caesura – an ironisation of the text, a campaign for semantic unreliability. But we shall have reason to revise this judgement.

Similarly, the 2+4+2+4 reading of the first line places it squarely within a certain scansional tradition designed to bring out its resonant orderedness, to bend the voice to its imperious repetition, to produce the pleasure of aesthetic fulfilment. But if we read it with a *coupe lyrique* (2+4+3′+3), we introduce the unstructuring consequences of purely vocal decision, where the e serves not syllabicity or rhythmic fluency, but the psychic in the phonetic: the 'choc funèbre' of 'automne', which 'clair et rose' cannot mask, because they themselves are dissociated by it, isolated in a purely decorative self-sufficiency.

This initial possibility of a *coupe lyrique* triggers others, even more disruptive, because not only do they likewise grow from a punctuational pretext (a comma, experienced as a moment of the voice recorded in *real time*), but they also and at the same time entail a hiatus, which breaks the bounds of the alexandrine syllabically (if this still matters) and produces the laryngal constriction, the frustration of vocal impulse, associated with glottalisation:

1.	Et laisse, en refluant, sur ma lèvre morose	2+4+3+3 BUT 3′+4+3+3!
6.	Ce qu'elle cherche, amie, est un lieu saccagé	4+2+3+3 BUT 5′+2+3+3!
10.	On s'y soûle, on s'y tue, on s'y prend aux cheveux	3+3+3+3 BUT 4′+3+3+3!

To these we might add the possible *coupe lyrique* in line 12, more muted, of the same kind as that in line 1:

12.	Ô Beauté, dur fléau des âmes, tu le veux	3+3+2+4 BUT 3+3+3′+3

These instances are made differently significant by the poem's pattern of articulated and elided word-terminal, non-clitic e's, traced in the following tabulation:

1. e // e	5. ~~e~~ //	9.	12. // e
2. ~~e~~ // e e	6. e ~~e~~ //	10. ~~e~~ //	13. // e
3. ~~e~~ // e	7. ~~e~~ // e	11. ~~e~~ // e e	14. e //
4.	8. // e		

[first hemistich = 10 (3 + ≠); second hemistich = 10 (10)]

Remarkably, none of the second-hemistich e's is elided. I have argued elsewhere that the alexandrine, as a 'vers composé' (created by two hexasyllables) not only encourages us to read rhythm in terms of paired measures, but to read each hemistich as a particular kind of vocal/expressive space (1998a, 70–2). One might feel, looking through the unelided e's of the second hemistichs that Baudelaire is encouraging the voice to indulge itself – in the wistful, the plaintive, the melodramatic – and to 'platform' simile. These kinds of tonal lyricism are, on the whole, suppressed in the first hemistichs, where a more matter-of-fact voice delivers unadorned statements. The poem is, in fact, a dialogue between a 'vous' and a 'tu' on another axis: the 'vous' perspective tends to occupy the first hemistich, the 'tu' perspective the second. The effect of the re-installation of 'e' at lines 3, 6 and 10, in our 'perverse' alternative scansion, acts not as the reintroduction of lyrical protraction, but as the notation of an emotional/experiential impasse, an exhaustion of possibility.

If the *coupe lyrique* tends to undermine the rhetorical integrity of the alexandrine, and its confidence as representative utterance, if it pushes the voice away from impersonation and towards self-intrusion, so, equally, recurrent phonemes can push one away from the tracing of patterns in carpets towards unpredictable and irregular acts of pronunciation, confrontations with nagging psychosomatic pulsions and self-generating associative networks. We have argued that /ɛ/ is a sound which, in the design of the poem, goes sour: the 'êtes' of 'vous êtes' becomes the '-êtes' of 'bêtes'. We might argue that the same is true of /m/, the /m/ of self and mother, but also the /m/ of 'femme' and 'amie' and 'limon amer' and 'mange' and so on. At the same time, like /ɛ/, the sound flits about the text as capriciously and erratically as a butterfly, so that its sound-symbolic value is never definitively established and can transfer itself to the reader/speaker's own existential and psychic preoccupations. Fónagy describes /m/ as the 'normalisation linguistique du mouvement de succion des lèvres' (1991, 76) [linguistic normalisation of the sucking movement of lips] (new light on 'ma lèvre morose'?) and quotes Ostwald, who notes among his schizophrenic patients 'une corrélation entre l'émission répétée de MM (humming) et un repliement sur soi-même, une régression narcissique profonde (qui les ramènent à l'unité duelle primitive de mère/enfant [. . .])' (1991, 77) [a correlation between the repeated uttering of MM (humming) and a withdrawal, a deep narcissistic regression (which brings them back to the primitive dual unity of mother/child [. . .])].

One might justifiably propose that there is nothing Baudelaire-induced about this shift from phoneme as element of textual design to phoneme as vocal discharge, as pronunciation, as timbre of reader/speaker. My argument is that there are signs of such textual engineering. What is curious about line 5, for example, is the sudden short burst of /ɛ̃/: 'main' > 'vain' > 'sein'. This phoneme occurs nowhere else in the text. Of course, it gives the line a peculiar acoustic density (along with /m/, /s/ and /i/), but this very density, so arbitrary in its imperious eruption, takes us to other places of fixation and psychic paralysis. Similarly, lines 12–13 play with /ø/ ('veux', 'yeux', 'feu'), adumbrated in the 'cheveux' of line 10, and the 'lieu' of line 6. But why? Again, despite the adumbrations, this relative concentration of the phoneme in a small space seems like a response to some pulsional imperative. Of course, we can make sense of it, by casting it as the antagonist, and destroyer, of /œ/ ('cœur'): both these vowels are front and rounded, but one is half-closed/high-mid and the other is half-open/low-mid. But we are still left with a significant margin of free-associative gratuitousness, of pure, unassigned vocality, with a sound which is expressive (of self), but still not quite the servant of articulacy.

One might want to make something of the same case about the punctuation. We have already had occasion to speak of the significance of the comma, as the intrusion into text of real time, a point of enunciatory indexicality.[3] And one may well feel that Baudelaire's insistent cultivation of the exclamation mark is less a consistent application of certain rhetorical pressures and more an unruly vocal impulse, not quite controlled, towards defensive or assertive self-amplification, towards imperativity, towards theatricality, towards the invocation or imposition of perceptions and desires. And there are other elements of punctuation that Baudelaire can use to multiply vocal inflexion, in particular the dash and suspension points.

Any idle reading of *Les Fleurs du Mal* might identify the dash with three *structural* functions: (1) to change the direction of address (here the dash may indeed be accompanied by inverted commas); (2) to set up a closing apophthegm or longer endgame; (3) more rarely, to introduce a brief, interpolated response, which the poet is as if powerless to suppress.[4] In 'Causerie', the two dashes look designed to alert us to a change of address. The difficulty is that we cannot see the extent of their applicability. Do we divide the poem, say:

ll. 1–4 Interior monologue ('vous' perspective)
ll. 5–7 Direct address ('tu' perspective)
ll. 8–10 Interior monologue ('vous')
l. 11 Direct address ('vous')
ll. 12–14 Interior monologue ('vous')
or perhaps:
l. 1 Voice I (direct address)
ll. 2–4 Voice II (soliloquy, aside)
ll. 5–7 Voice III (direct address or solil.)
l. 8 Voice I (direct address or solil.)
ll. 9–10 Voice II (solil., aside)

l. 11 Voice I (direct address)

ll. 12–14 Voice III (direct address or solil.)

or perhaps . . . All these attributions are highly uncertain, and it is impossible to tell consistently where the boundaries fall, whether at the next full-stop, the next stanza-end, or the next dash (which seems to be the case, for example in 'Les Petites Vieilles' and 'Un voyage à Cythère'). Baudelaire's own lack of clarity is perhaps testified to by the 1857 edition which, like its proofs, has a dash at the end of line 7. This makes more sense of the shift to the second person plural in line 8, but leaves the dash at the beginning of line 11 a puzzle. In similar fashion, Baudelaire requires a dash after 'nue' (line 11) in the first proof of the 1857 version. This further indication of line 11's isolation is hardly necessary and is ultimately replaced by suspension points. But the exact 'distribution' of discourse may not matter. What matters is the way in which the dash signals the labyrinth of voice, the shifts in vocal proximity and modality, and the unpredictability of the adjustments of level and threshold (genotext and phenotext, inner and outer voices, degrees of depth in the psyche) – the dash is the sign of the abrupt, the reflex, the peremptory, the disruptive, the impatient.

As far as the introduction of suspension points at the end of line 11 is concerned, we should first note Russell Goulbourne's general observations: 'They [suspension points] constitute a space, both visually and audibly, both literally and metaphorically, in which the reader is brought into play, invited to think, to use his/her imagination, to hear the unsaid, to read between the lines, or rather, to read between the points' (1999, 213). Goulbourne's words seem strikingly just, as long as the reader does not merely look to recuperate a suppressed message. Suspension points like these are the point at which the text falls into the hands of the reader; this space is explicitly the textual imaginary, the poem's blind field, endowed with greater or lesser intensity (Baudelaire uses, variably, between three and five suspension points). I say 'suspension points like these' because a check against variants tells us that the suspension points in 'Harmonie du soir' (5) and 'Ciel brouillé' (5) are similarly the replacement of a dash. In other instances – e.g. 'Les Petites Vieilles', 'Le Vin de l'assassin', 'Un voyage à Cythère' – suspension points make their first appearance in the 1861 edition as additions to text. This albeit undramatic gravitation towards suspension points seems to me to be motivated by the realisation that, in regular verse, suspension points can go beyond the linguistic (sign of elision) and the paralinguistic (suspended pitch, voice fade, drawl, pause, lightening of accentuation) towards vocal evaporation. This last phrase owes much to Ioulia Sarantou's illuminating analysis of punctuation in

'Épigraphe pour un livre condamné' (2004; see also Sarantou, 2001, for the erotics of Baudelairean punctuation), and is a vocal 'vaporisation du *Moi*' (Baudelaire, 1975, 676). The voice is in metamorphosis, not simply because it is in movement, but because it is passing through different manifestations of itself: the voice as practised by the dandy, on the one hand, and by the prostitute, on the other (the *flâneur* floats between the two), the voice of the *maître du jeu* and the voice of self-surrender. Insofar as the dash is a focusing of (vocal) consciousness (prelude to endgame) or a form of buttonholing (change of addressee), suspension points act against it.[5] Suspension points return the voice to the pre-verbal, to a state of availability to the self's vocal pulsions, and perhaps indeed to the pre-acoustic source of all being ('le langage des fleurs et des choses muettes' – 'Élévation').

The overall objective of this translation, therefore, is to transform a text orientated towards expressive delivery into something which invites timbre in all its versatility. This entails the sonnet's transformation into a free-verse form, which preserves the sonnet's stanzaic construction but which encourages the paralinguistic to invade the linguistic in the form of pausing, phrasing, etc. We also need to confront the task of turning the rhetorical – a code of figured speech, where figure supplants prosodic features – into the spoken, without having to descend to the colloquial:

Conversation

You're   an   (AUTUMN)   sky   BeauTIfuL,   unc.l.o.u.ded   **ro-syhued**
ButSadness   !sweLLS   [in]me   like   h/e/a/v/Ing   waVes
WHICH   asthey   ebb   a.W.a.y   leaveon my *SULLEN*   lips
The   Biting   **after**taste   of   BITter   *Silt.*

– Your hand glides:
            smooth across:
                        my breathless chest –
                                    it's all a waste of time

For what it's looking for:
            amie –
                        is a place already
                                    laid to waste

By others
            of your kind
                        red in tooth . . .
                                    and claw

Give up the search:
                    my heart's
                                long since
                                            been thrown to the dogs
                        My heart's a
                        palace ran-
                        sacked by the
                        mob, Drink sod-
                        den, they're at
                        each other's
                        throats, and hair
                        – A perfume
                        drifts around
                        your naked
                        breasts!...

Beauty
'unyielding
scourge of souls' –
that's how you want it!
Use your
fiery eyes, brightly lit
as if for
carnival
To incinerate
what's left of me
after the dogs
are done.

The first stanza attempts to establish the bearing principle of the whole translation: to free the voice as a projector of the text, setting the text in motion and at the same time being revealed by the text's movement. The juxtapositional strategies of the spatial text are thus supplanted by the metamorphic ones of the temporal text. But this textual temporality is not the quantitative, homogeneous and discontinuous temporality of metre, but, in the fashion of Bergsonian *durée*, qualitative, heterogeneous and continuous. Accordingly, I have created a line which, by filling the page's width and using uneven spacing and a promiscuous typography, frustrates any attempt to encompass it as a unit and requires the reader to *inhabit* its heterogeneous temporalities, loudnesses, acoustic associations. Instead of the time of the line being determined by the pressures of 'external' time (the surrounding space), it draws time into itself as the necessary medium of its own experience. Each reader/translator is thus at liberty to re-arrange layout and typography in order to register the *durée* and peculiar eventfulness of their own reading. In this sense, choices of layout and typography are, for the translator as reader, or vocaliser, of the source text (ST), more important than lexical choices.

Part of the strategy for decomposing the line as written, as rhetorically purposive, and returning it to the idiosyncrasies and pulsional turbulence of voice, is, as we have seen, the institution of a strong translinear, or intralinear, acousticity, which acts as dispersively, or disruptively, as it does integratively. While we may allow that acousticity orchestrates our hearing of the text, we must equally allow that we hear it, not as part of a formal design, but as the uncontrollable spray of the text, which the voice is attracted to/distracted by, in its passage through the text. This vision of acousticity is the compromise between the written and the spoken, the text read off (voice as instrument, which validates, endorses the text) and the text as stimulus or liberation of the oral (voice as that organ which explores its own psycho-physiology, through the text).

In my version of this first stanza, therefore, I have used the closing noun phrase 'bitter silt' as a rough target for sounds within the stanza, picked out by capitalisation. But these are competed with by other sounds whose purposes are not so clear, whose sudden projections are more darkly motivated. I have used italics and bold to rather the same effect: to create a text which is, above all, temperamental, or is made temperamental by orality itself. The task of the translator is not to promote in the target text (TT) a recognition of what is already there in the ST, but to use the TT to create the possibility of discoveries not yet registered. Translation is much more to do with the Barthesian *scriptible* than with the *lisible*.

And I have resorted to an alternative system of punctuation – slashes, brackets, 'misplaced' hyphens, preposed exclamation marks, suspension points within the word – in order to suggest that, in the 'new order', punctuation is not a servant of periodicity, the external classifier and guardian of the conventions of written utterance, but, on the contrary, an asylum-seeker from the written, withdrawing to the heart of vocal continuity, with which it has no wish to interfere, and where it can reinvent itself as the agent of vocal perception and projection.

Finally, another, related objective of this translation is to dynamise and heterogenise the metrico-rhythmic current. If I describe the final line of this quatrain – 'The biting after-taste of bitter silt' – as iambic pentameter, I am implying that it is made up of five rhythmically identical, isochronous units. This quantitative vision of iambic pentameter prejudices the reading voice and prevents our seeing the line as an accumulation of the heterogeneous, of elements all with different qualitative values, to wit:

amphibrach (x / x) + amphimacer (/ x /) + weak monosyllable (x) + trochee (/ x) + strong monosyllable (/)

The voice melts down iambic pentameter in order to find, in it its primary elements, these fragments of a *moi profond* which does not yet know what shapes it wishes to take, because it is a set of vocal/verbal reflexes. Like sadness, language swells in the poet and is brought to the surface by the voice in an indivisible act, where the sea of self seamlessly binds together its own flotsam.

The second stanza again maintains its 'quatrainness', but is designed principally to give a sense of the tetrametric movement characteristic of the alexandrine. There is no attempt here to limit the line to twelve syllables, nor to rhyme (what would be the point?). What is important is to provide a sense of a particular kind of rhythmic movement, in which each line has four measures whose lengths vary and solicit the voice in different ways: the slackening of tension, the diminution of concern in the longer measures (of five and six syllables); the moments of attentive poise in the amphimacers (/ x /) ('smooth across', 'laid to waste', 'red in tooth'); the suppressed bitterness or despair in the single iambs ('amie', 'and claw', 'my heart's', 'long since'). In other words, my version does not rely on rhetoricised patterns of paired measures, but looks to allow each measure to create its own intra- and interlinear affinities and conflicts. In this respect, it is truer to the rhythmic fluctuations and distributive rhythmicity of free verse, and a move away from the juxtapositional in the direction of the metamorphic and temporally irretrievable.

I have also sought to ensure that measures end on strong (accentuated) syllables, in the French manner, except at 'already' and 'others', where I have wanted to capture something of the *coupe lyrique*'s short moments of *repliement sur soi*, of loss of impetus, of the voice's brief inability to say what it is going to say. Two other features deserve comment. First, I have introduced further punctuation of a vocal kind: my colons in the first line are intended to express sensory breaks, those mixtures of the withheld or momentarily suspended and the about-to-be-given of erotic experience; these are impatiently interrupted by the dash which throws it all away. This movement is then imitated at a lower pitch in the line following. The suspension points in the third line mark the voice's resuscitation of a dead metaphor, an emotional reinvestment of the verbally automatic with the verbally intended, the recovery of a relish in uttering it. The colon of the final line is a last pale echo of the earlier ones: the note of stilled anticipation, arrested urgency, is now as if a memory, or something so abstract that the physicality of voice mirrors no other physicality.

Second, it would be usual to relate variety of margin to different psychic levels, gradations between the conscious and the unconscious, the enunci-ated and the thought. These differentiations do not really apply where the use of margins is, as here, merely a visual record of rhythmic segmenta-tion. But the fact remains that these lines look like a sequence of descents: each time the voice pulls itself back to the first margin, to make a new start in clarity of thought and purpose, so each time the baggage of the developmental or the circumstantial acts as a weight around the heart, and each time the line becomes a dying fall, an excursion of the voice into the modality of morbidity.

The columnar presentation of the first tercet presents a moment of vocal freefall. This is the point in the poem where the addressee is particularly difficult to identify: there are no indications of a second person, until, of course, the final, separated line. Are lines 9–10 spoken *à la cantonade*, to the reader, to himself . . . ? The layout is designed to convey the expressionless, a kind of no-man's land of utterance where the reader has no purchase on phrasing and finds it difficult to anticipate text with the eye. Reading becomes a series of sudden encounters with words or word-fragments. Significantly, this verse-column is rhythmically regular, at least insofar as each line, bar the last, is trisyllabic; and it is this insistent syllabic triplet which enforces the enjambements, so difficult for the voice to negotiate: rhythm and syntax are no longer mutually endorsing, but operate at cross purposes, at each other's cost. When the final line of the source-tercet arrives, it does not entirely escape the trisyllabic Procrustean bed, but it lies more easily than the previous lines, with less disruption of its phrasality, and its final word breaks into a space of its own: the rhythmical spell is broken.

The final tercet brings the translation further into English territory,[6] after the gallicised performance of the second quatrain. At the same time, it leaves the *terrain vague* of the mid-page and returns to a left-hand margin, where speech can once again improvise itself, develop its junctures, its tonal innuendoes, its variations of attack. True, each line of the ST is again bro-ken down into four segments, but there is no longer the 'lateral' music of a 'vers composé', with medial caesura. Instead we have English rhythm devel-oped as a modulating vocal trace. By this latter I mean: free verse allows English rhythms to re-establish contact between stress intensity, syllabic duration and pitch (metre has no interest in either the *nature* of stress or *degree* of stress). It also makes audible the unfolding of rhythmic variation as Heraclitian, metamorphic experience rather than as a sequence of adjacent similarities and differences. This series of lines begins with a trochee, but with the stressed vowel not insisted upon. 'Unyielding' provides the trochee with a 'prefix' and an extended stressed syllable. Thus, paradoxically, the negative 'un-' is swallowed and 'yielding' begins to acquire an optative flavour. 'Scourge of souls' reverses the previous line's amphibrach (x / x) into an amphimacer (/ x /), with more length in 'scourge' than in 'souls'. The fourth line might be read with a flattening iambic rhythm, rather matter-of-fact: x / x / x. I prefer the adonic configuration – / x x / x – because it makes better sense of the exclamation mark: of the poet's simultaneous realisation and acceptance of the pointlessness of further parleying. After the trochee and amphimacers of lines 5–6, the rhythm loses its focus and the weak syllables become more sapping. The second paeons (x / x x) of lines 9–10 (with a one-syllable upbeat –'To' – in line 9) eloquently capture the difficulty of generating stress and the ease with which the impetus falls off. The choriamb (/ x x /) of line 11 picks up the choriamb in the adonic of line 4, and the final iamb is like a reversal, gradually and variously engineered, of this tercet's initial trochee.

'Causerie', as we imagine it in our translation, is a proliferation of voices, and is so partly because we have sought to release within it the anarchic genotextual undercurrents which surface in the very resourcefulness of voicing, of paralinguistic (and indeed punctuational) versatility, and partly because we are writing against a certain translational tradition. Translation hitherto has concerned itself remarkably little with voice quality, as if poetic texts were not made peculiarly complex by paralinguistic potentialities, by the voice's construction of the text. It is assumed that the translator translates his/her reading of the text, where 'reading' means 'interpretation' and where the text is left in its writtenness, however much its 'music' may be referred to. But the music of the unspoken written is a far cry from the vocality of the spoken written; and reading, the psychophysiological inhabitation of the text, is a far cry from any interpretation which might be read *out of* a text. Translation, it might be claimed, has for too long had its eye on the wrong target. I want, as my final move in this chapter, to turn to a translational resource which acts out these particular issues, and which has already been playing a part, not least in crossing-out and in multi-sensory superimpositions, namely overwriting/overprinting. This topic will receive lengthier consideration in Chapter 8; in this first skirmish I would like principally to concentrate on its iconic functions (Fig. 14).

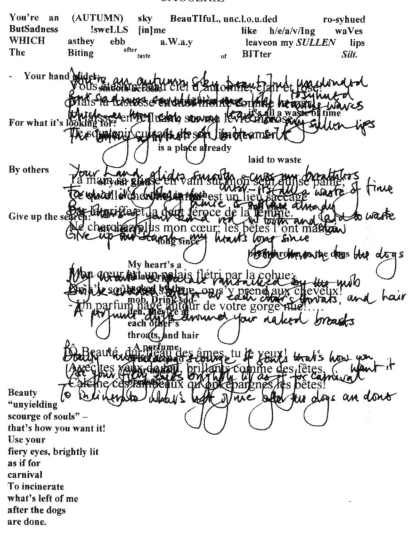

CONVERSATIONERIE
CAUSERIE

You're an   (AUTUMN)   sky   BeauTIfuL, unc.l.o.u.ded   ro-syhued
ButSadness   !sweLLS   [in]me   like h/e/a/v/Ing   waVes
WHICH   asthey   ebb   a.W.a.y   leaveon my *SULLEN*   lips
The   Biting   after taste   of   BITter   *Silt.*

- Your hand slides

For what it's looking for!

is a place already

laid to waste

By others

Give up the search:

My heart's a

long since

mob, Drink sod-

each other's

throats, and hair

Beauty
"unyielding
scourge of souls" –
that's how you want it!
Use your
fiery eyes, brightly lit
as if for
carnival
To incinerate
what's left of me
after the dogs
are done.

Figure 14 Overwritten translation of Baudelaire's 'Causerie'

Before turning to the specific issues arising out of 'Causerie', we might briefly outline overwriting's more general enactment of translation. Most obviously, the TT overwrites the ST, masking it without obliterating it, not a palimpsest so much as a sedimentation of texts, each layer concealing, the better to reveal as a bedrock, the originating ST. Overwriting is a textual geology, writing temporal accumulation into the page, its strata making visible different time-scales and historical tempi. But, at the same time, and with equal urgency, the two-dimensionality of the page asserts itself. This two-dimensionality not only allows the eye to see as reversible the process we have just described; it also allows all the texts included in the overwriting to affirm a simultaneity of appearance and activity. Texts vie with each other, or engage in well-orchestrated polyphonic choruses, as if by spontaneous combustion. The page does indeed become the stage of translation on which are acted out the protagonistic relationships of ST and TTs.

In my overwritten version of 'Causerie', I have simply superimposed upon the ST, printed in 16-point Times New Roman, a 'straight', hand-written rendering, and my subsequent, typographically 'managed' version, in 12-point Times New Roman. The choice of 16-point for the ST is designed to express something of the power politics in the relationship between text and page: the single text on the page, with the page to itself, looks to put itself beyond our reach. Holding the territory of the page in its sole possession, it seeks to exercise a non-negotiable authority. Paper is land rights. Over this is laid the tracery of handwriting, which has proportions, but these are elastic and do not necessarily equate with the space to be occupied; handwriting engages in guerrilla warfare with print, flexible in its adaptations, finding its advantage over the lapidary in capricious immediacy and movement. Out of this conflict comes a third text, with its unassertive 12-point default setting, but having caught the unpredictable waywardness and aggressive temporality of the handwritten in its typographical idiosyncrasies.

But, considered in its simultaneity, this overwritten presentation is a jumble of voices whose multiplicity might threaten grounded vocal identity, whose hubbub might constitute satanic solicitations or depredations:

Mon cœur est un palais flétri par la cohue

On the other hand, might it not be the voices of translation that lead us out of the inevitable, suicidal condition outlined in 'Causerie'? The poet is transfixed by his own text, caught in the formal imperatives of the sonnet; he is subject to the jussive tyrannies of vocal delivery:

Ô Beauté, dur fléau des âmes, tu le veux!

while timbre, the particular sound-quality of a particular voice, dies on his lips before finding utterance:

Mais la tristesse en moi monte comme la mer,
Et laisse, en refluant, sur ma lèvre morose
Le souvenir cuisant de son limon amer.

Accordingly, the practising voice of a new here and now, of being in the world, never manages to disengage itself from the already representedness of past and future, from memory which brings knowledge but no change, and seems only the more strongly to propel us towards a foregone conclusion. Translation, it seems, loosens this condition and, in its very procedures, endows texts with other options on themselves, simply by introducing an immediate present, a practising voice, into the construction of text, and by allowing, in its performative drive, timbre's return to the vocal mix, not merely as an isolated constituent, but as a presiding animator. In the world of the reader, there is no fear of vocal dispossession by vocal multiplicity; rather, vocal inhabitation of text derives directly from the experience of that multiplicity.

This may appear to be a very odd argument to pursue: translation releases us from the prison of the ST; in overwriting the ST, translation puts the ST on a new existential footing. But, after all, it is not so odd. Is it the purpose of reading and translation to *undergo* the ST, to relive its depicted predicaments, to act out some kind of fictional biographical transfer? No. Should we undertake to suffer with the poet (Baudelaire)? No. We read and translate in order to inhabit the language of the ST, to bring it to consciousness in our own perceptual world, to engage with it psycho-physiologically, performatively, in a constructivist rather than hermeneutic spirit. The value of the Baudelairean text lies in its power of self-reinvention in the hands of the reader, not in its reproducibility. Once again we must ask: if the translator translates for readers familiar with the SL and the ST, what is the point of translating a text back into itself? Thanks to translation, 'Causerie' remains an ongoing conversation susceptible of any number of revocalisations and performative reconfigurations.

CHAPTER 6

Free verse and the translation of rhythm

Chapter 2 posed the question about the part to be played in the translation of verse by metrical considerations. It concluded that, just as translation takes us from the linguistic towards the paralinguistic, so, correspondingly, it should take us from the metrical towards the rhythmic. This chapter is a further reflection on the translation of metre and rhythm. It proposes that, in relation to translation, metre is an unproductive distraction; rhythm is fruitful and conciliatory for the translator in a way that metre is not. To work through these arguments requires a broader exploration of certain prosodic characteristics of the languages involved in my chosen translational transactions, French and English. I should also reiterate that my approach to translation always presupposes that the reader of the TT is familiar with the ST. This presupposition makes the act of translation a linguistically dialectical act: acculturating the rhythm of the ST to the target language (TL) means *creating* the rhythm of the ST, since nobody else, including the metrical analyst, will do that for us.

We face the simplest of questions: how do we achieve an account of the metrico-rhythmic nature of verse which does not merely describe what the language of the printed text makes available, but which takes into consideration the readerly experience of text? The simple answer is to pass the text through a process of translation, itself understood as an account of readerly consciousness. To date, metrical analysis has been little interested in reading; indeed, metrical analysis has tended to imply that the reader *reads off* what have already been identified as the metrico-rhythmic givens. However, the real question is not what is there on the page to be read, but what is *activated by reading*, what resources does the reader bring into play. And the task of the translator is, equally, a participatory one: actively to read the ST into another language.

Metrical analysis tends to equalise values because its underlying interest is quantitative, and because it is driven by the iso-principle (isochrony, isosyllabicity, isoaccentuality); thus the relative relationships of weakness/strength of stress are converted into absolute ones, to ensure a binary contrast. If metrical analysis were to take the reader into account, what changes of approach would be involved? First, and most fundamentally, such an analysis would acknowledge that rhythm is a negotiation of dialectical inputs between text and reader, between the linguistic and the paralinguistic (both verbal and visual), between the metrical and the rhythmic, between chronometric time and the inner duration of reading, and that, in performance, this negotiation of dialectical inputs will tend to supersede the metrical givens, however much it might initially be guided by them. Readerly input into the construction of the metrico-rhythmic being of a line concerns the infusion of the qualitative and the relative (i.e. the breaking of the iso-principle) and the valorisation of the features of voice. When one speaks of the 'qualitativisation' of accent/stress, one does not merely mean the activation of qualities of accent/stress other than intensity (i.e. duration and pitch), which are difficult to evaluate without technical aids; one means the quality of accent/stress – and indeed of syllable – more generally, what they mean *in perception*, as an instrument or object of perception. Hopkins had begun to think about this in positing a stress driven by 'instress':

> Since, though he is under the world's splendour and wonder,
> His mystery must be instressed, stressed
> ('The Wreck of the Deutschland', ll. 38–9)

As Storey (1981, 61) explains, 'instress' has two senses: '(1) the energy or stress that "upholds" an object's inscape [selfhood, quiddity], that gives it its being . . . ; and (2) the force which the inscape exerts on the minds or feelings of the perceiver'. Instress is thus as much in nature as it is in verse; in a wood of bluebells, Hopkins speaks of 'the blue colour/of light beating up from so many glassy heads, which like water is good to float their deeper instress in upon the mind' (Phillips, 1986, 215). Rarely does the metrist think of stress or accent as the vehicle of specific expressive energies acting in the word or through the word; and more rarely still does the metrist think of stress or accent as the fusional meeting-point of those energies and the touch – in a pianistic sense – of the reader's voice. Once we adopt a scansional or paralinguistic approach to stress or accent or syllable, we naturally treat these things more inclusively, that is to say that the experience of them is not only connected with intensity and pitch and duration, but with grouping and pausing and tempo and loudness and vocal timbre, and what these features contribute to the phonetic quality of the language.

This latter must be emphasised, simply because the greatest involuntary crime of metrical analysis – if one can call it that – is the wedge it has driven between the raw, phonetic data of particular poems, and abstract patterns, whether of weak and strong syllables, where 'weak' and 'strong' tell us about the enunciatory intensity of syllables and nothing about what they sound like; or, as in French, of the number of syllables, where number likewise tells us nothing about acoustic values. Even where the device in question is explicitly acoustic, the same process of de-acoustification takes place: an interest in rhyme resolves itself into an interest in rhyme-pairs as semantic conjunctions, or as manifestations of rhyme-degree or rhyme-gender, or as the source of stanzaic structure, in which case, equally: 'En effet, les rimes structurent les strophes par leur récurrence, non pas du point de vue de leurs timbres, accidentels et non-périodiques, mais de celui de la structure qu'elles rendent perceptible' (Peureux, 2009, 234) [In fact, rhymes structure stanzas by their recurrence, not from the standpoint of their timbres, which are accidental and non-periodic, but from that of the structure they make perceptible]. A newly conceived metrical analysis, or scansion, must find a way of doing justice to the acoustic particulars of any given poem, not just the repetition of sounds but the dynamic of the relationships of sounds: open/closed; front/back; voiced/voiceless; rounded/spread; so that, as with accent, sounds are treated as colour-values.

It seems possible, on the above evidence and adopting the currently orthodox French view, to argue that a syllabic metre like French has, metrically, periodicity but no rhythmicity.[1] It lacks rhythmicity, because syllabism reflects the fact that French is an accentuable language but not an accented one. Accents are created by syntactic configurations, processes of phrasing and grouping (linguistic), and by paralinguistic and vocal input (*accent oratoire, accent d'insistance,* etc.). But agreement about the principles of the application of accent is so difficult to achieve that no metrical rule can be based upon it. Some would say that French verse is numeric-syllabic and would have nothing to do with accent (accent is either an unavoidable concomitant of the end of a syllabic sequence, or an accidental and uncontrollable accompaniment of the speaking of verse). Others might say that accents at the end of numerical sequences are metrical, while other accents are not (i.e. group-terminal accents *within* the line or hemistich are not metrical, but are dictional or rhythmic, in the same way that word-internal and phrase-internal accents are). However, to say that French verse is non-rhythmical, even though rhythm is not part of its metricality (periodicity is), would clearly be false. How to put this anomaly right should be a central preoccupation of metrical analysis; but early attempts to install a metric of *vers mesurés* (late sixteenth century, with resurgences of interest in the seventeenth and eighteenth centuries), the practice of *vers mêlés*, and subsequent proposals for accentual models of the French line, have had no lasting progeny; French metrical analysis is left to nurse a profound unease with its rhythm-generating non-rhythmic syllabism.[2]

The standard translational policy in verse, particularly for the reader ignorant of the source language (SL), is, regrettably, one of preservation: to preserve as much of the original as possible, within a certain play of equivalences and compensations. But if rhythm is not textually there, or perhaps *is* there, but not reliably so, then it cannot be preserved/translated. If metre is there, on the other hand, and demonstrably so, then it should be translated, even if its translation prevents us from moving the text forward in terms of its rhythmic possibilities. This policy of preservation has other disqualifying drawbacks:

(i) It necessitates a sub-policy of sacrifices and priorities: if one chooses to answer rhyme with rhyme, then some other factor, semantic perhaps, or syntactic, must be correspondingly sacrificed. This separation of constitutive elements is what Bonnefoy attacks in his defence of free-verse translations (see below).

(ii) It makes the assumption that constitutive elements are the same from language to language, if adjusted by a touch of equivalence. The iambic pentameter is metrical in the same way that the alexandrine is metrical (though this is clearly untrue). Rhyme in English is the same as rhyme in French, even though rhyme in French recognises different degrees of rhyme, makes alternating rhyme-gender a principle of construction, and rhymes on endings and suffixes, which necessitates a certain practice of avoidances, all features unknown to English rhyming. To encourage readers to think of French and English rhymes as equivalent is seriously and irresponsibly to mislead them.

(iii) To translate alliteration by alliteration, or assonance by assonance usually entails two second-bests: (a) one does not alliterate the same sounds (i.e. alliteration is more linguistic mechanism, indifferent to the phoneme that constitutes it, than anything to do with phonosemantics); (b) one cannot alliterate in quite the same textual location. This again implies that alliteration is more an isolatable rhetorical figure than a location-specific psychophonetic drive or physio-acoustic imperative. It encourages the view that a poem is a sum of particular devices and figures, and if these can be satisfactorily ticked off on a list of translational obligations, then the literary is saved.

To date I have canvassed two broad directions for the translation of verse: first, following Bonnefoy, to translate verse, whether regular or free, into free verse (Scott, 2000). As translators, we are constantly invited to re-imagine ourselves, and equally to re-discover ourselves; we need the kind of medium responsive to the multidimensionality of the translational experience; as Bonnefoy puts it:

Free verse is poetry, in its necessary freedom of expression and research. And one of the consequences of this ... is that it is as such the only place where the contemporary poet can define and solve the problems he meets in his existential or cultural condition: for instance, in his relationship with the poets of the past and his task of translating them. (1979, 378)

And not only with the poets of the past, one might add.

Ironically enough, it may be free verse, more than regular verse, which can re-establish the textual integratedness of a regular-verse ST. One can broadly agree with another of Bonnefoy's propositions, that translation too often involves a process whereby form and content become divorced from each other:

We must understand that writing, the act of writing, is in itself an unbreakable unity whose formal operations are conceived and executed in constant interaction with, for example, the invention of images and the elaboration of meaning ... But this necessary freedom is not, unfortunately, within reach of the translator. In his case, meaning, the whole meaning of the poem, is already determined; he cannot invent anything about it without betraying the intent of the author. Consequently, were he to adopt the alexandrine or the pentameter, this regular pattern would be for him nothing but a frame to which the meaning would have to adjust itself, obliging him to pure virtuosity. (1979, 377)

We would say that the translator, with each translation, re-invents the act of writing; that the translator is not bound by the intent of the author, since (a) authorial intent does not survive beyond the time and place of the ST's writing, and (b) the translator's obligation to what the ST makes possible in the way of a new text is greater than his obligation to the ST's author. As Bonnefoy suggests, in these circumstances, the translation of metrical form is an empty gesture. To translate the numero-syllabic alexandrine into an accentual-syllabic pentameter is to confirm a cultural separation, a border to be crossed by the good offices of systematised equivalence, but at the expense of the dialogue of rhythmicity, at the expense of the idea that translation is not a spatial juxtaposing of texts (ST and TT), but the temporal and existential progression of one text to another. In a translational policy which believes that this progression is best envisaged as a progression from the linguistic to the paralinguistic and performative, from the metrical to the rhythmic, metrical translation would be a step backwards, a stalling of onwardness. It is by translating the metric into the rhythmic that the text is opened up to readerly input. What the translator is attempting to do is not so much to translate a text, but to translate/transform the way a text lives, has its being, in the consciousness of a reader.

There is a sense, anyway, in which metrical analysis, as presently prac-tised, is obsoletist: it insists on linguistic inherency as a value, and thus implies not only that paralinguistic accidentals are without value, but that value of any kind – literary, aesthetic – must be demonstrably *already* in the text, rather than ever-renewable and bestowed by performance.[3] Metrical analysis will not venture into speculation, is descriptive, analeptic, casts its poems as documents. And thus it gives the reader no help in making the most of variables, possibilities, the fund of vocal resource.

We may have felt, from time to time, the push towards a new foundation for metrics, a metrics based perhaps on breath (Charles Olson's 'projective verse' (1966), the Allen Ginsberg of *Howl* (see Ginsberg, 1994)), or on pat-terns of intonation (see Cooper, 1998). Denis Roche suspects that metrical rhythm is no more than a support mechanism, of purely practical and limited interest; instead, rhythmic analysis should attend to the pulsional dynamic of the verse:

déroulement de l'écriture, rythme d'arrivée des enchaînements métaphoriques et des ellipses, rythme de déroulement de la lecture, rythme des thèmes, de leur apparition et de leur destruction, rythme des structures du discours, de leur arrivée et de leur disparition, rythme de disposition, d'étalement, d'enserrement, d'écoulement des textes imprimés, rythme de succession des pages et de leur imbrication possible et de leur succession comme autant d'*empreintes* (au sens biologique). (1968, 13)

[unfolding of the writing, rhythm of arrival of metaphoric series and ellipses, rhythm of the unfolding of reading, rhythm of themes, of their appearance and undoing, rhythm of the structures of discourse, of their emergence and disap-pearance, rhythm of layout, of spreading and compression, of the flow of printed texts, rhythm of the sequence of pages and their possible overlaps and of their sequencing as so many *fingerprints* (in the biological/genetic sense).]

Accordingly, scansion should cease to have as its business the evaluation of verse measures, whether quantitative or syllabic, and should, rather, trace the pulsions (units of energy) propelling the verse, or what Roche calls the '*bousculade pulsionnelle*' (1968, 16; original emphasis) [*pulsional jostling*]. Translation might take upon itself not only the reinstatement and elaboration of the art of scansion, but might advance scansion-based kinds of metricity, maximalist, rather than minimalist, and thus ready to incorporate a higher degree of elasticity into the description and notation of what constitutes the measurement of verse.

But there are other reasons for opting for free verse as the medium for the translation of verse:

(1) Free verse has a versatility, a polymorphousness, which increases its cultural range, its capacity to create multi-metrico-rhythmic landscapes. Translation's aim is not perhaps so much to transport a text wholesale into the modern age, but rather actively to measure the distance between then and now, there and here, acting out that distance with its mass of intertexts. Translation should perhaps, in limited fashion, enact the temporal mutability of the work it translates. Free verse offers an inclusive medium with a great deal of formal and generical flexibility.

(2) Another way of putting this is to say that free verse is a coming to form which never, quite, comes to form. It thus allows the translator to work in the very medium of the problematic, of that which does not quite declare itself, or cannot be quite declared.

(3) Free verse makes visible, in the dispositional and typographic options it offers, the sense in which translation is linguistic and formal engineering.

(4) Free verse has the ability to identify and express its author (the translator) in the singularity of its layout and rhythmic configurations, without necessitating radical transformations of the existing textual material.

(5) Free verse changes the temporality of text. Where regular verse may seem to wish to dam up time, to hold it suspended, free verse keeps time with temporal flow. Free-verse translation draws a text into the present of the translational act. We remember D.H. Lawrence's words: 'But in free verse we look for the insurgent naked throb of the instant moment' (1967, 88). We would argue, however, that this 'instant moment' is interwoven with Bergsonian (inner) duration.

Second, I have argued for both a more extreme and a more general version of free-verse translation: the translation of the linear into the tabular (2009). There is not space here to outline that argument in detail: in my rough tally, the shift from linear to tabular entails some twenty corresponding shifts of readerly mindset (2009, 42–7). But from that argument I would like to rescue three points for present purposes:

(i) The shift from linear to tabular text produces a cinematisation of discourse. Verse sacrifices the articulation of discursive syntax to the splicing together of cuts, to 'editing' by 'shot'. The tabular introduces the ethos of montage: anything can enter, can be montaged into its self-adapting structure (expanding text). This rhythm of adjustment, this preparedness to re-orientate structural and emotional drives, is the essence of the kind of reading I have in view. Rhythm lies not in syntagmatic continuities, but in the enchained discontinuities of shot. We shall further explore below this shift from enjambement to *découpage*.

(ii) The tabular pushes time almost exclusively in the Bergsonian direction. Time is no longer teleological, forward-driven, but is made up of digression, distraction, unresolvability. The unicursal labyrinth of the linear gives way to the multicursal labyrinth of the tabular. The linear page is the page we pass through; the tabular page is the page we spend time in.

(iii) There is no accepted way of either writing or reading the tabular; we do not know how to do either. Each time we have to reinvent our perceptual behaviours, our itineraries through language. Translating into the tabular is translating away from the interpretative and towards the phenomenological, away from the gathering of meaning and towards the palpation of language.

Additionally, in order to institute what I have called 'the dialogue of rhythmicity', and to explore the ST in all its genetic phases and variant options, verse-translation needs to draw on prose-versions, as a pre-textual ground in which all is still possible, latent, awaiting the multitude of readerly/speakerly self-explorations and their rhythmic realisations (a proposition already set in motion in our treatment of Henley in Chapter 2). In French metrical commentary, the identification of verse-lines, or verse-fragments, in passages of prose has been the source of unnecessarily hot dispute. Antoine Fongaro's listing of 'segments métriques' in the *Illuminations* (1993) has called forth responses of deep scepticism (Cornulier, 1994; Murat, 2000, 273),[4] which are, from a platonic point of view, justified; but these pseudo-lines deserve to be thought about differently, in ways more in tune with prose's equivocating malleability:

Néanmoins, il faut souligner que les compétences métriques et l'oreille des contemporains de Montaigne puis de Molière, jusqu'à Hugo au moins, leur permettaient peut-être de percevoir dans la prose des constructions qui pouvaient leur rappeler des vers familiers, *a fortiori* puisque ces propositions peuvent se lire en langue des vers. Dans ce cas, il y aurait un effet de citation possible, une connivence culturelle. Cela ne fait pas de ces énoncés des vers, mais il est donc envisageable qu'ils aient étés identifiables comme tels à certains moments de l'histoire. (Peureux, 2009, 12, footnote 1)

[Nevertheless, it must be emphasised that the metrical competences and the ear of the contemporaries of Montaigne then of Molière, up to Hugo at least, perhaps allowed them to perceive in prose constructions which might call to their minds familiar verse-lines, all the more so since these constructions can be read as verse-language. In that case, there would be a possible effect of quotation, a cultural connivance. This does not make these constructions verse-lines, but it is thus envisageable that they were identified as such at certain points in history.]

There is some pussy-footing here. Why the qualifications? Why stop at Hugo? Why say 'perhaps', 'envisageable' and so on? 'You are not justified in calling these constructions verse-lines, but I cannot prevent you from perceiving them as such.' This storm in a tea-cup is avoided, as Peureux's words imply, by Murat's notion of '[L]a prédominance du rapport mémoriel sur le rapport contextuel' (2008, 136) [the predominance of a relation of memory over a relation of context], interpreted perhaps more loosely than Murat would wish, and with this proviso: recognition by memory (of previous examples) does not necessarily make the fragment recognised the citation of a (past) form; it may also make it the potentiality of a (future) form, as happens in the case of Apollinaire's 'La Maison des morts' (*Alcools*, 1913) – murky though the genesis of that poem is – and in Cendrars's many re-castings of prose texts as *vers libre*. We shall see prose in action as a re-geneticisation of text below.

Armed with these initial reflections and resolutions, let us begin to imagine what new styles of notation might reveal within a translational process. I take the first line of Baudelaire's 'Chant d'automne', accompanied by a standard metrical notation:

> Bientôt nous plongerons dans les froides ténèbres   2+4+3+3
> (Baudelaire: 'Chant d'automne', l. 1)

The plus signs between the syllabic groups suggest recuperative stasis, measures marked off and juxtaposed with each other, a process of adding units together to make the desired number: twelve. This anti-Bergsonian, spatialist view of verse-structure is reinforced by the terminological habits that have come to us from linguistics: Peureux, for example, does not speak of the phonemes which *precede* or *follow* the rhyming vowel, but of the phonemes 'à la gauche et à la droite de la dernière voyelle masculine' (2009, 244) [to the left and right of the last accentuable vowel]. But if, instead,

I write 2>4>3>3, I am already suggesting that sequence is not a process of addition but of metamorphosis (including morphing into something numerically the same but constitutionally different), an ongoing dynamic of measures finding their way, of verbal decisions on the wing.

Soon we will plunge into the cold shadows / x x / x x x / / x

One might think of this line as an act of simultaneous interpreting, which is only interested in the words and their meanings, not in the rhythm. But we can become interested in the rhythm:

Soon ... ... we will plunge/intothe *cold shadows* 3 ... 214/311431

And then turning back to the twelve syllables of the French:

Soon ... ↑ plunge/>deep↑ into
soon we will *chilly sha-*
dows ↓ 4 3 1 1 3 4 1 1 4 1 3 2
/ / x x / | / x x / x / x

In these two re-writings, the minimal diacritical notations are: suspension marks = drawl and pause; ↑↓ = rise and fall in pitch; reduction to ten-point = recession of voice; /> = caesura (/) with syncopation (>) (and silent off-beat) + thrust forward on to following word; *scriptio continua* = accelerando; italics = rallentando; numerical notation = different degrees of stress on a rising scale of one to four. The diacritical marks, it should be emphasised, are not designed as *accurate* notations of pitch, speed and so on, but an indication that these features are *in action* at these points, and are an invitation to the reader to exercise him/herself in them.

This view, where translation operates as a process of rhythmicisation, or enrhythming, of the text (not *necessarily* at the expense of the metrical background), naturally attracts back-translation as the mapping out, by intertextual dialogue, of a widening rhythmic field, in which a continual process of metamorphosis expands the rhythmic parameters of the 'shared' text. When I first asked the computer for a translation, I left in the diacritical marks, and it replied with a linguistic hybrid, bilingual and sharply fragmented:

Bientôt ... ↑ deep↑> de plongeon dans
bientôt nous *sha-frais*
dows ↓

For me, this hybrid is powerfully telling: it acts out a hand-to-hand collision of languages, unresolved, unresolvable, and yet bespeaks the self-insinuative capacity of language; it acts out, too, a writerly predicament: unde-cided, caught between languages, the writing shudders forward, through a sequence of false starts. In short, the line has taken a genetic step backwards, towards the stuttering rhythms of the pre-articulate. Translation has this capacity to investigate the ways in which a text finds its rhythmical way. In this sense, translation is a process of textual becoming, of text coming to itself, *as the psychologisation or existentialisation of the reader.*

In my second back-translation, I removed the diacritical marks and re-aligned the text on a single level. What emerged was a seventeen-syllable line:

> Bientôt bientôt nous plongerons profondément
>   dans les ombres fraîches

Its measures, for me, run : 4>4>4>3>2. So I have printed it here as a 'tailed' *trimètre* (three-measure alexandrine, with added, hypermetrical syllables), where the tail describes a movement of syllabic diminution. 'Bientôt'/'soon' now has a new impulsiveness: where my English version has an 'inflated' first 'soon' which then recedes, here we have a first 'Bientôt' reaching impatiently for the second in which an accented pitch-peak is reached. And now the acoustic range is dominated by a nasalised /ɔ̃/, and by the shifts between voiced and voiceless (/b/ : /p/, /t/ : /d/, /ʒ/ : /ʃ/), as if the conflict between heat and cold, light and dark, were playing itself out in the throat.

The final back-translation appeared without my quite knowing where from or how:

> Profondément nous de plongerons de bientôt de Bientôt
>   fraîches d'ombres de les de dans

This line, punctuated by 'de', gradually undoes syntax and disappears into the sand. This is a line heading towards glossolalia. As we have seen, trans-lation is a naturally self-polarising enterprise: it must institute a productive interaction between languages, whereby the expressive range of the lan-guages involved is reciprocally extended and refined; but, at the same time, translation re-investigates language as a medium, challenges its acoustic and syntactic assumptions, tests its limits, explores its pathologies. This 'vari-ant' is the Baudelairean line seen as the divagation of a disturbed mind, the step-by-step descent into the inarticulate, the gradual evacuation of lan-guage's semanticity. But it may equally be translation into a new language, a new syntax, a twelve-tone music of syntax, in which words live different lives and come into perception from unfamiliar angles.

This set of translational moves is instructive. It is not just that a single line can be read in many ways; it is that translation compels text constantly to re-imagine itself from its putative conception to any number of alternative realisations, so that a complex rhythmic portrait develops, a gradual rhythmic sedimentation, or sedimentation of rhythms, rhythmic impulses, rhythmic re-configurations.[5] A perusal of Cocteau's poetry, for example, tells us that what may have been conceived initially as regular verse, a sonnet even, can easily morph into free verse (*poèmes scindés, poèmes éclatés, poèmes démontés*) or prose (see Purnelle, 2003, and Gullentops, 2003). Here is part of the attempt, by redistribution, by devices of *emboîtement*, of imbrication, to overcome the inevitable partnership of linearity, monotemporality and chronometricity, and to internalise rhymes. Correspondingly, in translation, the TT is what the ST might have found its way to, if it had taken a slightly different route through language. The translator's task is to restore the ST to activity in the activity of translation, and to translate rhythm, because rhythm is the way in which the reading of the ST registers *its* activity.

As we move on from the translation of a single alexandrine to the translation of free verse itself, we should first explore the French analytical predicament when confronting free verse. It may well be justified to trace the emergence of free verse back to a certain relationship with syllabic metricity and to claim that 'le rejet de la versification se fondait sur elle' [the rejection of versification was based upon it [syllabic metricity]] (Peureux, 2009, 25); but to read free verse as an 'objet-limite pour l'étude métrique' [outer-extreme/outer-limit object for metrical study] (26) encourages not only this retrospective reading of *vers libre*, but also a reading of it which inevitably casts it as the negation, or transgression, of a certain perceptual system. Free verse certainly needed to find its way out of metrical assumptions, but only to establish itself as a real perceptual alternative, not as an absence of rhythm, or as a *subversive* rhythmicity, but as a *relocated* rhythmicity.

Nor is there any need, in free verse, to outlaw syllabic number; one only has to treat it differently, not as metre-giving but as rhythm-making, not as something to be adhered to, but as something which emerges as the text unfolds, not as a monopolising consideration, but as one aspect among many in an inclusive view of verse-constituents (accent, acoustic landscape, intonation, tempo, pausing, etc.). Laforgue may, famously, have forgotten to count syllables,[6] but syllabic numbers are an inevitable concomitant of the lexicon and syntax he chose, a property of his texts. And the argument that counting is unreliable because of doubts about the status of the mute e (syncope, apocope), and about synaeresis and diaeresis, is not disqualifying, when one is experimenting with reading rather than trying to establish a metre; one reads the text now one way, now another, to explore its rhythmic possibilities and to discover what kind of reading does best justice to one's own textual perceptions at a particular moment.

In his treatment of Valery Larbaud's *Barnabooth* poems (1908), Murat (2008, 215–34) initiates his study with this affirmation: 'il s'agit bien chez Larbaud d'un vrai vers libre, non compté et non rimé. Bien que les poèmes contiennent un grand nombre de mètres virtuels, le principe d'équivalence en nombre syllabique cesse de s'appliquer; la périodicité, c'est-à-dire la récurrence systématique et exhaustive des formes, est abandonnée' (2008, 223) [with Larbaud, it is a matter of true free verse, not counted and not rhymed. Although the poems contain a large number of potential metres, the principle of equivalence in syllabic number ceases to apply; periodicity, that is to say the systematic and exhaustive recurrence of forms, is abandoned]. One might immediately object that the notion of a 'true' *vers libre* is as chimaeric as it is undesirable, just as Murat's construction of a 'forme standard' of *vers libre* takes it into platonic realms which are alien to its ontological relativity and elasticity. Additionally, one should say that the importance of rhyme to the definition of free verse is negligeable, while the definition of free verse is crucial to rhyme. The absence of rhyme does not help to install *vers libre*, even in France; *vers libre* simply changes the function of rhyme: its role is no longer structural/structuring, but psycho-physiological. And this reveals the more fundamental burden of my argument: *vers libre* has certain prosodic characteristics by which it is customarily defined; but their significance is no longer prosodic so much as cognitive, perceptual and psychological.

In his account of the first stanza of Larbaud's 'Ode':

1. Prête-moi ton grand bruit, ta grande allure si douce,
2. Ton glissement nocturne à travers l'Europe illuminée,
3. Ô train de luxe! et l'angoissante musique
4. Qui bruit le long de tes couloirs de cuir doré,
5. Tandis que derrière les portes laquées, aux loquets de cuivre lourd,
6. Dorment les millionaires.

and despite his affirmation that syllabic number is no longer pertinent for free verse (2008, 50), Murat provides a standard notation of syllabic values, with indications of caesuras or structural *coupes*: 6–7, 6–8, 4–7, 4–4–4, 10–7, 6 (2008, 226). We might disagree with such a notation on two grounds: (a) some of the numbers seem wrong: line 2 = 6–9, not 6–8; line 4 is more

like 2–6–4; line 5 = 11–7, not 10–7 (Murat seems to be counting the mute
e in the traditional way); (b) it continues to suppose that these are *vers
composés*, pivoting around a structural juncture; first hemistichs of 4 and 6
thus identified condition reading towards a recognition of 'virtual' metres,
blurred by the syllabic 'débordement' of their second hemistichs (2008,
227). But there is no obligation to read in this fashion, no obligation to
make that kind of choice. I read these lines with this rhythmic disposition:

$$3>3>4>3$$
$$4>2>5>4$$
$$4>4>3$$
$$2>6>4$$
$$8(2>6)>3>3>4$$
$$1>5 \qquad\qquad = 75$$

which, in turn and leaving aside consonants, produces a foregrounding of
the following vocalic elements:

$$/a/>/i/>/y/>/u/$$
$$/ā/>/y/>/ɔ/>/e/$$
$$/y/>/ā/>/i/$$
$$/i/>/a/>/e/$$
$$(/i/>/ɔ/)>/e/>/ɛ/>/u/$$
$$/ɔ/>/ɛ/$$

Even though, technically speaking, the poem is not rhymed, line-terminal
echoes help to project and shape the phonic manifestations of accent;
as Eliot puts it: 'Rhyme removed, much ethereal music leaps from the
word, music which has hitherto chirped unnoticed in the expanse of prose'
(1978, 189). Rhyme no longer generates repetitive structures and does not
therefore establish particular kinds of intonational pattern. It does not
have a role independent of other acoustic structures in the verse.[7] It does
not endorse metrical structure, although it may endorse the line-ending.
Above all, it is not the agent of memory/reflection, but the instrument of
the association of ideas, propulsive rather than recursive, but propulsive
without anticipation. Put another way, one might say that it is involuntary,
a linguistic compulsion, not listened for but recognised. It is an element of
verbal psychology rather than of aesthetic structure.

To use a prose version of the ST as an initial relay-station on the way
to translations is to return to the inchoate of language, to rhythmicity as a
shape-shifting miasma, where all is yet to be conceived, drawn out, where

the multiplicity of virtual verbal trajectories, expressive configurations, seg-
mentations and groupings, is at a maximum, where vision is unprejudiced
by the already-arrived-at:

prête-moi ton grand bruit ta grande allure si douce ton glissement nocturne à
travers l'Europe illuminée ô train de luxe et l'angoissante musique qui bruit le
long de tes couloirs de cuir doré tandis que derrière les portes lacquées aux loquets
de cuivre lourd dorment les millionaires

Once folded into prose and re-virtualised, verse can be folded out again, but
in many re-configured forms. Prose is a medium which multiplies verse; it
asks us to see the possible patterns in the carpet, to make varieties of choice,
and varieties of choice about literary value. That is why prose itself needs
always to be re-translated. Sadly, our sensitivity to prose's multiformity is
little developed. From this prose I take:

prête-moi ton grand		3>2
	bruit	1
ta grande		2
	allure	2
	si douce	2
ton glissement nocturne		4>2
à travers		3
	l'Europe illuminée	2>4
	ô train de luxe	4/2>2
et l'angoiss-		3
	ante musique qui bruit	4>3
le long de tes couloirs de cuir		2>4>2
	doré	2
tandis que		3
derrière		2
les portes lacquées aux		2>4
loquets de cuivre		2>2
	lourd	1
dorment		1
	les millionaires	4 = 70

In regular verse, there is much difference in the significance that enjambement has in French and English. Being a 'foot' prosody (recurrence of
metrical unit) rather than a line prosody, being a motor-metre rather than
a metre of boundaries, English regular verse has few inhibitions about
enjambement; it may produce marked expressive effects, effects which
grow from the kind of syntactic rupture, or from the kind of loading of
juncture, which it produces, but it is not *metrically* subversive. In French

regular verse, on the other hand, where the line-ending is a boundary reinforced by rhyme which establishes the line's numericity and is thus 'naturally' the location of a tonic accent, enjambement threatens to undo that metrical order. Enjambement may provide the same expressive effects as in English, but here there is potentially a metrical price to pay and correspondingly a nuance of transgression in the effect. In free verse, on the other hand, where the line in both languages is not a metrical product so much as a typographical one, enjambement, by its arbitrary intervention, establishes the formal imperativity of the line; or, alternatively, it defines the line as a palpation of junctures: the line comes to an end when it has identified the juncture most apposite for its expressive agenda; or, alternatively, it helps to generate the meaning of margins. As we move further into these new functions, the notion of enjambement becomes increasingly inappropriate: no metrical boundary is being straddled by a syntactical unit whose very integrity is crucial to the force of the enjambement. In the new dispensation, syntactic integrity is not at stake; language's raison d'être is its fragmentation, its denaturalisation of syntax and parts of speech, its promotion of the morphemic and phonetic at the expensive of discursive continuity. Line-endings are no longer sites of completion, but rather of rupture and dislocation. Enjambement cedes its place to *découpage*.

In my re-writing of the Larbaud stanza, *découpage* clearly has an overall rhythmic significance: instead of long lines imitating the expanding trajectory of the train, gliding smoothly across measures, we have a choppier, staccato movement, as if the train's impulsiveness were being dammed up, frustrated, only periodically released in rather longer measures, or combinations of measure. In this process, by virtue of being line-group-terminal, some syllables attract degrees of accentuation they would not normally enjoy; and the increase in line-group-terminal mute e's means that this version of the stanza, by 'standard' metrical rules, has only seventy counting syllables, where the original has seventy-five, which itself impairs the stanza's pronunciatory flexibility and fluency. In the end, the train is almost immobilised by the inertia of its heavy fittings ('lourd') and the sleep ('dorment') of its millionaires.

This *découpage* also creates a pattern of margins in which the fourth margin attracts post-posed adjectives, the third nouns, and the second, not surprisingly, prepositions and pre-posed adjectives. It is as if the train were passing through a sifting device, its progress along the lines disaggregated and scattered across grammatical categories. This pulverisation of the train journey leaves the translator thinking of the entropic rhythms of energy-dispersal, rather than the purposeful ones of unidirectional momentum.

As I turn to an English rendering, I return to the bath of prose, reflecting upon the process of re-writing I have just passed through:

lend me your great noise your great so soothing motion your nocturnal glide across Europe in lights o train de luxe and the harrowing music which reverberates along your gilt leather corridors while behind the lacquered doors with their heavy copper latches the millionaires slumber on

From this emerges:

LEND↑ me . . . .

       your GREAT↑   //   **NOISE**↓
       your **GREAT**   **MOTION**↓
                       so soothing

       your noc**TURN**al → ≈   **GLIDE** →
       across **EUR**↑**O**pe
                 in **LIGHTS**↓
             O train de **LUXE** →
                  and
          the HARrowing MU↑**sic**
               which
        *re***VERBerates** →
             along
         your **GILT LEA**ther
            COrridors →
   While be**HIND**↑ the **LAC**quered **DOORS**↓
With their HEAvv↓ **COpper**↓ **LAtches**↓
The million**AIRES** →
                    SLUM↓*ber*
                        ON↓

[Additional diacritics: // = a resistance to the voice, which holds the voice up and requires an effort of the voice to overcome; ≈ = an undulation in the train's glide, a wiggle of the vocal hips]

At first glance, regular verse is made up of units whose raison d'être is independent of any typographical disposition, but which typographical disposition serves the function of making formally visible: layout makes rhyme patterns easy to recuperate; indentation facilitates the identification of heterosyllabicity. In free verse the relation between typographic disposition and inherent (linguistic) feature is much more crucial and problematic. What we can claim, in very general terms, is that metrists have continued to look for the answers of free verse in the *linguistic* givens, and thus correspondingly insufficient attention has been paid to typographic disposition as verse-constitutive – lines define the relation of margins as much as vice-versa; language releases the play of fonts, of bold, of roman and italic, as much as vice versa. One might argue that, in adopting this particular disposition of Larbaud's lines, we are enhancing the cosmopolitan spirit of his verse, and, in the process, subscribing to the view, expressed by Murat, that the arts of typography and layout promise an international verse-language:

D'autre part, le découpage et la mise en page du vers libre sont des processus indépendants de la langue du poème (de sa phonologie, de sa prosodie et de sa syntaxe) ainsi que de la tradition métrique qui s'est développée dans cette langue. Ils peuvent être adoptés pratiquement sans apprentissage, transposés d'une langue à une autre. (2008, 216)

[On the other hand, the line-divisions and layout of vers libre are processes independent of the poem's language (of its phonology, its prosody, its syntax) as of the metrical tradition which has evolved in that language. They can be adopted almost without any need for initiation, transposed from one language into another.]

But in fact our view is very different. While typography and layout may be international as a language, as a resource, they reach, *in every particular application*, deep into the phonology, prosody and syntax of the particular language concerned, multiply their aspects, and exercise, and perhaps extend, their expressive range. Typographical disposition is important precisely because it is able to embody those paralinguistic features which metrical analysis leaves totally out of account, and to act, if need be, as a visual/vocal prosthetic, to create 'signs' which might push the voice in the direction of the non-vocal, or conceptual (the mental-acoustic). Because of these capacities, a set of typographical and dispositional features cannot simply be transposed from one language to another, as Murat suggests, but on the contrary, must be translated into different forms of themselves in order to capture the rhythmic, acoustic and syntactic shifts which occur as one morphs from one language into another (see Scott, 2002). And because of these capacities, we are reminded that typographical and dispositional change is the device by which a text can constantly be called back into time, into the time of its making and of its being read anew, and the infinity of possible typographical and dispositional permutations brings home to us that translation, no less than writing or reading, is an activity continually at work on itself.

This version of these lines draws on nine typefaces: Engravers MT, Copperplate Gothic, Bauhaus 93, Bernard MT Conder, Wide Latin, Broadway, Algerian, Stencil, with Times New Roman as its default position. It is easy to think that language in tabular texts has a greater power to act imitatively, iconically or transcriptively, and this is undoubtedly true. But more valuable, perhaps, is the new sense that language is not the secretary of another order of reality, but an investigative equipment, the instrument of a neuro-surgical exploration, and the sense that it is more diverse in its enunciability, in its range of function and expressiveness. The tabular page can explore the whole gamut that runs from the lyrically voiced to the non-vocal or non-vocalisable (i.e. noise), via the speakable (but devoiced) through the oral (sounds vocalised, but without vocal continuity). And these different degrees of vocalisation and non-vocalisability can be conveyed by variable fonts. Fonts can also suggest decorative, sculptural or architectural styles (Algerian, Bauhaus 93), lifestyles (Broadway), spatial pressures, like the compression of Bernard MT Conder, or degrees of amplification, as in Wide Latin. The buccal cavity and the mechanisms of articulation add up to actualisations of the voice in shapes, volumes, intensities, structures. In the end, we may dream of the whole family of fonts as an intricate system of diacritics, conveying voice quality and phonetic values.

When we listen to language, we can listen phonetically or phonologically, that is to say, we can either listen to language as raw sounds, as *origins*, or we can listen to it as a string of phonemes, as determiners of meaning, as *destinations*. In our translation, typographic foregrounding helps to engineer this phoneticisation of the phonological, governed by no particular obligations to standard morphology, so that the text releases not only a suggestive new lexicon, but also the poet's song of himself, what Larbaud refers to as the 'borborygmes' [intestinal rumblings], the 'chuchotements irrépressibles des organes' [irrepressible whisperings of the organs], the 'inévitable chanson de l'œsophage' [unavoidable song of the oesophagus] ('Prologue').

Finally, and briefly, we should notice that in the translation of lines 3 and 4 of the original stanza, the lateral patterns based on the left-hand margin give way temporarily to a vertical, middle-axis sequence (as in our translation of 'Adlestrop' in Chapter I); that is to say, there is a point at which this stanza breaks away from the left-hand margin of authorial textual possession, of authorial enunciation, the place where the linear ever seeks to re-establish itself, and installs an alternative consciousness, a consciousness which sinks into the centre of experience, and which expands from the middle, spreading out in a movement of bi-lateral encompassment. This is a consciousness without a psychology, driven forward by a pure receptivity to phenomena, but finally intruded upon and effaced by the sleeping millionaires.

It is usual to think of translation as the servant of prevailing critical circumstances and attitudes. Literary translation mirrors the situation which obtains in the critical marketplace and gravitates towards those available approaches which best serve its purposes (postcolonial studies, cultural studies, cognitive poetics). If one supposes, however, that translation is designed as a critique of critical methods, if one assumes that translation, as a record of a particular kind of creative reading, is to be valued as a counterweight to interpretative reading, then one might call upon translation to re-orientate our thinking about the ways in which texts can be most fruitfully absorbed. In the case considered here, and supposing that translation is reading across languages, rather than converting one language into another, translation reveals what metre obstructs in the interchange of texts, in the reader's negotiation between texts, and what it discourages in the reciprocal, performative inhabitation of texts. As our knowledge of a poem deepens, so the centre of metrico-rhythmic interest and activity shifts, outwards, from processes of recognition and identification towards processes of diversification, differentiation, modulation. Rhythmic choices – choices with any number of visible and invisible motivations – individuate the reader; by that I do not mean 'individuate the reader's interpretation', but individuate the reader's consciousness as a consciousness-of-text, act as 'footprints' of a changing readerly metabolism.

Translation should thus have as its business the development of new kinds of rhythmic analysis, new languages of scansional notation. What we have yet fully to realise is that inasmuch as translation, as experimental writing, is the art of typeface and layout, the poetics of the page, it seeks to activate in the eye and the ear degrees of awareness and responsiveness which the eye and ear only too readily fall short of. We have to re-imagine the participatory arts of the eye and ear, and exercise them in our reading and writing with a physical immediacy we are unaccustomed to.

CHAPTER 7

The reinvention of the literary in
literary translation

The main purpose of the present chapter is to pick up and develop an argument adumbrated in the main text and note 9 of Chapter 4, to wit, that the literary is not a stable value, that it tends to be limited, unjustifiably, to a certain range of features, and that it is subject to historical erosion and conventionalisation. It needs, therefore, constantly to be re-defined or re-invented. And, as a consequence, we should understand the ways in which literary translation is a translation *into* the literary. As ever, my particular concern is translation into performance, into the performed text, and I would like to begin this re-theorisation of the literary in literary translation with Virgil, and more particularly with the *Aeneid*.

As a verse-line for translation, Virgil's dactylic hexameter has a certain degree of expressive elasticity built into its structure; given the possible exchange of dactyl for spondee, it may vary between twelve and seventeen syllables, with the Latin hexameter tending towards the lower end of the range and the Greek towards the higher (Gasparov, 1996, 72). I am taking as my point of comparison *Aeneid* XII, 903–14, the passage in which Turnus, in his duel with Aeneas, loses all power and momentarily enters a dream-like state of dulled activity:

SED NEQUE CURRENTEM SE NEC COGNOSCIT EUNTEM
TOLLENTEMVE MANU SAXUMVE IMMANE MOVENTEM;
GENUA LABANT, GELIDUS CONCREVIT FRIGORE SANGUIS.
TUM LAPIS IPSE VIRI VACUUM PER INANE VOLUTUS
NEC SPATIUM EVASIT TOTUM NEQUE PERTULIT ICTUM.
AC VELUT IN SOMNIS, OCULOS UBI LANGUIDA PRESSIT
NOCTE QUIES, NEQUIQUAM AVIDOS EXTENDERE CURSUS
VELLE VIDEMUR ET IN MEDIIS CONATIBUS AEGRI
SUCCIDIMUS; NON LINGUA VALET, NON CORPORE NOTAE
SUFFICIUNT VIRES NEC VOX AUT VERBA SEQUUNTUR:
SIC TURNO, QUACUMQUE VIAM VIRTUTE PETIVIT,
SUCCESSUM DEA DIRA NEGAT.[1]

Of the relatively free-rhythmical versions of this passage in English, Cecil Day Lewis (1966, 527, ll. 903–14) uses 12 lines, with a syllabic average of 14.50 and a stress average per line of 6.00; Robert Fagles (2006, 385, ll. 1048–61) uses 14 lines, with a syllabic average of 12.00 and a stress average of 5.64; Frederick Ahl (2007, 326, ll. 903–14) uses 12 lines, with a syllabic average of 15.92 and a stress average of 6.50. Robert Fitzgerald (1992, 401, ll. 1227–40), for his part, uses 14 lines of iambic pentameter. Then there are the prose versions (e.g. W.F. Jackson Knight (1958, 337), David West (2003, 289)). In other words, we move from a verse whose explanation and literary justification is inbuilt, in its metre, dactylic hexameter, to mobile heterosyllabic rhythmic structures whose rhythmicity, and perhaps literariness, is revealed principally by vocal realisation. As we move from metricity to rhythmicity, the source of rhythm is less exclusively linguistic and more paralinguistic; in other words, freer rhythms demand a wider range of vocal effects if they are to be properly embodied. But wherein lies the literariness of the spoken word? Perhaps in the quality of silences; or in the degrees and patterns of juncture; or in the shifts of tone; or in the play of intonational shapes; or in the expressive manipulation of tempi and loudness.

Those who have concerned themselves with the speaking of Classical Latin (e.g. W. Sidney Allen, 1965; Clive Brooks, 2007) have concentrated their reconstructive energies[2] on the pronunciation of individual phonemes and on the nature of Latin accent/stress. Brooks feels able to affirm: 'Great strides have been made in recent years towards establishing the real pronunciation of ancient Roman Latin' (2007, 4), but the isolation of phonemes leads to repeated acoustic definitions which take the form 'as in English'; one is thereby led to believe that, when these phonemes are combined into words and sentences, the corresponding accent of speech will be English. Latin stress is reckoned to be principally a stress of intensity, and the laws of its placement – including the so-called 'Penultimate Law' – seem confidently possessed. But doubt surrounds the part played by pitch: we rely for much of our knowledge of these matters on comments made by post-classical grammarians using a terminology derived from Greek (Allen, 1965, 83–4). And when it comes to the operation of word-accent in verse, further doubts come into play. What is the relationship between word-accent and quantity in the speaking of verse? Is this relationship further complicated by an ictus, or metrical beat, on the leading 'heavy' (Allen) or 'large' (Brooks) syllable of the foot (if dactylic hexameter is the metre)?[3] While commentators agree that there is coincidence of accent and 'heavy' syllable in the final two feet of the dactylic hexameter, the vocal conduct of the rest of the line remains suppositional; Gasparov (1996, 86), for example, suggests that ancient readers *pronounced* verse according to the natural stresses in the language, but *heard* the rhythm of longs and shorts.[4]

But the real problem for the performance of Latin verse, rather than for its recitation, is the absence of any indication of suprasegmental or paralinguistic features, of what one might call its 'vocal envelope'. Brooks (2007, 29) shows plenty of awareness of these kinds of feature, but they play no part in his central investigation. And the live readings that accompany his book are characterised by a general consistency of tone, and intonation patterns that respond to the inserted 'English' punctuation. The question of national styles of pronunciation – Allen devotes an appendix of *Vox Latina* to 'The Pronunciation of Latin in England' (1965, 102–10) – and the historical evolution of habits of pronunciation – Brooks (2007) traces pronunciation through to the eighteenth century – only complicate matters further.

The example of Latin reminds us of two truths, not sufficiently attended to perhaps. The first is that our sense of the vocal envelope does not stretch very far, that even reading our own language of 200 years ago, we do not stop to wonder what our grasp of that envelope is. Are we, even among the modern languages, surrounded by dead languages? We might regret that readers of translations, and perhaps translators themselves, are little worried by that fact, for, after all, texts are being translated out of the texts' time and into our own. Put another way – and this is the second truth – because translators do not concern themselves with the vocal envelope of either ST or TT, languages are becoming dead languages by virtue of the very act of translation. But for the translator who wishes his/her version to be read in sight of the ST, the reader's ability to compare changing vocal envelopes is a matter of some concern, as we saw in the previous chapter, a matter that is both to do with translation as an intensification of our historical and geographical sense, as an intensification of our sense of the changing anthropology of voice, of evolving conceptions and practices of voice in its relation to metre, rhythm, prosody, expression, and also, and thus, of our sense of the changing location of literary effects. Our fundamental proposition continues to be that all literary translation should translate from the linguistic towards the paralinguistic, from script towards dict, that is towards spoken or performed text (see Beardsley, 1977). What we want to imagine is a set of translations which generate their own oral tradition, which are closer to each other than to the source text, and which constantly require a re-positioning of the literary.

The processes of digestion and playing over and experimenting, that reading and listening are, need to be recoverable from translation. When, for instance, I read a version of our *Aeneid* passage, I need to be able to recover, by a process of readerly scansion, the possible shifts of tone and speed that indicate shifts of consciousness between narrator and Turnus, between the agents of speech and perception; I need to register the gradations of stress, the slurring together of syllables, the pauses, the changes in clarity of articulation, the notes of urgency, surprise, effort, self-satisfaction. And, consequently, I begin to look for a new system of notation, which will turn my reading, appropriately, into the equivalent of the Roman practice of *praelectio* (to which we have already made reference in connection with the notion of pre-textual translation – see Chapter 2) and thus help me towards the most effective oral delivery of the text.

We may continue to regret that the sounds of a text in script are 'limited to phonetic considerations which represent little more than a systematic adaptation of the Latin alphabet' (Tedlock, 1977, 508), that pause, tone, loudness, tempo of delivery and so on, are silently erased. But even *within* the limits of the script, there are ample signs that the literary has fallen victim to 'the same old alphabetic ear' (Tedlock, 1977, 508). I want to consider three features, again in the light of Virgilian translations: rhythm; acousticity; punctuation.

In considering rhythm, I want to turn to prose, because prose, as we tend to understand it, is a potentially infinite, linear, non-spoken extension of language, folded backwards and forwards across a page, a pure invention of writing, that cannot find its way to the oral. As such, as the extremely scriptual, it has produced a very low sensitivity to its literariness *as a medium*, other than at the lexical, word-selective level. Penguin's other current *Aeneid* translation, beside that of Fagles, is a prose version by David West, dating back to 1990. West defends his choice of prose in these, laudable, terms: 'Received wisdom, as represented by *The Proceedings of the Virgil Society* 19 (1988), 14, states that "to translate poetry into prose is always a folly". I believe that this view does less than justice to the range, power and music of contemporary English prose' (2003: xlv). But, looking across at Jackson Knight's Penguin Classic of 1956, also in prose, West reckons its language is dated, and agrees with Sandbach that over-preoccupation with its lexical fidelity puts 'sentence rhythm and cohesion and the emphasis that goes with form' (2003, xlv–xlvi) at risk. The argument that translations are subject to the ravages of time, in a way that source texts are not, has been part of the mythicisation of 'pure' literature at translation's expense, and should be firmly rebutted. Sandbach and West's judgement, however, bears on another crucial question, namely the relation between readerly tolerance, the perception of literariness and the mode of reading. I want to take a few sentences from Jackson Knight's prose account (1958, 117–18) of Book IV and provide a self-consciously scanned reading of them. Dido has just fallen on her sword:

A cry rose to the palace-roof.	3>5	x / / x x / x /
Carthage was stricken by the shock	5>3	/ x x / x x x /
and Rumour ran riot in the town.	6>3	x / x x / x x x /
Lamentation and sobbing and women's wailing	4>3>5	x x / x x / x x / x / x
rang through the houses,	5	/ x x / x
and high heaven echoed with the loud mourning;	6>5	x / / x / x x x / / x
as if some enemy had broken through	6>4	x x / / x x x / x /
and all Carthage, or ancient Tyre,	4>4	x / / x x / x /
were falling, with the flames rolling madly up	3>8	x / x x x / / x / x /
over dwellings of gods and men.	4>4	x x / x x / x /
Her sister heard, and the breath left her.	4>5	x / x / x x / / x
Marring her cheeks with her finger-nails	4>5	/ x x / x x / x /
and bruising her breast with her clenched hands,	5>4	x / x x / x x / /
she dashed in frightened haste through the crowds,	6>3	x / x / x / x x /
found Dido at the very point of death,	3>7	/ / x x x / x / x /
and cried out to her	5	x / / x x

(Virgil, *Aeneid*, IV, 665–74)

[iambic: x /; anapaest: x x /; third paeon: x x / x; bacchic: x / /; ionic: x x / /; antispast: x / / x; antibacchic: / / x; I refer here to groupings of weak/unstressed (x) and strong/stressed (/) syllables using a classical quantitative terminology, that is, a terminology designed for short and long syllables, rather than weak and strong. Many might reckon this practice to be misleading, but the classical terms provide a much neater way of classifying rhythmic segments than imaginable alternatives]

This piece quite clearly does not deserve Sandbach and West's judgement. What I hear, evident in the way I have disposed the passage, and metrico-rhythmically analysed it, is a set of dyads, whose paired elements rock between three and six syllables, polarising in 3>7 at the touching discovery: 'found Dido at the very point of death', but which elsewhere play with repetitions and reversals within a narrower syllabic range; the unit of four stabilises the passage just after the mid-point. Rhythmically, the passage is constructed on variations of measure involving adjacent stresses – the bacchic, antibacchic, ionic and antispast – and a recurrent third paeon, with leavening from iamb and anapaest.

But there are two larger points to be made. First, the translation of verse into prose is, as we have heard, much sniffed at, unless it has the express function of a crib. But, in fact, and as we have argued in Chapter 6, the translation of verse into prose is translation into a medium which virtualises verse and allows verse, once folded into prose, to be folded out again, but in many re-configured forms. Prose is a medium which multiplies verse; it invites us to see all the possible expressive paths through the thicket, to test the different options; and these are different options on literariness. That is why prose itself needs always to be re-translated.

The second point is equally simple: if these same lines were read less *in*tensively, more *ex*tensively, more prosaically, they would have noticeably fewer stresses, so that we would be less aware of rhythmic distribution and more aware of stress highlights; thus my voice might pick out: cry – roof – Carthage – stricken – shock – Rumour – riot – Lamentation – sobbing – wailing – rang – houses – heaven – mourning – enemy – through – Carthage – Tyre – falling – flames – up – dwellings – gods – men (i.e. up to that point in the text, twenty-four stresses rather than thirty-seven). At the same time, a different set of reading tolerances is brought into play. A different manner of reading, we might say, presupposes a different register; or we might say that the number of possible relations between lexical register and vocal register is much greater than we think. Interestingly perhaps, C. Day Lewis says of his own translation: 'I have weeded out from the *Aeneid* some of the modernisms and colloquialisms which, though they may have served a purpose for *broadcasting*, now seem to me unacceptable in *print*' (1966: v; my emphases). Reading-mode makes its own kind of literariness, activates its own kind of literary resources and expectations.

But if we must increase our sensitivity to the relationship between reading styles and rhythms and registers, we must, at the same time, on the acoustic level, update our ears; we must assimilate into our hearing of text all the contemporary sound-worlds that new typographies, and new serial or electro-acoustic musics, have added to our aural capacities. We must break out of a hearing situation in which the literary acoustic depends on our conversion of individual sounds into rhetorical devices (alliteration, assonance, rhyme); at the moment, we sacrifice our perception of particular sounds to the discovery of a structure, to a *given*, rather than created, literary resource. The trouble is that this already-given stock of literary resources is extremely limited and has held the ear caught, for decade after decade, century after century, in the same crude auditory routine. Worse still, and as we have already pointed out, the translator who is not able to answer alliteration with alliteration at a particular point in the text invokes the principle of compensation and introduces an instance of alliteration at the earliest opportunity, at some *other* textual point. This is a ludicrous policy; and instructive, in that it indicates a naïve belief in the (uninspected) literary value of a small number of devices, which must be salvaged at all costs from the process of translation and be allowed to maintain their monopoly. The idea that alliteration might be translated into a *different* literary effect is simply not entertained.

In examining translations of Virgil, therefore, I listened to Iannis Xenakis's *Persepolis* of 1971, a fifty-six-minute, eight-track tape piece of *musique concrète*, performed through fifty-nine loudspeakers scattered in circular arrangements throughout the audience. The methods and vocabulary of electronic music seem highly suggestive for translation: a language of engineering, editing, modulating, modifying, of mixing and re-mixing. Xenakis's *Persepolis* is accompanied in my recording by nine remixes, four by Japanese composers, two by Americans, and one apiece by a Spanish, a Polish and a German composer. During the course of this chapter, I am undertaking remixes of some of the available translations of Virgil, which themselves constitute remixes of the source text. Since I envisage these translations constructing their own oral tradition, their own family of performances, out of the Virgilian source text, I would also argue for the continual translation and re-translation of the translations themselves.

The passage I have chosen acoustically to remix is Fitzgerald's version (1992, 401, ll. 1232–8) of the latter part of Turnus's physical and psychological undoing:

> Justasindr EE *ms* **W** henthe n **i** ght-**s** **W**oonof **s** lEE **pp**
> **W** *ai* yson **ou**r **i** sit **s**EE*ms* **W** EE tr**i** inv *ai*n
> Tok EE**pp** onrunningtr **i W** ithall **ou**r *m***i** ght
> Butinthe*mid***s**tofe **FF** ort **FF**a*i* ntand **FF**a*i*l
> **ou** rtongueis **pp**o **W**erle **ss** **FF** a*m*iliar **s**trength
> **W** illnotholdu **pp** **ou**rbodynota **ss** **ou** nd
> Or **W** ord **W**illco*me* ju**s**t**s**o **W** ithTurnu **s**n**ou** **W** [5]

Here represented is a kind of pathology of listening. When sounds in language are heard without reference to the word which makes them and by which they acquire their raison d'être, then they become part of the pathology of listening and hearing, equivalent in the ear to the pathology of speaking (glossolalia, echolalia, Tourette's syndrome). This is to place the literary squarely in the activation of poorly controlled associations and subconscious pulsions. These are not sounds artificially isolated for the purposes of identifying pattern, structure, acoustic hierarchy; these are sounds isolated by a kind of psychophonetic attentiveness, aural neurosis, as audiences of modern music might be prompted to listen to a particular arrangement of separated timbres, or the vocal range of a particular instrument, or to a melody as a discontinuous string of notes. Translation, let us not forget, is a recording of a reading, of a listening, which has within it the invitation to further elaborations, the invitation to further translations.

In this text I have highlighted some of the strings of voiceless consonants: we are in the wadded atmosphere of dream, of the voice that cannot enter the throat, cannot find its vibrations; and the isolation of sounds acts out the disintegration of Turnus's belief in himself and in his bodily capacities. I have used variations between roman and italic, between bold and unbold, between different fonts – Broadway, Wide Latin, Bauhaus 93, Franklin Gothic Medium Condensed, Bernard MT Condensed – to try to capture the different ways in which these sounds might materialise themselves in the voice, or in different voices. The visual is a new kind of acoustics, in the sense that a typeface may project its own paralanguage of, say, tone, or loudness, or enunciation. And where I have not isolated sounds but rather kept to the default setting of Times New Roman, I have fallen into *scriptio continua*, as a reminder that, in text-presentational terms, Virgil predates the kind of textual Virgil *we* are familiar with.

Next, I make an interlinear addition of the Latin text:

Justasindr EE *ms* **W** henthe n **l** ght-**s** **W**oonof **s** lEE **pp**
AC VELUT IN SOMNIS, OCULOS UBI LANGUIDA PRESSIT
W *ai* yson **OU**r **l** sit **s**EE*ms* **W** EE tr**l** inv *ai*n
NOCTE QUIES, NEQUIQUAM AVIDOS EXTENDERE CURSUS
Tok EE**pp** onrunningtr **l** **W** ithall **OU**r *ml* ght
VELLE VIDEMUR ET IN MEDIIS CONATIBUS AEGRI
Butinthe*mid***s**tofe FF ort FF*ai* ntand FF*ai*l
SUCCIDIMUS; NON LINGUA VALET, NON CORPORE NOTAE
OU rtongueis **pp**o **W**erle **ss** FF a*mi*liar **s**trength
SUFFICIUNT VIRES NEC VOX AUT VERBA SEQUUNTUR:
W illnotholdu **pp** **OU**rbodynota **ss** **OU** nd

Or **W** ord **W**illco*me* ju**sts**o **W** ith**T**urnu **s**n**OU** **W**
SIC TURNO, . . .

By this device I seek to do two things; first to both highlight and scumble chronology: if *scriptio continua* allows the English translation intermittently to predate the familiar Virgil, the interlinear translation makes Virgil now a version of Fitzgerald, now the other way round. This would square with the Borgesian view of translation, where translations may from time to time turn the tables on their originals.[6] At the end of the passage, Virgil outpaces Fitzgerald, waits for him to catch up; so we feel something, too, of Virgil's or Latin's economy, his/its narrative impatience. Secondly, it helps me to imagine the relevance to translation of the electro-acoustic notion of 'morphing'. In a recent radio programme (*Discovering Music*, BBC Radio 3, 17 February 2008), the composer Jonathan Harvey, in conversation with Alwynne Pritchard, described how, in his work 'Mortuos plango, vivos voco', a tolling church-bell morphs into a boy's singing voice and vice versa; at the same time, one might add, the medieval church morphs into an electro-acoustic studio. At the moment, our view of translation is too much governed by the *jump* rather than the *morph*; bilingual dictionaries, notions of equivalence, of transferring text from one synchronic language-system to another, of updating or modernising, are all governed by the jump, by this sudden, peremptory, hygienic process of substitution. Jump-thinking subscribes to a view of time and space which nullifies time and space as a gradualism of lived experience; the past, for example, is something that one leaps back to, as if time were constantly being left behind. The morph, on the other hand, thrives on a Bergsonian view (1984, 495–500), in which, on the contrary, time always catches up with us; the past is merely a coexistent part of an accumulated present, the snowball in the snowman. But we can only express Virgil's being contemporary with us if we equally express the cumulative and assimilative process itself. And this again argues for a practice of translation in which the source text expands, to absorb all that has accrued to it in the unfolding of time, a translation practice that is temporally and spatially ragged, heterochronic and multidimensional, and never done with reconfiguring the distance between source and target.

In his preface to *Vergil's Metre* (1986, v), Nussbaum breezily affirms: 'In some ways, learning to read Latin hexameters should be easier than Greek. The script and punctuation are familiar.' But what punctuation does Nussbaum mean? Malcolm Parkes (1992, 13) tells us that the earliest surviving codices belong to the fifth and sixth centuries AD, including Turcius Rufius Asterius's copy of Virgil, which Asterius punctuated – as a reader of course, not as a scribe – when he was consul in 494. The punctuation we now have in Virgilian texts is in no sense Virgilian, but is an accommodation to modern linguistic expectations, developed across the years by editors.

Punctuation 'is a phenomenon of written language' (Parkes, 1992, 1). The development of the written language is, however, in part, a development from the written as transcription of the spoken to the written as a source of both vocal and non-vocal information; the written word becomes peculiarly poised between a text which is performable by the voice (i.e. with signs to guide that performance) and a text whose signs tell us about performance inscribed *in* the text, which may have more to do with the psyche of the writer and reader than with the vocal organs of a potential speaker. Vocality may be a demonstration of the expressive resources of the voice, but vocality may also be an embodiment of what are essentially non-vocal events. Correspondingly, punctuation has enlarged its range, to include alongside the grammatico-syntactical and respiro-intonational functions, the task of representing response, thought, subdiscursive pulsions, and so on – in short, punctuation has at its disposal the ability to register the temperamental and psychic landscape of the writer and reader, over and above the service it could render to a text's purely linguistic constitution.

It was only with the introduction of print that there was any real pressure to standardise the signs of punctuation and their use. In modern writing, non-standard practices have again taken some hold, not now to be explained by the absence of standard practice, but by an exasperation with it, and by a desire to exploit punctuation's mind-shaping capacities. Punctuation does not require to be rationalised by phrases and clauses; it operates as much alongside them, releasing a hooded horde of unspoken reflexes. More recent French enquiry has served to emphasise the stylistic, as opposed to the grammatico-syntactical, functions of punctuation (see Lorenceau, 1980; Gruaz, 1980; Catach, 1996, 111–19; Popin, 1998). We learn, for example, that neither Mallarmé nor Claudel had any time for suspension points; that Giono was hostile to the semi-colon; that Michel Tournier prefers brackets to dashes, because they are 'less traumatising' (Catach, 1996, 113); that colons proliferate in Sartre's *Les Mots*. Just as modern music has found available notation inadequate for its purposes – Varèse observes: 'As frequencies and new rhythms will have to be indicated on the score, our actual notation will be inadequate. The new notation will probably be seismographic' (Cox and Warner, 2004, 18) – so contemporary writers, according to Catach (1996, 113), ask for new punctuational and diacritical resources.

Let us return to the passage describing Turnus's being overcome by a corrosive weakness, at the end of Book 12. This is a re-disposition of West's prose version (2003: 289), which I have tinkered with, changing words or syntax here and there; I am, after all, translating West:

But he had no sense
                    of running
                              of going
                              of lifting
                                        of
moving; the huge rock.
His knees gave way. His
          blood grew chill
and froze – and the rock rolled
away   under its own momentum . . .
                        over the open ground . . . between them.
But it did not go/the whole way
it did not/strike
                                                  its target
Just   as when we   sleep
          when in the weariness of night
                              rest
                              lies
                              heavy on our eyes:
we dream, we,, are,,, trying   desperately
to run further and we are not succeeding
till   we fall   exhausted
                        in the muddle of our efforts.
The tongue   useless
The strength (we know we have)   fails the body.
                        no voice
no words to obey our will –
this is how it was
              with   Turnus.

My translation of West combines punctuation, in elasticated form, with
paginal space, as two systems of communication, each concerned to explore
the continuum between specific vocal effects and the multiple ways in
which a mind inhabits a text as it reads, the ways in which inner duration
expresses itself in changes of perceptual pace and perceptual focus, as a
voco-psychic and voco-affective dynamics. What the page maps out in its
two non-verbal languages is both a vocal adventure *outside* the text, in
performance, and, at the same time, a sub-vocal, or voco-visual adventure
in the text, in which voice is, as it were, conceptualised, and in which
we hear the mental processes behind voice: doubt, anticipation, digestion,
puzzlement, movedness, associative reverberation.

Throughout this book, more or less explicitly, I have been pursuing an
argument that one of translation's preoccupations should be the translation

of the linear into the tabular, where linear and tabular are to be understood as mindsets towards text and language, as much as realisations of text on the page. Our tabularisation of West's text is not an extreme example; so I offer a further version, which will perhaps allow us to see more clearly how the tabular text lets the reading consciousness into the heart of the text, and squares with modern theatrical and musical attempts to destroy the idea of a performing space, a stage, specially set aside and at a distance from the audience:

```
          But he                                      His knees
    had no sense                      of          gave way. His
                    lifting
           of                                    blood grew chill
running                                               and froze
                               of                – and the rock
               of            moving;            rolled
going                    the huge rock.                  away
                                                      under its
      own
      momentum . . .
                                                       in the
                       rest         muddle of our efforts.
             over the                                    The
open ground . . . between                            tongue
them.                       lies                      useless
        But it did                                      The
    not go/the whole                              strength (we
    way                 heavy on our              know we have)
          it did    eyes:                         fails the body.
not/strike                   we
                     dream, we,, are,,,            no
                     trying                        voice
          its target    desperately
                           to run              no words to obey
        Just         further and we            our will –
    as when we       are not                            this is
    sleep            succeeding                 how it was
                          till
      when in the    we fall                    with
weariness of night   exhausted
                                               Turnus.
```

Verbal sounds, dispersed in space as here, relativise hearing and mean that different ears have different mixes of the same sounds. And if the reading eye constantly adopts new positions within the text, the text becomes a multidimensional acoustic experience, made up of shifting proximities and distances.

A striking advantage of tabularity is that it undermines the distinction between poetry and prose. When Mallarmé proposes that all writing is verse, he assumes that immediately writing, prose included, becomes self-aware, so it naturally gravitates towards rhythm, wrought-up diction, acoustic patterning;[7] this is what takes place in my translation of Jackson Knight's version. But tabularity creates a more complete ambiguation of the two mediums, and in so doing withdraws a literariness specific to each. Instead it re-installs the literary in our own making of the text, in our negotiation of it, in our choices of reading itinerary and textual construction, in the rhythms of attention we wish to activate.

If remixing and morphing have been our metaphor for translation to date, I want now, as a coda, to turn to another metaphor, a culinary one: translation is a recipe in which the source text is the main ingredient, the meat. Other ingredients, the translator's ways of reading and hearing the source text, are designed to infuse the meat with particular flavours and provide accompanying sauces. At this point, too, we move forward in history, to Apollinaire, to his poem 'Zone' from *Alcools* (1913). If, in my translation, 'Zone' is my meat, then my other ingredients are perambulatory writing,[8] Situationism (1957–72),[9] and street photography. In this short and fragmentary glimpse, I want to shift more firmly from the oral to the visual as another locus of the literary, remembering, however, that the visual will ever remain an inner resonance of the oral.

We think of Situationist psychogeography as the psychological climates and affective ambiences generated by different urban spaces, from which the drifting walker can, as it were, take passing nourishment. As Apollinaire, in 'Zone', strolls through Paris, towards the early morning in Auteuil, I imagine him responding to the changing psychogeographic atmospheres with different feelings, actions, memories. I express these different psychogeographic atmospheres in different fonts:

Zone

$$ \$ \$ \$ \, ° \mp \sim \Upsilon \sim \mp \cdots \searrow \mp \sim \Upsilon \doteq \frown \$ \cdot \text{\textperiodcentered} \mp \text{hùùuyàùʌ}$$

[symbolic text in various fonts — 9 lines]

[Bookshelf Symbol 7]

···· ≭ ∼ ⌒ ⌋
∼Ġ⌒V̆œ̇ó
≭····∾ ﹨◡Ġ····
ŕ····∼⌋ Ẋ̣
ŕ⌒ŕ≑∓◡
h····≑

Yes,
In the end
You're tired of
This antiquated world
[Papyrus]
Shepherdess O Eiffel Tower
The flock of bridges bleat
This morning

You've done with living
In antiquity
Greek and Roman

φηγλφυ χλυψγγβ./   :κκ   η/4λκλ;
Σψμβολ [Symbol]
.,φκνφκηκιρι3ιλρλ:κλ;λ;φγθμ;ι   ορ̄τ
νδωφυδνηδψγ   εμξ;πολ   δμφ
.θ   μν,κνσ/κσ;λ2ιεφΔΜ≅∀![πρμφΣΑ
ΜΝΞΜΣΜδ;δνκ3ο3ι≅∀;ε

Here even the motor-cars
[Wide Latin}
Look out of date[10]

There are two things I would like the reader to notice in this rendering of the poem's opening lines: first, as we have already insisted, these fonts are different languages, with different expressive ranges: some remind us of architectures, some of art-styles, some of behavioural characteristics, some of bodies in different states of compression, expansion, elongation. All fonts enjoy their own specific temperaments. It is for this reason that I have named them in the text. These are languages we still do not know, but when we do, their manipulation can become a true source of the literary. Second, when I say that fonts are languages, I also mean that quite literally: we have on our computers repositories of symbols which may be alternative alphabets, or may remind us of lost hieroglyphic languages. I have opened the poem with a language on the point of shifting from the hieroglyphic to the alphabetic; and, a few lines further on, I have indulged in a pseudo-Greek, the kind of Greek that a modern computer would want to write if the Symbol font was chosen and fingers were left to play randomly over the keyboard, an automatic cyber-writing.

But in tracing this sequence of different psychological climates across Paris, I want also to refer to the Situationists' love of alternative map-making, maps devoted precisely to 'drifting' and psychogeographic experience. These maps register the pathways of a kind of insubordinate walking, which subverts canonical maps and encourages experimental behaviour. Best known of these maps are perhaps those of Guy Debord and Asger Jorn, *The Naked City* (1957) and its predecessor the *Guide psychogéographique de Paris* (1956), whose subtitle – *Discours sur les passions d'amour* – not only alludes to Madeleine de Scudéry's *Carte du tendre* (1656), but is also particularly apt for Apollinaire's amatory preoccupations. My presentation of maps of the brand-new street whose name the poet has forgotten ('Zone', ll. 15–24)[11] –

```
                        PESME
                        A       A
                        C       SPANKING NEWAND
                        S       Y
                        E       O
                        E       N
                        M       T              C
                        A       HYGIENE-CLEANTHE
                        N       E              A
                        E       E              R
            T           S       Y              I
          H         O   E
          E     H       F              NUSEHTFO
      THIS MORNING I SAW A STREET
      A                   O           G
      N                   M           N
      A                   M           I
      G                   O                N
      E                   N           E
      R                   D           V
      SHORTHANDTYPISTSPASSBYFOURTIMESADAY
      T                   Y                Y
      H                   M                A
      E                   O                D
      W                   R                R
      O                   N                U
      R                   I                T
      K                        NGTOSA
      ERSTHE ELEGANT
```

Figure 15 Calligraphic translation of a section of Apollinaire's 'Zone', ll. 19–24

– (see Fig. 15) takes two forms which are designed to create connections between psychic mapping and the Apollinairean calligram, whether printed or handwritten. They are also designed to show how new experience, new itineraries of psychic or affective adventure, might re-write language and suggest new syntaxes. But I also want the printed and the handwritten to play against each other in two related senses: first, I want to suggest that with the technologically and industrially advanced new street, with its regimentation of managers, workers and shorthand typists, the individual soul, the eccentric and idiosyncratic, still have freedom to express themselves; and second, at another level, I want to suggest that if the first map has much in common with Futurist views of street-life as a complex dynamic of lines of force, in the second, Apollinaire is able to re-affirm his belief in the continuing centrality of the intimate lyric voice (1991, 971).

Finally, I want to argue that the spirit of documentary photography – the spirit of the conditioned, the transfixing, the confrontational – dominates in *Alcools* (1913), even though the street-photographic, that celebration of coincidence, distraction, transformation, which comes into its own in Apollinaire's second collection of poems, *Calligrammes* (1918), tries from time to time to assert itself.[12] In 'Zone', for example, the street-photographic tries, initially, to establish itself as the spirit of the new; but, as the poem proceeds, it is restrained, then suppressed, by the documentary. I have chosen two passages to exemplify, first, this eruption of the street-photographic, and then its suffocation by the documentary, the one being the passage about which we have already been speaking, the brand-new street (ll. 15–24), the other the passage about Jewish emigrants (ll. 121–34).[13]

For my street-photographic version of ll. 15–24, I might simply fall back on my cartographic and psychogeographic account; but I have another version in view:

1. this morning
   1. i saw a street
   2. whose name escapes me
   3. easy on the eye
   4. spanking new and hygiene-clean the clarion of the sun
   5. the managers the workers the elegant
   6. shorthand typists pass by
2. four times a day
   1. from monday morning to saturday evening
   2. and three times every morning
   3. the siren wails
3. while at about midday
   1. a bell beside itself
   2. clangs clangs clangs clangs
   3. the SIGNS the **graffiti**
   4. nameplates and notices
   5.   screech like parrots
   6. i love the supple ease of this industrial street
4. in Paris somewhere between
   1. the rue aumont-thiéville and the avenue des ternes.

This passage does not share with the emigrants passage the same complexity of perceptual position, the same play of personal pronouns. It is governed by the first-person singular – 'J'ai vu ce matin' and 'J'aime la grâce' – which conveys that uncommitted but responsive presence of the street-photographer before the inexhaustibly changing spectacle of the street. This changingness is partly expressed in the changing typefaces, with their changing acoustic frequencies and modalities. But it is the numbering which constitutes the most significant super-structure of insinuations, including the following effects:

(i) Bullet-points. This is the street of managers and young executives. The bullet-point is the reduction of argument to act, to the setting of targets; it is the promotion of clarity of mind and the achievability of objectives. This passage becomes a structure of headings and sub-headings which give the street its crisp orderedness, which create the sense of its constituents and habits as epitomes and exemplarities.

(ii) The numerical layout also enacts a gradual focusing of temporal events – 'this morning' > 'four times a day' > 'while at about midday' – which, at the close, suddenly tips into space, a location both vague and exact. Space, Paris, in line with the rest of 'Zone', has a huge appetite for time, has many times and differing durations, both digested and undigested, both inscribed and at play, within it. These lines have something of Lefebvre's rhythmanalytic approach to ambience (see Chapter 4).

(iii) The numbers suggest the numbering of stanzas and of the lines attached to them. This stanzaic structure is irregular – 1 + 6; 1 + 3; 1 + 6; 1 + 1 – adaptable to the life of the street, not subject to a borrowed formality, but responsive to every shift in time and space, constantly remoulding itself to incoming phenomena. The poetry of the modern city is a record of the chances of the street, of the street's own protean imagination and creativity. The literary is born in the same haphazard way.

In order to express the documentary spirit in the emigrant passage, I wanted a verse-form which would enact the repetitive cycles of aspiration and resignation, which would capture the mirage of change that masks debilitating routine, but which, at the same time, would distil a predicament, and block further metamorphosis. I chose the terza rima sonnet. I wanted terza rima to embody mindless reiteration, as it is does in Hugo von Hofmannsthal's 'Ballade des äusseren Lebens'. I wanted the final couplet to act not as a moment of invocation, stock-taking, exhortation, as it does in Shelley's 'Ode to the West Wind', but rather as a movement of entropic congealment. And I was reminded that Robert Frost's terza rima sonnet 'Acquainted with the Night' draws on the motions of perambulation. This is what emerged:

> Believer-emigrants; you watch them; tears well
> Up. They pray. The women suckle their young. At Saint-Lazare,
> The station hall is seasoned with their smell.
>
> They, like the Magi, are following their star,
> Looking to earn some silver in the Argentine
> And then come back to where they are.
>
> You transport your heart, a family transports its eiderdown,
> Bright red. Our dreams, that eiderdown, are all untruths.
> Some stay, in shabby digs in town,
>
> The rue des Rosiers or des Écouffes.
> Often, at evening, I've seen them in the street.
> Like chess pieces they seldom move.
>
> They're mostly Jews. Their wives wear wigs.
> And, pallid, in the backs of shops, they sit.

I begin to imagine 'Zone' as a cycle of poems in the way that other poems in *Alcools* are: 'La Chanson du mal-aimé', for example, or 'Le Brasier', or 'Les Fiançailles'.

As a further step in this dramatisation of the conflict between the street-photographic and the documentary, I have produced two photo-poems (Figs. 16 and 17). My design here is threefold: first to generate differential interactions between colour and black and white (unfortunately not visible in the black-and-white illustrations); the documentary is traditionally associated with black-and-white photography (Fig. 17), because black-and-white is reckoned to have the ability to reach through the colour of appearances to more essential truths; black-and white seeing is unflinching and undeflectable; black-and-white guarantees a certain dose of gravity, a certain level of intellection. Colour (Fig. 16), on the other hand, is there to seduce us, to distract us, to catch our eye, to draw reality out of its tonal uniformity; in that sense it suits a street-photographic mentality. The only colour in the emigrant photo-poem is the grubby façade of a concrete housing block. Second, I wanted to use proxemics, spatial relationships, to generate perceptual attitudes. The sights and events of the brand-new street (Fig. 16) are in close-up, the layout emphasises contiguities, the images convey an activity, or potential for activity, which refuses to identify specific human agents (absence of faces). The spectator is immersed in the

Figure 16 Photopoetic translation of Apollinaire's 'Zone', ll. 15–24

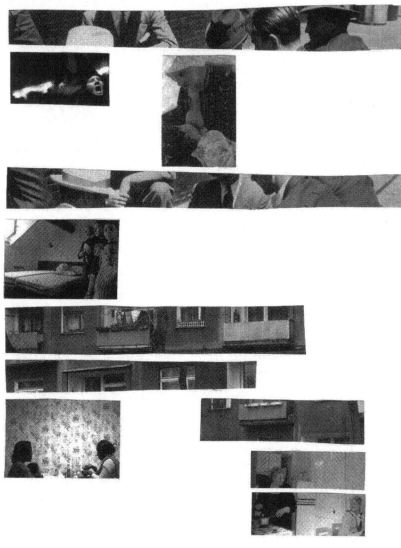

Figure 17 Photopoetic translation (with unattributed photographs) of Apollinaire's
'Zone', ll. 121–34

dynamics of the street. Conversely, the photo-poem of the emigrants
(Fig. 17) sets its images at a distance from the spectator and isolates them
from each other, even when the images constitute different parts of the same
whole. In this world, persons are identified, cannot surrender identity to

participation, to a unanimistic psychology, are often, instead, confined to interiors. Finally, I wanted, as we have already seen, to impute to the two passages different attitudes to verse-form, the brand-new street more tabular, the emigrants more linear. The linear locks us into a status quo, gives authority to verse-conventions rather than to the writer, implies that the disposition of text is a given and that the 'reading' of it must therefore be, in some sense, a compliance, an assent to the known. The documentary attitude, however indignant, is coloured by the fatalistic. The tabular, on the other hand, bestows freedom, if not authority, on the reader, implies that dispositional sense is still to be made, that text is an ad hoc and improvised arrangement, that creative play is possible, that knowledge is yet to be invented. The street-photographic attitude believes that destiny can be re-arranged, that we can outwit our condition. If we translate words into images, the images we produce can continue to project the modalities of the words we have left behind, by their very dispositions.

The wordless photo-poem is a translational genre that deserves to be explored and developed: translation means for us the task of embodiment, both in the sense of the injection into text of the translator's body and in the sense of the transformation of printed text into performance. One might suppose that our approach is designed to distance us as much as possible from the opticality of the printed word, and that the photographic would only be an exacerbation of that opticality. But the photographic, quite apart from its aptness to our present theme, ties opticality to indexicality and thus elicits a world beyond the text, the environment, precisely, of its potential performance. Furthermore, by the logic of our present approach to translation, a purely paralinguistic version is the ultimate desideratum. A text made of purely visual paralanguage – as one might say of sign-language – is quite as envisageable as a text made of purely verbal paralanguage.

My abiding image of the work of literature is of something orphaned and nomadic, something which, from the moment of its production, has a diminishing comprehension of itself. This runs against a view that the measure of a work of art is its adaptability and assimilative capacity: the work of art indefatigably imbibes all that time and change throw at it. No. Works of art constantly become discrepant with themselves, understand themselves less and less, as they pass through time and space. What did Madame de Lafayette intend for the reader of 2012? What does Ian McEwan intend for the reader from Ulan Bator? Translation re-settles these nomadic works into new modes of being, new kinds of literariness. That literariness must be shifted from textual features and devices which are no longer relevant to the TT, or which have lost all literary efficacy by their conventionalisation, to features which express our active engagement with the text. Inasmuch as translation is an account of a reading and listening process, then the literary should be installed more in this readerly procedure than in the text itself, and this requires me to give more literary weight to verbal and visual paralanguage, to performance values, whether that performance be of the text or in the text. And what is the literary? The literary lies in the excess of the signifier over the signified, and that excess is created by literature's maximisation of the materiality and conceptuality of language, so that both the body and the psyche of the reader are maximally involved. And this excess may derive, in a performance-based text, from vocal complexity, from the dynamics of acoustic fields, from the languages of punctuational and diacritical marks, of fonts, of paginal disposition, and indeed of photographs.

CHAPTER 8

Writing and overwriting the sound of the city

Criticism is largely a consensus art. It looks to create conditions of textual assimilation (reading, study) which are shared by all, and to arrive
at interpretative conclusions that can be agreed to, on evidence that is
textually available. This is praiseworthy, and vital where any evaluative
ambitions are in play. But it is also self-deluding. We do not all read with
the same even level of attention, the same even speed, the same perceptual
sensitivities and understandings. Indeed it is doubtful whether we could
achieve this state, even if we wanted to. The kind of reading this book is
concerned with attempts to do justice to the variables and imponderables
which make reading a positive enrichment of the text as it stands, and
the literary a mobile and conferable value. We are trying, too, to develop
forms of translation which, for example, register the fact that we all hear
and listen differently, as a result of our education, culture, language; we
must combat the assumption that we listen to text as a steady sequence
of sounds from the International Phonetic Alphabet (IPA) unfolding in
an anechoic chamber; we want translations that are earwitness accounts of
text in concrete contexts (Schafer, 2005, xiii). To say that we are witnesses
to a text, both by the eye and by the ear, is unashamedly to make a virtue
of first-handness, the exercise of individual perception, a constant coming
to a singular consciousness: 'sound also is shaped subjectively, depending
on the auditory capacity, the attitude, and the psychology and culture of
the listener. There is no universal approach to listening: every individual,
every group, every culture listens in its own way' (Augoyard and Torgue,
2005, 4).

It is fitting that we should quote from Jean-François Augoyard and Henry
Torgue's *Sonic Experience: A Guide to Everyday Sounds.* This concluding
chapter returns to the preoccupation of Chapters 3 and 4 – reading and the
environment – and it does so under the auspices, so to speak, of CRESSON,
the Centre de recherche sur l'espace sonore et l'environnement urbain, to
which Augoyard and Torgue belong, the inheritors of R. Murray Schafer's

167

mantle in the field of environmental acoustics (see Chapter 4, note 3). As we have already observed, the reader's body is the point of intersection between, on the one hand, the inside world of the text and the energies it lets loose in the reader, and, on the other, the outside world which provides the context of reading and which both infiltrates, and is marked by, that reading.

What I want here to consider is the way in which the language of text itself can be turned outwards, can achieve a certain extra-textuality. In order to do this, language must escape its founding condition, to be heard semiotically, as designating signifiers with a *known* code of decipherment, for even onomatopoeia *means* the sound it imitates rather than making that sound. To prevent language reaching too quickly for its known stock of signifieds, that by which language becomes conceptual, that by which language adopts the role of intermediary, it must be 'détourné', so that rather than being a code, it is a raw material in the real world, and so that its users feel that its ability to have sense is yet to be identified or properly activated. There are many ways to effect this diversion: one shifts one's acoustic perception from the phonological to the phonetic; one lets words inwardly ramify through the autonomisation of phonemes, syllables and morphemes; one liberates language from the categories of parts of speech and necessary syntactical relationship. This is very much the programme of the Russian Cubo-Futurists. This is language-use informed by *zaum* (transreason). The Cubo-Futurists felt free creatively to manipulate orthography, and, like Marinetti, rejected the worn-out Symbolist mechanisms of alliteration and assonance in favour of dissonances and other devices of 'alphabetation'; vowels and consonants were prized as sources of multi-sensory and multi-dimensional experience (vowels = time, space; consonants = colour, sound, smell). In their effort to deflect language from its rational functions and to block automatic routes to signification, the Cubo-Futurists also looked to that store of graphic and typographic resources (illegibility, doodling, typeface, crossing-out) which we have been at pains to promote as translational aids. In an early manifesto of 1913, *A Trap for Judges 2*, over the signatures of members of the Hylaea group, including David and Nicholas Burliuk, Vladimir Mayakovsky, Velemir/Viktor Khlebnikov, Benedict Livshits and Aleksei/Alexsander Kruchenykh, we find this declaration:

5. We modify nouns not only with adjectives (as was usual before us), but also with other parts of speech, as well as with individual letters and numbers:
(a) considering as an inseparable part of the work its corrections and the graphic flourishes of creative expectation.

(b) considering handwriting a component of the poetic impulse.
(c) and therefore, having published in Moscow 'hand-lettered' (autographic) books. (Lawton and Eagle, 1988, 53–4)[1]

Many might argue that all these devices serve only the autonomy of the word, that they do not stand in any relation to the world, but, on the contrary, establish language as a self-gratifying, self-renewing medium pursuing its own agenda. Our argument is different: these devices are the means by which language extricates itself from the business of text-making and weaves itself into the texture and perceptual experience of the everyday. These are the moments at which we become most acutely aware of those expressive effects inalienably possessed by language as a raw material, rather than as achieved discourse. One may indeed begin to think that, paradoxically, the signifier is most rich when it turns away from the text, and that the literary lies in the extra-literary.

The translational device I wish to return to in this chapter is overwriting/overprinting, whose significance for voice we briefly explored in Chapter 5. But first we must explore the source text (ST), in this instance Baudelaire's 'À une passante', as itself an out-turned text, listening to, and absorbing into its textual being, the ambient noise of the street. In order to do this, and as already acknowledged, I will draw on the arsenal of sonic effects identified by the CRESSON researchers. It seems almost incomprehensible that we have no terms to describe acoustic effects to be found in language other than those which relate to the repetition of individual sounds (phonemes, syllables). This implies that we have no broader or more dispersed experience of verbal acoustics, no perception of, say, dissonance or cacophony, or acoustic foregrounding, or crossfade. Of course it might be argued that we hear the 'music' of language only in a single, constantly self-superseding line. But this is to take no account of the enveloping acoustic of a particular voice, or effects of reverberation and 'remanence'.[2] Of all the supplementary translational resources which print should add to its stock, overwriting/overprinting, with its compacted text, most obviously promises that density of competing utterances, that play of simultaneous audibilities which might most effectively project or synthesise the larger acoustic experiences concealed in linear writing. All tabular writing, as we have already observed, tends towards the simultaneous apprehension of different textual elements; only overwriting makes that desire explicit.

Baudelaire's 'À une passante' (1975, 92–3) might be considered to present sonic effects which are textually produced, but which make the text work as if it were an urban event, as if poetic language and urban soundscape were inextricably fused together:

1. La rue assourdissante autour de moi hurlait.   2>4>4>2
2. Longue, mince, en grand deuil, douleur
                                    majestueuse,   3>3>2>4/1>2>3>2>4
3. Une femme passa, d'une main fastueuse   3>3>3>3
4. Soulevant, balançant le feston et l'ourlet;   3>3>3>3

5. Agile et noble, avec sa jambe de statue.   4>4>4
6. Moi, je buvais, crispé comme un extravagant,   4>2>6(1>5)
7. Dans son œil, ciel livide où germe l'ouragan,   3>3>2>4
8. La douceur qui fascine et le plaisir qui tue.   3>3>4>2

9. Un éclair... puis la nuit! – Fugitive beauté   3>3>3>3
10. Dont le regard m'a fait soudainement renaître,   4>2>4>2
11. Ne te verrai-je plus que dans l'éternité?   6>6

12. Ailleurs, bien loin d'ici! trop tard! *jamais* peut-être! 2>4>2>4
13. Car j'ignore où tu fuis, tu ne sais où je vais,   3>3>3>3
14. Ô toi que j'eusse aimée, ô toi qui le savais!   2>4>2>4

The first line is what, in the language of Augoyard and Torgue, we might identify as a 'drone', of mixed high and low frequencies – /R/, /a/, /u/, /y/ – and of both the voiced and voiceless – /d/, /t/. This is endorsed by a visual effect: the double s's of 'assourdissante' act on the eye as instruments of acoustic diffusion and homogenisation. We might add that the lower frequency /u/ helps to make the overall sound more ubiquitous, less easy to locate, but that the relatively higher intensity of /y/ adds an element of positive 'de-localisation' and disorientation. At the end of the line comes 'cut out': a full stop, the drone disappears, yielding to another, more muted soundscape. The chiastic structure – /y/ > /u/ > /u/ > /y/ – which initially bespeaks envelopment by sound, and in the course of which phonemes are rearranged (La rue > hurlait), becomes a process of turning on in order to turn off. As we read on, we might believe that this sonic effect has more to do with 'crossfade' than with cut out, that the passing woman had absorbed into her very figure and gestures and clothing the ambient sound. True, there are the beginnings of a new sound-set (/ɛ/, /ɔ̃/, /ø/), but the double s of 'passa' still seems imbued with 'assourdissante', and the /ɑ̃/ is picked up in 'grand' and the participial endings of line 4. /u/ and /y/ continue to exercise their changes of pitch. Nonetheless, the more the woman detaches herself from the acoustic background, the more her presumably silent movement suggests its own sound world in lines 3–4: a rhythmically regular 3>3>3>3. This effect might be associated with what Augoyard and Torgue call 'anticipation' (2005, 25–6): the poet pre-hears 'the expected signal, even though no sound has been emitted . . . It happens as if the desire of the event was creating its own sound envelope'.

As we pass from the first to the second quatrain, however, an effect of 'desynchronisation' occurs, described by Augoyard and Torgue as 'a temporal decontextualization effect' which 'characterizes the emergence of a sound emission that breaks the regularity of a rhythm or a well-established sound structure, creating a feeling of incongruity' (2005, 38). The sonnet is our well-established sound structure (4 lines + 4 lines + 3 lines + 3 lines), and the 3>3>3>3 rhythm of lines 3–4 our regular rhythm. Line 5 disrupts both these patterns: the intrusion of street noise in line 1 means that the first quatrain has not been able to complete itself by line 4; it needs line 5 to find its true full-stop. The whole structure is thus shunted forward, syncopated against itself. Additionally, line 5 puts an abrupt end to the tetrametric rhythmic regularity of lines 3–4, with a 4>4>4 trimetric syncopation, and verbless telegraphic syntax.

In this second quatrain, it is not so much crossfade as 'metamorphosis'[3] which predominates, creating unsteady relations between woman and environment, but also between woman and poet. A sound – /i/ – that we have heard only once in the first quatrain ('assourdissante'), is activated, and occurs eight times, with one instance of the semi-vowel /j/ (/sjɛl/). This high-frequency sound combines with the equally high-frequency /y/ to characterise the woman in her urban guise. And the poet is marked in his turn by both these sounds, in 'crispé' and 'buvais'. 'Douleur' morphs into 'douceur', but a 'douceur' heightened by /i/ ('qui fascine'). What we might have believed to be a benign combination (/uR/), becomes, along with the equally positive /ā/, a renegade in 'ouragan', picking up the unrealised, or momentarily deflected, threat in 'assourdissante'.

Within all these sounds there is always the chance of 'anamnesis'. We walk the city, slip by many potential encounters, enter soundscapes of all descriptions, and within that web any sound is likely to trigger an involuntary memory. In language, sounds and their associations may find themselves located in any words, as if the words were not primarily chosen as words, but grew uncontrollably out of their sounds. But the anamnesic effect in language is unmeasurable:

Two people listening to the same sound environment can develop very different evocations, but these effects could not happen without the occurrence of sound. The anamnesis effect merges sound, perception and memory. It plays with time, reconnecting past mental images to present consciousness, with no will other than the free activity of association. (Augoyard and Torgue, 2005, 21)

Here, we might draw two conclusions, both based on the obvious proposition that language tirelessly engineers, in its various acoustic figures (alliteration, rhyme, paronomasia), the wider anamnesic effect of sound; and that therefore personal memory is peculiarly ready to exercise itself in its encounters with these figures. This process may take us directly out of text (textual sound > extratextual sound), but equally, as here, a textual sound may involuntarily and anamnesically conjure up another textual sound, in the same text, and may then, beyond that, connect with extra-textual sound. So my first conclusion is an inevitable one: that the poem itself is a memory generated by the sounds of the first line, in particular, the acoustic collocation /u/, /R/, /d/ – sources of 'douleur' and 'ourlet' and 'douceur' – and /i/ and /mwa/, whose significance is explored below. The second conclusion is equally inevitable: that the woman has two aspects, corresponding roughly with the first and second quatrains, and belonging to the poet's pre-natal and post-natal memories, two aspects which ultimately cannot be put apart – the woman is an alter ego of the poet (/u/, /ɑ̃/), and an embodiment of the city (/y/, /i/).

I want briefly, by way of testing supposition against text, to consider the former of these aspects. In the first quatrain, the only reference to the first person is 'moi' (/mwa/), which remembers itself in 'majestueuse'. This word in itself embraces /m(w)a/ and /ty/, but it also gives us the first inkling of /ʒə/, here as /ʒɛ/. /m(w)a/ is also heard, in a more dispersed form, in '*m*ain f*a*st*u*euse'. The sounds of the self hear in themselves the woman and a condition of high-styled melancholy and elegant widowhood, that social status that presupposes absent otherness. Finally, '*fes*t*o*n' gathers into itself 'maj*es*tueuse' and '*fas*tueuse'. Subsequently, in the second quatrain, /ʒɛ/ does become /ʒə/, but it has already heard itself in other guises: /ʒi/ ('Agile'), /ʒɑ̃/ ('jambe'); /ʒɛ/ returns in 'germe'. In the sestet, along with /ʒə/, /ʒi/ recurs in 'Fugitive' and 'j'ignore', /ʒa/ appears in '*jamais*', and /ʒy/ in 'j'eusse'. On this showing, /ʒ(ə)/ acts as a point of attraction for multiple, remembered selves, a phoneme which the poet cannot avoid producing.

The Parisian soundscape creates a situation in which relationships cannot establish a stability, in which acoustic change and acoustic pressure create and compel conditions of continual transition. The players in the urban drama are in flight, protean, 'comme un extravagant', because the sounds they hear, and the language they hear, are generators of hallucination. The ear may selectively isolate certain sounds, as here perhaps the vowels /i/ and /y/ and /u/ and /ɑ̃/, as figures on a ground; but the ground, as here perhaps the consonants /f/ and /b/ and /st/ and /l/, interferes with the figure, so that it will not hold still, but takes on variable colouring.

The sonnet's sestet is governed not by crossfade or metamorphosis, but by the 'ubiquity' effect,[4] partly because the unfolding narrative of the quatrains is immobilised in the questions, implicit and explicit, and the exclamations, of the tercets, partly because, to my ear at least, the half-open, unrounded /ɛ/, which has emerged from the second quatrain – 'avec', 'extravagant', 'ciel', 'germe' – proceeds to dominate the final six lines – 'éclair', 'fait', 'soudainement', 'renaître', 'éternité', *jamais*, 'peut-être', 'sais', 'vais', 'savais'. Additionally, this /ɛ/, so often expressed graphemically by ai, draws in other lexemes even though, in their case, the ai does not express /ɛ/: 'plaisir' (/e/), 'Ailleurs' (/aj/), 'aimée' (/e/).

Here we must be careful to distinguish between ubiquitous sounds and sounds that create a ubiquity effect. Many sounds may be experienced as ubiquitous and dismissed from consciousness, without producing a psychological condition in the listener. With the ubiquity effect, on the other hand, 'we must consciously look for the source location of the sound, and fail, at least for a moment, to identify it' (Augoyard and Torgue, 2005, 131). Our own psychological well-being, our peace of mind, depends on our being able to identify sound-sources, or their location. The woman evaporates, or proliferates, at the moment of contact. In the same moment a choice must be made, and choice becomes impossible.

What one then might propose is this: the ubiquity effect produces spatial and temporal disorientation, such that space and time expand and become meaningless:

> Ailleurs, bien loin d'ici! trop tard! *jamais* peut-être!
> Car j'ignore où tu fuis, tu ne sais où je vais

At the same time, the loss of knowledge and ability to localise generates a corresponding belief in the activity of a transcendental or omnipotent power:

> Ô toi que j'eusse aimée, ô toi qui le savais!

The woman, despite her apparent ill-adaptedness to the city, bound up as she is in her 'douleur majestueuse', is in fact an agent of the city, as the second quatrain makes clear, complicit in its seductive stultification of its citizens. Characteristically of the ubiquity effect, a communication takes place which is a failure of communication, or a communication not brought to realisation. A sender and receiver come into contact, but the message sent loses its potential source and thus its relevance to anything. What is left is a vague sense of anxiety, excitedness, puzzlement. Ubiquity, then, has two major effects: it marries the single and the multiple, singularises the multiple and multiplies the singular; and it provides a metaphysical dimension. This latter is evidence of a deeper collusion between the city and the sonnet, if David Scott is right in observing that, in Baudelaire's work, the sonnet's sestet is formally conditioned to turn towards the metaphysical (1977, 47–56).

As the poem ends, we might refer to the 'release' factor, 'the residual duration of a sound, from its cessation until silence or background noise' (Augoyard and Torgue, 2005, 87). As the poem ends, we re-enter the context of reading, the outside world, in a process of auditory re-adaptation. Such a release might happen at the end of any stanza or indeed line, or at any point in the poem – these are the moments of looking up from the text explored in Chapter 3. What is curious about tabular writing, of whatever kind, is that no point of release is designated in the text, that the relationship between the textual and the extratextual is not formally inscribed in the text, is not part of the text's rhythm.

What, then, in this initial analysis have I been suggesting, or, rather, what does the analysis itself suggest? It suggests three degrees of relationship between the text-internal and the text-external:

(1) The infiltration of a (fictional?) environment into the making of text.
(2) The inextricable blending of environment and text/language, so that they act as an indistinguishable partnership.
(3) Language/text itself is an acoustic environment and acts according to principles which are comparable to extra-textual/extra-linguistic sound effects.

In other words, text and environment have three different levels or modes of interaction, the final one of which suggests that the acoustics of language itself is not just affected by, but may be modelled on, or has the capacity to model itself on, patterns and effects obtaining in the acoustic environment.

Sean Bonney's translations of *Les Fleurs du Mal, Baudelaire in English* (2008) (Figs. 18–19), are typewritten verbal constructions/sculptures whose lines and words and punctuation marks and deletions are so closely printed that they often overlap. The collection is preceded by four photographs of the nondescript, derelict interiors of abandoned buildings (shed? garage? office?), three of which appear with others in the Notes at the end of the collection, a piece of experimental prose without beginning and end. I say 'without beginning and end' because these Notes are apparently made up of fragments, (so far) numbered from 1 to 63 (as far as we can tell), but in a random order and with several missing (though 6 appears twice). This prose

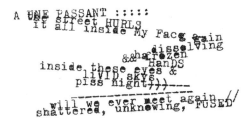

Figure 18 Overwritten translation (1) of Baudelaire's 'À une passante' by Sean Bonney

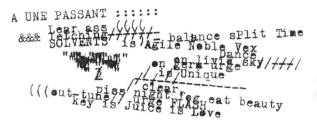

Figure 19 Overwritten translation (2) of Baudelaire's 'À une passante' by Sean Bonney

is, in its own way, 'assourdissante'. It paints a picture of a contemporary London which is a modernised echo of Baudelaire's Paris: the spirit of Haussmann has simply become a carefully engineered bio-genetic-medical capitalism. But it is a prose whose pandemonium is frequently illuminated by insights which take one to the heart of the translator's preoccupations. About the photographs, for example, we pick up the following explanation:

The photos were interesting to me because they were of the 'invisible', both in terms of being rooms I couldn't see, and of being of an asocial, abandoned space in the inner city / rapidly being cleared in the last push of the alleged creation of a smooth-surface postmodern city / safe for faux-bohemian yuppies. The 'invisible' is not some other-worldly visionary realm, it is just these abject spots / these gaps in the safely constructed social text, tenuously analogous to 'poems', where nothing 'useful' can happen ((1))). (2008, 86)

These rooms, then, are the poems, situated not on the periphery of the city, but at its inner interstices, the 'unofficial parts of town' (87), repositories of an equally unofficial knowledge, 'the occult secret at the heart of the society's discourse about itself' (88). They are still presided over by a lyric 'I', 'a potential parasite within the clean capitalist body' (85), an 'I' which has had its day, which is erased from the new alphabet. Baudelaire is an inhabitant of these abandoned office spaces: 'not so much a decadent as a disgruntled office worker' (85). He

mingles his voice with the roar of the city as one might mingle one's voice with the breakers on the shore. His speech is clear to the extent that it is perceptible. But something merging with it muffles its sound. And it remains mingled with this roar, which carries it onward while endowing it with dark meaning (((23))). (87; original emphasis)

The poems (STs and target texts (TTs)) are, it seems, difficult of entry, protected against all but the initiated, all but those who have business with them: 'each poem as a map / impenetrable chart of (a) no admittance except on business (b) username and password (c) human beings & their luminous explosions in space (((15)))' (86). But that difficulty of access can increase as the poems are invaded by noise, as they become illegible:

Finally, as the poems are in danger of absolute illegibility, they become places that cannot be entered: or at least, not everything that's going on in them is ultimately available to the reader. I could print the poems neatly, but I choose to let them be swamped by static and interference /// these are polluted poems ///. (89)

With the switchover to digital, the animating presence of static on radio and television will be removed: 'Without mess and stains, static and interference, the poem is in danger of becoming an overly smooth surface fit only for the lobbies of office buildings and as illustrations' (90).[5]

As we turn to Bonney's versions of Baudelaire, we are already in two dimensions of readerly experience. First, we have a text buffeted by an environment, encroached upon by a sound-world full of urban turbulence – the language, as we have just seen with the ST, is both affected by forces external to it and is itself a language which expresses that urban tumult. Second, this text is also the product of the reader – a translation of the ST, a translation of the reading of the ST – the record of a mind seeking to establish a footing, a location, an orientation, in a text which gives him no rest.

For some readers, Bonney's choice of the typewritten as his graphic medium will constitute a pointed allusion to Charles Olson's 'projective verse' essay (1966, 15–26). What is curious, as Olson himself points out, is that his call for the restoration of the breath, of the voice, to verse should coincide with his warm welcome for the typewriter, as the ideal partner for his new poetic:

The irony is, from the machine has come one gain not yet sufficiently observed or used, but which leads directly on toward projective verse and its consequences. It is the advantage of the typewriter that, due to its rigidity and its space precisions, it can, for a poet, indicate exactly the breath, the pauses, the suspensions even of syllables, the juxtapositions even of parts of phrases, which he intends. For the first time he can, without the convention of rime and meter, record the listening he has done to his own speech and by that one act indicate how he would want any reader, silently or otherwise, to voice his work. (1966, 22)

The typewriter, 'the personal and instantaneous recorder of the poet's work', can be used 'as a scoring to his composing, as a script to its vocalization'; it has the advantage of supplying marks (e.g. the slash) more sensitive than traditional punctuation, and of facilitating the multiplication of margins.

Looking at Bonney's versions, one might suppose that the typewriter had found, in Baudelaire the office worker, an incompetent or subversive operator. Far from aiding the voice, the typewriter seems to frustrate its every effort to find itself. Bonney has an angle on the typewriter very different from Olson's, but one just as concerned with the revolution brought about by keyboard writing. The keyboard presents the writer with a re-ordered alphabet, with a new linguistic matrix, with a way into linguistic construction which seems undetermined and full of dizzying possibility. We have already suggested a connection between the impulses of the keyboard and automatic writing. We have suggested, too, that the keyboard is not only our alphabet re-ordered – rich though that facility might be in discoveries of the unexplored dimensions of our own language – but also the repository of the alphabets and hieroglyphs of countless other languages. Translation with a typewriter, as with a computer, takes one immediately into an interlingual realm, into the machine's own Babel. In the machine there are no territorial barriers or borders, no insuperable dividing lines between the givens of different cultures. In this sense, the typewriter is equally the writing instrument of a single inclusive language. And it is the powerfully dissociative nature of keys on the keyboard which opens the way into the elaboration of avant-garde verbal musics: the detachment of sounds from specific instruments or words (acousmatics); the detachment of punctuational and diacritical (notational) marks from a certain grammar and syntax of lexemes/notes; the undoing of the compact locatedness of the orchestra (linear writing) and the redistribution of sound sources across space (tabularity), so that distances/intervening spaces and spatial changes in acoustic relationships become vital elements in the composition. This is a world, then, as Olson himself implies of the slash, in which punctuational and diacritical marks can achieve a new expressive subtlety, by virtue of their enjoying, thanks to the independence of the key, an unusual self-sufficiency.

In Bonney's translations, the slash is a new kind of all-purpose punctuation of juncture, more or less strong depending on the multiplication of the mark, but also, on occasion, a gesture of strike-through, of exasperation, of textual self-mutilation. The repeated bracket, on the other hand, is something that buries things even deeper in the hidden heart, security walls, but at the same time, and ironically, the measure of resonance and reverberation activated by that hiddenness. The repetitions of the colon are likewise two-edged: either they express the strength of the revelation to follow, or the repeated failure of the illumination to produce itself – a mark of postponed explanation, exemplification, disclosure. Repeated hyphens, which, in the Notes, initiate utterances, are the white noise, or silence, or psychological elsewhere, from which utterance emerges, and have additionally in the translations the function both of suspension points (used only twice in the Notes and in only two of the translations ('Le Cygne', 'Spleen' ('J'ai plus de souvenirs'))), that undefined psycho-physiological realm into which language fades, and of an armature for the poem's physical construction, guiding the verbal material along particular diagonals and horizontals. The important factor in all these signs is their infinite repeatability. If we read these signs as anti-linguistic, or as the language of the secret police, then they have at their disposal inexhaustible resources, against which language can only gesture in fragmentary ways. Alternatively, these signs are what is left after linguistic dispossession. This is borne out by the inverted commas, for example, which, though they play their conventional role in the Notes, appear in the poems in frenzied clusters, unable to attach themselves to words, performing, as it were, a feverish hum which cannot find its way to articulacy. But we must be careful as we draw these parallels with known usage. This may be another language, a diacritical (hieroglyphic) language with which we are not yet familiar, a language whose expressive inflexions we have not yet caught.

The idle reader of Bonney's two versions of 'À une passante' might derive satisfaction from identifying some of the transpositional techniques used: anagrammatic rearrangement (Lear ass = 'La rue' minus u + 'ass/ourdissante'); homophonic approximation (solvents = 'soulevant'; Juice = 'j'eusse'; vex = 'avec sa'; key = 'qui'; fog eat = '*Fugit*ive'); homographic approximation (urge = 'ouragan'; piss = 'puis'; HURLS = 'hurlait'); direct appropriation or translation ('Agile'; 'Noble'; 'livid sky'). But it is a mistake to suppose that, in uncovering potential sources and linguistic mechanisms for Bonney's translation, one has somehow 'solved' them. For, in many senses, one has already taken a wrong turning. The question is not how the text was created, but how it should be read, and here, the frustration of the attempt to read in one direction must be treated as the encouragement to read in another; one might say to read not for words in syntactical discourse, but for the total page: to read the text as a physical construct in a certain kind of space; or as the exploration of a range of vocality. But as with all tabular writing, the idea of the verbal construct is misleading: it too much implies a stasis, when the task is to find the new linguistic kinesis. This kind of text is not, of itself, an invitation to read, does not draw the reader along familiar paths, does not seek to engage the reader's subjectivity; on the contrary, it looks recalcitrant, unaccommodating, rebarbative, discourse reduced to the rubble of language.

Deprived of syntactic channels along which to discharge their semantic load, words and phrases constitute a milling crowd in the act of demonstration or brewing riot. Verbal relationships are dammed up and at the same time multiplied. In this paradoxical situation, in which the kinesis of visual structure is paralysing for the reader without reading routes, temporality itself is as if stalled, or compelled to mark time. But this relative stasis is also the condition of explosive excess, of a huge pressure applied by formal kinesis. Language is on the brink of running out of control; without the discipline and direction of linearity and syntax, the whimsical (puns, acoustic affinities) run riot, urging language towards centrifugal eruption.

Overwriting may indeed suggest an invasion of noise, ubiquity effect, drone, interference, a jamming of communication; but a utopian view would place it at the centre of another of our abiding concerns: the generation, out of the alphabetic, of multi-sensory and synaesthetic experience. The problem is that the utopian shares the same ground as the dystopian. Bonney's versions look just as plausibly like mockeries, like grotesque disfigurements, of the Baudelairean dream.

I want now to offer a second account of 'À une passante' based on two translations of the sonnet into a villanelle – one in the strict nineteen-line English form,[6] the other in a sixteen-line free-verse version[7] – which I made for my *Translating Baudelaire* (2000, 97–105). I have taken two printings of each version, in different typefaces (Britannic Bold, Gungsuh, Lucida Console, Verdana), and superimposed them (see Fig. 20). I have then added doodles and handwritten fragments from three other translators (Richard Howard, James McGowan, Walter Martin). In this instance, I do not wish to examine the relationship between overwriting and sonic effects, but rather the relationship between overwriting and textual/extratextual status.

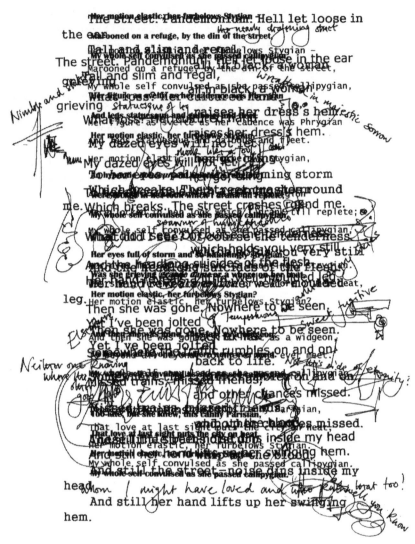

Figure 20 Overwritten translation of Baudelaire's 'À une passante'

In my original account, I described my intentions thus:

what I felt the villanelle made necessary was the projection of the encounter, not, as in the sonnet, as a unique, once-and-for-all event, but as something repeated, habitual, as a kind of Muybridgean cinematic sequence, a series of frames slightly differentiated from each other, where the repetition itself takes the woman away, confirms her in an otherness. It is in this sense that I imagine the villanelle as something new, as a traditional Renaissance fixed form reborn as minimalist music, a kind of Nymanian experience designed to accompany the theatrical spectacularity of Greenaway cinema. (Scott, 2000, 99)

In this new version, I have sought to intensify this sense of the same ground being endlessly gone over, albeit with slight variations (of typeface and formulation), both in memory and in fact. The doodles are intended as indications of a resigned frustration, of a paralysed incapacity – either to come to the end of this encounter, or significantly to rewrite it – expressed in the idle meanderings of the hand. I also wish, by the very fact of overwriting, to imply that the sheet of paper has itself become a fetishised object, that the process of writing has not, as it were, disappeared in the text, to become a self-justifying and self-sustaining alternative reality beyond the page, but rather that the process of writing has *literally* disappeared into itself, without managing to become text, as an index of its failure to transcend the physicality of the paper on which it inscribes itself. Repeatedly caught in this failure to cross the threshold from the external world of the paper into the inner world of text, we gradually cease knocking at the door and live out the condition of being marooned on this side of literature, in the world of repeated but fruitless physical self-inscription. Correspondingly, reading, too, stays in the realms of desultory decipherment, is unable to engage in psycho-physiological processing, has only glimpses of what its true destiny should be. Words, phrases, clauses, stand off from the page as unassimilated citations or tags, in a reversal of the natural order of things; for, here, assimilation means the assimilation of language into illegibility, rather than the assimilation of the reader into a viable text. The reader/writer remains exiled in the environment of reading/writing, out of reach of textual fulfilment.

Since this chapter is tantamount to a conclusion, I would like to close with two general visions of the reading/translation act, visions which might seem to be further metaphorisations of the process of translation, but which are, in fact, expressions of reading/translation's deeply synaesthetic and intermedial nature: walking and drawing. Thanks to the writing of Certeau (1984, 91–110), and of Augoyard (2007, 23–76) after him, we have grown used to the treatment of walking as a rhetoric (bypassing, shortcutting, giving prominence, digressing), as a syntax of itineraries; conversely, we might suppose that linguistic use is a reflection of the styles and psychology of walking, and in this latter respect, we might say that Bonney's translations are translations into kinetic stasis of a perambulation that found itself without a destination, locomotive power trapped in continual replay.

Walking is the same kind of reading-writing that translation is: 'The analogy with graphic expression is unendingly striking. Just as a book is read in company with a motionless (re)writing and is written at the same time that it is read for oneself and for others, *walking resembles a reading-writing*' (Augoyard, 2007, 25). A map always presents passages, routes, as unproblematically traversable; we choose our itinerary. We might say that linear writing is like the map, in that the pursuit of unfolding syntax, as it moves along one line and turns into the next, is clear of obstacle, a free passage. Tabular writing catches some of the existential complexity of wayfaring: the strategies of avoidance and cutting through, the polysemous nature of choice, the management of speeds. How does walking adapt itself to the surrounding architecture? What cues does it take from the buildings? 'One and the same object takes on several meanings. For the inhabitants questioned, a given site can be walked through in several ways at the same time or one time after another' (Augoyard, 2007, 41). What we are clearly not very cognisant of, in our assessment of the reading experience, are the ways in which the reading mind encounters language, and constantly renegotiates that encounter, changes the angle of view or approach. Or rather, tabular writing dramatises the encounter, brings it out into the open. Walkers are constantly breaking down the monosemantic functions that town-planners might have ascribed to buildings or monuments.

One might think it hardly plausible to speak of a poem as a planned environment. But any use of pre-existing forms and metres will imply a choice made with a certain mode of inhabitation in view. And the ascription of intention to a text will inevitably imply strategy. Print, and linear writing in particular, suggest an organised space, a having-been-put-in-place; but a system of paths or thoroughfares, and of buildings, cannot predict the walks taken through them, or the manner of their inhabitation. If reading is inhabiting, then it reconfigures the spaces and pathways presented to it; it modalises percepts and inflects sense with the senses. These processes are what we have casually termed 'autobiography': 'Every walking, every inhabiting gives itself out not only as structures, figures, but also as *configuration, structuration*, that is to say, deformation of the built world such as it was conceived and re-creation of space through feeling and motor function' (Augoyard, 2007, 128). Inasmuch as text is 'the built world such as it was conceived', reading is its deformation and re-creation. Inasmuch as the ST is a 'built world', translation is its deformation and re-creation. We have seen it as being one of translation's principal tasks to relocate the ST, not just in modernity, but in the urgently here and now, to ensure that it is embedded in, and subject to the pressures of, time. For us, performance and environmental assimilation are ways of guaranteeing this subjection to lived time. Lived time in reading and translation is the guardian spirit of the phenomenological, the refusal to let the spatialism of criticism re-establish itself. Criticism itself is a mapping of what is there, fixing relative positions, recovering structure, counting, measuring units; reading and translation are configurative, the continuous production of morphologies, the capacity to dynamise space with time.

Even at the level of the phoneme, this configurative process takes place: standard critical procedure, which we have ourselves employed in search of sound-patterning, retrospectively isolates phonemes or phonemic clusters, transcribed in the sign-system of the International Phonetic Alphabet. But the sounds of language are not isolated in our vocal delivery or auditory perception of them; print alone makes that isolation possible. Sounds spoken are inhabited by a voice which gives a particular colouring to the IPA abstractions, and, in turn, these sounds, heard, are inflected by the listener.[8] It is perhaps not so much about acoustic distortion in itself that we are speaking, however significant that may be, as about the adaptation of sound to different acoustic and auditory needs and pressures, the shaping of sound to a perceptual consciousness which synthesises the environment and its own imaginary. Any treatment of reading and the ambient should take account of the way the ambient acts at the microscopic textual level, drawing the text's very sound-system out of IPA into a specific milieu of resonances, acoustic refractions, acoustic hierarchies and competitions.

Translation has within its resources, and quite literally, as we have seen, various forms of drawing: handwriting, overwriting, doodling, crossing-out. The 'graphicisation' of translation, the incorporation into translation of the creative movement of the hand, not only reminds us of its homology with constructivist reading, but also reveals to us what distinguishes translation from criticism: translation is a genetic or generative perception of the ST, rather than a recuperative one:

It is the actual act of drawing that forces the artist to look at the object in front of him, to dissect it in his mind's eye and put it together again; or, if he is drawing from memory, that forces him to dredge his own mind, to discover the content of his own store of past observations . . . A drawing is an autobiographical record of one's discovery of an event – seen, remembered or imagined . . . A drawing is essentially a private work, related only to the artist's own needs . . . (Berger, 2008, 3–4)

Drawing is not about the depicted subject so much as about the experience of looking. Or rather, what a drawing tells us about its subject is coterminous with the experience of looking. A drawing brings its subject into being; it is not just copying or reproducing; the draughtsman has to make his subject, so that each stroke or line engenders or releases the next, in a self-generating sequence occurring in real time. A drawing preserves the real time of its execution so that a making, a perceptual process, is still rediscoverable in it. And this time is not an easy time, a time of unimpeded one-after-the-other; it is a cumulative time, increasingly heavy with thickening perception and broadening consciousness.

One must draw in order to see; and then one must see more and more 'drawingly' in order to draw. One must translate in order to read; and then one must read 'translatingly' in order to translate. An image of a standard translational procedure might look like this:

$$\text{read}$$
$$\text{ST} \rightarrow \rightarrow \rightarrow \text{ meaning} < \text{meaning} \leftarrow \leftarrow \leftarrow \text{TL} \rightarrow \rightarrow \rightarrow \text{TT}$$

One reads the ST to extract its meaning. The meaning of the ST must search out target language equivalents, which can then be shaped into a TT. An over-simplification and over-systematisation of the translation process perhaps, but the basis of a possible model. What we, on the other hand, are searching for is something more like this:

$$\text{reading}$$
$$\text{ST} << \quad \uparrow \downarrow \quad << \text{TT}$$
$$\text{translating}$$

What does this figure intend to mean? That the process of translation never comes *away* from the ST, but always moves back towards it, whatever expressive distances are interposed. That reading and translation are a dialectical or integrated activity – it is often difficult to tell which – which need each other in order to reinvest the ST with a readerly consciousness. The product, a TT, is the translation, not of a text, but of the process of reading a text: one translates reading into a translation which is still reading. The TT, therefore, does not stand off from the ST as a substitute or an autonomous piece. The TT is a (re)inhabitation of the ST which continues to depend on the ST and which, correspondingly and conversely, makes the ST dependent. The continuing survival of the ST is to be measured by its continuing dependency on new readers.

We must in these closing paragraphs reiterate, in the light of drawing, what has been an underlying tenet of our translational position: the active agency of the support, the blank sheet of paper. In standard views of translation nothing intervenes between the ST and the TT, no third party, apart from the translator. But the blank sheet of paper has questions of its own to ask and negotiations to demand. James Elkins describes a drawing as 'the invaluable record of the encounter of a moving, thinking hand with the mesmerizing space of potential forms that is simply called "a blank sheet of paper"' (in Berger, 2008, 106). It may be fairly apparent how drawing is impelled by, and feeds off, its support; how, in constituting itself, it constitutes its support; how, in inscribing material on the support, it draws material out of the support:

A blank page of a sketch-book is a blank, white page. Make one mark on it, and the edges of the pages are no longer simply where the paper was cut, they have become the borders of a microcosm . . . That microcosm is filled with the potentiality of every proportion you have ever perceived or sensed. That space is filled with the potentiality of every form, sliding plane, hollow, point of contact, passage of separation you have ever set eye or hand on. And it does not stop even there. For, after a few more marks, there is air, there is pressure and therefore there is bulk and weight. (Berger, 2008, 102–3)

It is easy enough to imagine how these plastic values might be elicited and activated, the more text moves from signification to onomatopoeia, from alphabet to pure graphism. The more language as signifying code is de-realised or de-naturalised, the more one can envisage 'truthfulness' to a linguistic material, to a linguistic materiality, and, correspondingly, the more the support materialises as an extension of, or counterpoint to, it. In tabular writing, one might say that the page *is* tabularity, and all the forces – non-chronometric time, variable tempo, non-perspectival space, etc. – that tabularity unleashes. Our argument is that, in translation, the blank page should be not only an answering plasticity for language, but also, and even in conventional modes of translation, the point of engagement of translational consciousness, of whole-body consciousness, somewhere that has to be crossed into from the ST, and inhabited. In drawing, I do not look for likeness, but for knowledge of the model, that particular knowledge that only the draughtsman has in his/her drawing. The model (ST) was already in a context, prior to the drawing (translation); the paper then was blank. The paper becomes a new context, the edges the outer limits of the draughtsman's (translator's) coming to knowledge, or the compositional reference points within which the play of consciousness of the model (ST) is performed. At the same time, the paper, as a physical object in a partic-ular place and time, however much imprinted with drawing or text, is a force-field open to the world, and able to occupy any number of locations within the world. As we saw in our treatment of collage in Chapter 3, when a text becomes a-text-on-a-sheet-of-paper, when our consciousness of the support is activated, text and paper have a new currency, have compelled upon them a part to play.

Our final objective, then, is to achieve some kind of 'total translation'. If we borrow this term from Jerome Rothenberg (2004, 201–15), we do so with a sense of a difference of application. For Rothenberg, the term relates particularly to his ethnopoetic translations from Seneca and Navajo Indian, and concerns the translation of an oral poetic event into a full re-animation of that event in a cultural elsewhere. For us, it is an ongoing project in which tireless translation aspires to the 'totalisation' of the textual experience generated by a ST. To achieve this end, translation must give more prominence to certain experimental techniques, in particular those that tend to dissociate language from established codes of meaning, or that promote the materiality of language. Totalisation of the textual experience offered by the ST can only be accomplished by the multiplication of translations, because totality itself is Heraclitian flux. We act so that things can move on, so that the place we are at can be renewed. Translation should, as far as it can, situate itself in time, in a cumulative Bergsonian time, so that it becomes itself the willing instrument of time's impatience to generate *from* a text an ever-expanding psycho-sensory immersion *in* text.

Epilogue: portrait of a reader – Malcolm Bowie in search of the critical interworld

This book is concerned to argue that translation should encourage the reader of a source text (ST) to write his/her responses, his/her own particular insights and associations, into the quick of the target text (TT), so that the TT can be seen as the ST re-textualised, given new expressive coordinates, in the here and now of the reading act. In the work of Malcolm Bowie, the subject of this chapter, the process of translation does not end in a translation (TT), but in a piece of critical writing in which interpretative moves are deeply and ineradicably imbued with phenomenological *Einfühlung* [empathy]. I do not want to suggest that the hermeneutic and the constructivist, the interpretative and phenomenological, should seek to come to some understanding, their antagonism transcended; their interests are too invigoratingly conflictual for one to wish that. But I do want to suggest that in some readers, in gifted readers like Bowie, readers for whom translation in its 'literal' sense is not a favoured form of self-expression, critical discourse is permeated with the phenomenological, with a practice of translation which crosses media and disciplines to create a critical language imbued with a sense of expanded and expanding sensory awareness.

It may seem odd that, in introducing a new translation of Flaubert's *Madame Bovary* by Margaret Mauldon (2004a), Bowie should give so much attention to Flaubert's writing, in all its stylistic detail, since 'Flaubertian' is presumably not a language accessible to his readers, other than in an English approximation. This partly expresses Bowie's unwillingness to let translation compel any compromising of the source language's text-originating energies. But, more important, it makes clear Bowie's fundamental devotion to a criticism which flows from an engagement with the dynamics of writing – the syntactic rhythms, the lexical interactions, the labile tonal nuances – and from a corresponding 'critical sympathetics' of reading. Bowie's own practice makes this coinage necessary. He himself refers to the 'imaginative absorption' that reading demands (2004a, xviii); and elsewhere (1999, 21), he taxes a critic with not 'immersing himself in the phonic, lexical, and syntactic substance of his writers' words as they unfold in the real time of reading'. This sympathetics is something deeper than the quality of detailed attention; let us not overlook that reference to 'the real time of reading'. This sympathetics is more like the mobilisation in the reader of a kinaesthetic empathy, which makes fluid the boundaries between subjects, installs the intersubjective, and activates a psycho-perceptual participation in 'style'.[1] This of itself, perhaps, triggers a synaesthetisation of readerly experience. We might say that such a readerly posture *necessitates* comparatism; that is to say, necessitates a language that will do justice to multi-sensory and multi-cultural promptings, and to conceptual shape-shifting.

Bowie's contribution to *The Cambridge Companion to Proust* (2001), 'Postlude: Proust and the Art of Brevity', begins with an exquisite commentary on Canaletto's *View of the Grand Canal from S. Vio* (prior to 1723): 'The sweep's gesture repeats that of the water workers beneath him. He is a gondolier of the rooftops' (2001, 218). Canaletto, as Bowie points out, has only the slightest of parts to play in Proust's published work, and one might wonder what makes him the apposite parallel for a consideration of Proust's art of brevity. Admittedly, the final and most substantial Proustian example treated by Bowie has Venice as its setting, but it is not as a painter of Venice that Canaletto earns his inclusion. Nor by virtue of the fact that, with age, he loses his appetite for detail, where Proust's writing follows the opposite trajectory. It is only after Canaletto has left Bowie's text that he comes to inhabit it, as a language of painterly perception applied to narrative construction:

The phrases, sentences and episodes that have been rapidly reviewed in these pages all occupy tension-points in the texture of the novel. They direct the Proust reader towards a far horizon of narrative closure while detaining him or her in an incident-filled foreground. They are micro-dramas taking place in a grandly unfolding festal pageant. (2001, 229)

Where are we to find a language that brings home to us the play of proxemics, the restless modulations of focus, which assail the reader of Proust, if not in Canaletto? And this is not a language supplied *directly* by Canaletto's painting, but by someone *writing about* Canaletto. We would be wrong, however, to imagine that this interfusion of critical languages has anything to do with borrowing, as if one might casually, as the occasion demands, appropriate the odd term or concept. This is a process of translation, or, more accurately, transubstantiation. Bowie is particularly drawn to the last paragraph of *Wuthering Heights* (see both 1994, 33 and 2001, 228), where Heathcliff and Hareton are reborn in the heath and harebells that surround

Heathcliff's grave; in this passage, protagonists are absorbed into landscape, figures into ground, the terms of one order (proper nouns) are transformed into the terms of another (common nouns), just as the language of one medium or writer may become the language of another.

The instrument of comparison (Canaletto), then, has a more active, a more crucial relationship with the critic (Bowie) than with the subject (Proust); comparative literature is not in the text, but in the reader. The critic summons, voluntarily or involuntarily, the instrument, in order to elicit from himself the desired perception of the subject. But the very appropriateness of the instrument may, on occasion, be an obstacle. In Bowie's approach to the poetics of Mallarmé's late prose (1994), for example, the perceptual detour is provided by Borges's Pierre Ménard. But here Ménard's thinking, as described by Borges, anticipates, pre-empts Bowie's own ruminations on Mallarmé. The task then is the recovery of one's own perceptions, the retrieval of one's own words, touched as they may be by a predecessor's inescapable formulations. This is another sense of translation, if you like, one in which the target text (Bowie) attempts to escape the source text (Borges), not by radical changes of insight, but by subtle repossessions, so that the source text becomes a text shared with the subject (Mallarmé) rather than resorted to, as a guide, by the critic.

Bowie's masterly contribution to *A Short History of French Literature* (2003) leaves him little room to develop these reflective spaces so welcoming of artists from elsewhere. But we may recognise as particularly significant the section entitled 'Beyond the Literary Profession' (306–9), in which he considers those ostensibly outside the institution of literature (e.g. Bergson, Foucault, Lacan, Lévi-Strauss, Leiris), those in whom the brilliance of their writing is proportional to the *performance* of their ideas, those who write themselves into thought:

The traffic in fact flows in both directions between literature and the 'other' discipline. In each case the author concerned takes us, by way of his writerly display, into his innermost intellectual workshop. The sensation, as unmistakable here as in Proust or Valéry, is that of witnessing the act of creative thinking as it takes place. (2003, 306–7)

Throughout Bowie's work, the art of critical writing has been the fundamental key to the very perception of art, because one writes into one's own writing the very quick of one's insights, as if either one's style gave rise to one's perceptual biases and strengths, or seeing something in someone else's work inevitably resonated through the whole of one's own writerly metabolism. This writing is also a process of self-elicitation: as we write about something, all our perceptual habits, learning, education, become available in suggestive ways, with different kinds of adaptation to the subject being considered. Thus, in Tovey's account of Beethoven's piano sonata Op. III, 'Thanks to the discreet ingenuity of Tovey's writing . . . an existential choice that figures prominently in the works of the Church fathers and in the history of European monasticism has been brought to bear, in a miniaturised and intensified form, on three bars of keyboard music' (Bowie, 2007, 68).

This makes the map of comparative literature infinitely extendable and its time-sequence constantly re-imaginable. Here the time-sequence is the sequence of critical consciousness rather than that of history, or is the re-writing of history by critical consciousness. This is to contest a positivistic comparative literature which believes that critical scrutiny draws the map which settles works and determines their coordinates and network of activities.

One might hazard that the temporal medium within which Bowie's acts of comparison take place is, like Proust's treatment of Italian painting (see 2004b), unnervingly but richly dialectical: it becomes difficult to tell whether the painting that seems uncannily to anticipate some modern gesture, or expression, or dress, is not drawing the modern back into its own pastness. Such collusions of the proleptic and analeptic are at once anachronistic and powerfully apposite. Literary history is an autobiographical ordering of mental events in which chronology is reversible, and is constantly to be re-written as the occasion demands.

But it is not just the progress of the work in (a)historical time that matters, but also the forward-movingness of the text itself: 'Literature, and criticism in its wake, are all to do with meaning on the move, in transit, in transformation from moment to moment inside a signifying flux' (2007, 72). What Bowie is afraid of is a writing that can write about the techniques at the source of, say, a musical experience, but cannot write about musical experience itself. Bowie often expresses regret about critical writing's impotence in the face of the intimate, intricate operations of text. Criticism may trace, as in slow motion, the dynamic of thought and feeling; but it is dedicated to separation and immobilisation, to juxtapositions rather than to transitions and metamorphoses: 'We need an analytic method that, having frozen the poem's individual moments and tendencies, can unfreeze them again in order to rediscover its dialectic' (1990, 241).

As we have already supposed, and despite his contribution of a translation of Mallarmé's 'Le Mystère dans les lettres' to Mary Ann Caws's *Mallarmé in Prose* (2001, 46–51), Bowie seems sceptical in his attitudes to conventional translation: too much is at stake in what he often refers to as the 'local textures' of writing, for translation to be anything other than a last resort. And he has every reason to be familiar with the ways in which Freud's thinking, for example, has been given a 'scientific' colouring and re-inflected by translation. Consequently, one may also suspect that he has more sympathy with translation as a crib than as a substitute: feeling one's way back from a TT to a ST can bring revelations vouchsafed perhaps neither to the reader of the ST nor to the reader of the TT.

In view of these considerations, it comes as no surprise that Bowie should be attracted to Pierre Ménard's translation of Cervantes, the translation that is textually identical, but profoundly different in regard to the spirit by which it is informed, and to the way in which the reader responds to it: 'Here again text is stretched upon text; Ménard's eventual reader would encounter the same work twice over, but made different and incommensurable by the passage of time' (1994, 35). According to this principle, all reading is an intralingual translation, as it seeks to re-plot the work's coordinates, its expressive range, its relationship with ambient media and disciplines.

Alternatively, as in Ménard's translation of Valéry's decasyllables into alexandrines, the work is shifted into another scale, another amplitude, another tempo, another rhythmic and conceptual framework; but the source text is in no way superseded:

This was not an attempt to destroy or replace the poem but an attempt to make it vibrate in a new way. Between the dodecasyllabic version and the earlier decasyllabic one, which remains intact and in force, a grid is formed, and a new, severe and playful form of poetry – over which neither Ménard nor Valéry has proprietary rights – comes into being. (Bowie, 1994, 35)

This is all to show that translation's principal virtue is as a response to the ST's compulsive reaching for futurity, and for a futurity in which it can live out its desire to be other, repeatedly and unconditionally.[2] The dangers which beset translation are twofold: (i) to carry within itself an agenda of retrospective closure; (ii) to translate in such a way that the ST's desiring condition is stifled or frustrated. Ménard's translation of Cervantes maintains the ST's textual 'futurity' word for word, even as it makes *Don Quixote* temporally other; Ménard's transposition of Valéry respects what Valéry himself in fact wished for the decasyllables of *Le Cimetière marin*, that they should be raised 'to the power of twelve'.[3]

But the kind of translation that is closest to Bowie's heart is not the conventional kind, between or within different national languages; it is the translation between different arts, or different media within the same art, where the art's critical language may matter as much as its creative language, since the critical language generates the art's thoughtfulness. This kind of translation finds its place more fittingly in the consideration of Bowie's comparatism/interdisciplinarity that follows.

Perhaps Bowie's most direct confrontation with the 'question' of comparative literature occurs in the 1993 article 'Comparison between the Arts: A Psychoanalytic View'. We should begin by noting what constitute for him the privileged sites of comparatism: he implicitly counts himself among 'those who concern themselves with the migration of meaning between art forms, and with the often obscure structural kinship that exists between works in different media (between literature and painting, say) or between the different elements of a composite medium (opera, ballet, "performance", say)' (1993a, 81). One might safely conclude that Bowie is more interdisciplinarian than comparatist, or, rather, more intermedial than interlingual comparatist. It might also lead us to suspect, as already intimated, that, under his pen, every medium is likely to become composite, that meaning itself is the desire to be medially other; one art has the other arts as its 'blind field', as that area around it into which it has an innate yearning to expand.

For Bowie, the underlying problem relates to language: to find the critical language which will spare us the 'loose metaphorizing of one medium at the hands of another' (1993a, 86) and engineer smooth transitions and exchange between the different arts:

There are two obvious ways of thinking comparatively in these border territories. On the one hand, the structural vocabulary and syntax of one art can be put to work upon another; on the other hand, a diplomatic language can be assembled by observing and comparing a wide variety of artistic practices. The latter would be a structural Esperanto of sorts, a lingua franca in which the transactions between, say, poetry and painting, music and drama, or sculpture and narrative could be accurately described and boldly theorized. The second of these options strikes me as much more promising, even if more laborious, than the first. (1993a, 86)

The first option is a translational mechanism, and loose metaphor is the risk it runs, unless the translation is sensitively managed. The second is an interlanguage, a 'third place' between the two media/arts concerned, and it is Bowie's hope that a language like that of psychoanalysis can occupy that space. This option is presumably more laborious, because the ability of psychoanalysis to negotiate between two arts depends on its preliminary ability to be appropriate to each of them individually. Bowie seems doubtful that his hopes can be realised, because of the qualifications that must be placed on psychoanalysis: it functions best with works that belong to its own cultural context; it functions best with works that have particular kinds of structure (1993a, 99–100); more fundamentally perhaps, aligning psychoanalytic perceptions with the critical idioms of the arts is, inescapably and already, governed by the principle of translation: 'The psychoanalytic account of mental process is combinable with, and to some extent translatable into, the analytic idiom appropriate to each individual art-form' (1993a, 89). But if this looks like a setback, we should not be discouraged. For one thing, psychoanalytical concepts and language often do prove their worth.[4] For another, Bowie himself is a pastmaster of intermedial translation; and for another, comparison, in his handling of it, is not a be-all and end-all, but a relay-station, impulsive, provisional, virtual; it is, as we have observed, the performance of an idea.

Bowie's own practice shifts easily between his two options or seeks some merger. Translation continues to be central to the critical enterprise – 'Good criticism is an art of translation – from language to language, or from level to level, or idiom to idiom, within a given language' (2007, 72) – and, ultimately, one of Bowie's abiding preoccupations remains the contribution that can be made to one art by the language of another, regardless of any comparative or interdisciplinary ambitions:

What I have been suggesting is that a willingness on the part of writers on music to use a more varied verbal palette can actually bring us closer to the real world of musical experience, and to the wonderfully impure acts of translation, of provocation, of risk taking, and of abyssmanship that musical experience involves. (2007, 72)

Elsewhere (1998c, 114), Bowie praises a skill in Proust – navigating between art and the thought-animated ordinary world – that might be an account of his own intermedial practice:

In doing this he [Proust] relies upon a special vocabulary of what might be called 'switch-words' or 'crossover-terms'. These often originate in a localised semantic field, and seem in some cases to belong to the jargon of a single art, craft or intellectual pursuit, but their role is a mobile and diplomatic one. They make disparate fields of human activity intelligible to one another. Such negotiation has its own Proustian lexicon: *transition, transposition, transmutation, substitution, transformation, transmigration, modulation, traduction* ('translation').

Here, then, the notions of diplomatic language and translation become potentially co-terminous. But what further emerges from this discussion are the senses in which comparatism and interdisciplinarity are worthwhile undertakings for Bowie. Comparatism is the instrument whereby different arts or different works are made intelligible to each other, or whereby one art might make another intelligible to itself. Comparatism is justified to the degree to which it can deepen our immediate, 'lived' experience of the work or works concerned; and it is more the critical languages involved, than any specific virtues of the medium or the artists, which allow this end to be achieved.

When Bowie compares Proust with Fauré (1993a, 95–9), the question is not whether Vinteuil's music owes something to Fauré's, but whether Fauré's compositional techniques might help us to capture the elaborative processes at work in the Proustian sentence. There is no question of debt, influence, allusion; the accident of their being contemporary promises an insight into something shared by them and lying beyond either of them, a structural principle: dedifferentiated flux silenced by a large conclusive gesture.

In similar fashion, Bowie's triumvirate of Freud, Proust and Lacan (1987) are not explored for what each might tell about the others, but because their writerly trajectories are all sighted on 'the *intermundium* between theory and fiction' and make it the source of crucial revelations to the human scientist (1987, 7). One should also add that this partnership is Bowie's safeguard against having his words pre-empted by any author studied singly; comparison is a strategy in the power struggle between the critic and his subject, an alliance which safeguards the critic's writerly autonomy.

Again, when Bowie 'compares' word-play as he finds it in Mallarmé and Lacan (1998a), it is in terms not of what one might owe to the other, but of what they *converge in*, and they converge in a critical practice governed by its underlying riskiness:

Their own word-play takes place under conditions of great stress: on the one hand it is reduced at a culminating moment in each text to an intimation of empty, contentless structure, and on the other hand it becomes a variety of passion and sensual engagement with experience. Word-play itself is subject to the Freudian *fort/da*, to a rhythmic intermittence, to an interleaving of sense and nonsense, sensuality and anaesthesia, gravity and levity. Dare one imagine a theoretically self-aware criticism in this mould? One that resisted as well as endorsed its master texts? (1998a, 80)

What is further remarkable about this comparison is its 'could' modality and Bowie's need ultimately to resist its siren-call: 'The comparison between

Mallarmé and Lacan could be taken much further in this direction. We could examine... We could set... and we could see both authors' (1998a, 77). Bowie implies that comparison is a choice that should always trigger an awareness of other possible comparisons. And he warns the reader that, for him, the comparative relationship is a tangential one in that, beyond it, are activated both a sense of *differentiae* and a sense of the extendability and reversibility of the points of comparison. Reciprocal illumination is fine as long as it is bought at the expense neither of mutual contestation and diffraction (1987, 68), nor of 'the complex middle-distance' (1987, 76).

Viewed from a converse position, the writer seems to keep his position permeable to other systems of thought, other stylistic or ideological models, as the occasion arises, so that the presences in his work are not those of occupants pressing their proprietary rights, but temporary squatters, whose only rights are precisely those of presence to the viewing consciousness. When considering Lacan's intoxicating, inclusive account of Truth, Bowie remarks: 'An ecstatic sense of plenitude is being sought. Gaps and spaces of all kinds are to be filled. Besides Erasmus, Lacan's kinsmen at these moments are Rabelais, the Apuleius of *The Golden Ass* and the Joyce of *Finnegans Wake*' (1991, 116). The comparatist, then, sets out to establish points of contact, shifting, unfixed, temporary, unpredictable, where the solicitations of intellectual autobiography are freely responded to. Comparative literature of this kind, as we have said, is not so much in a text or a discipline as in a person, in that person's unique literary education and the kinds of reading that that education produces. And, of course, relationships of quotation and elective affinity are very different from relationships of influence.

All in all, the nature of Bowie's comparatism, we might argue, is intimately bound up with his attitude to meaning, which is itself psychoanalytically grounded:

Meaning is to be had in psychoanalysis only intermittently, as a momentary purchase achieved upon a constant interplay of levels, systems, structures, registers, intensities and investments. Psychoanalysis is a theory of meaning not simply arrived at and grasped but dawning and expiring, still out of sight or already on the wane. (1993a, 90)

Bowie more comfortably occupies a Kristevan/Barthesian world of *significance* than of *signification*, and in such circumstances comparative literature becomes a play of shifting interfaces and overlappings, which momentarily reveal makeable meanings, but just as quickly withdraw the desirability of pressing too hard to establish them.

To attempt to enter the 'innermost intellectual workshop' of a distinguished scholar is not only a mightily presumptuous undertaking, but one which is likely to convince us that the gifts and persuasions of an individual mind are not generalisable.

Bowie's writing is steeped in his dealings with psychoanalysis, but he is never a psychoanalytic critic. What concerns him is not psychoanalysis as an interpretative key, with all its threats of impoverishing the reading experience, but as a theory and methodology profoundly implicated in the processes of linguistic production. There are three related aspects of his intellectual engagement with psychoanalysis which seem to be of importance to his own comparative and interdisciplinary method, all touched upon in his paper 'On Proust and Psychoanalysis' (1998). The first lies in the dialogue between the analyst and the analysand (Freud's *Übertragung*: transference, transferential interaction): 'the patient transfers on to the person of the clinician feelings that come from elsewhere' (1998b, 22), particularly from childhood, which the clinician is able to transform, render intelligible, render assimilable. In Bowie's literary-critical reading of text, the roles of analyst and analysand become merged, even reversible, in the sense that those connections which spring to the reader's mind – read Michaux (1973), and Bosch or Blake or Rilke or Wordsworth or De Quincey may erupt into consciousness – do so either as if spontaneously generated, or as if elicited or projected by the text under scrutiny. And in this dialectical, dialogic relationship, these 'eruptions' find their level, their appropriateness, their true, relativised effectiveness; we are witnesses of the transformations 'that take place when different arts are brought into alignment and caught up in each other's signifying field' (1993a, 86).

This transferential dialogue between reader and text is, in turn, underpinned by a critical posture that is also that of the Freudian clinician. When Bowie sees Mallarmé's late prose as 'requiring of the reader that he evenly suspend his attention' (2000a, 7), he is alluding to Freud's 'gleichschwebende Aufmerksamkeit' (1998b, 22). It is this even distribution of attention that gives access to what Barthes calls the 'formes laïques' [lay forms] of the unconscious: 'l'implicite, l'indirect, le supplémentaire, le retardé: il y a ouverture de l'écoute à toutes les formes de polysémie, de surdéterminations, de superpositions, il y a effritement de la Loi qui prescrit l'écoute droite, unique' (1982b, 229) [the implicit, the indirect, the supplementary, the delayed: listening is open to all forms of polysemy, overdetermination, superimposition, there is erosion of the Law which prescribes focused, single listening].

Finally, Bowie finds his natural critical space in the *intermundium*, whether we think of it as Rilke's *Zwischenraum* or Merleau-Ponty's *intermonde* or Winnicott's 'transitional space' (1998b, 26). Here creative forces, ideological postures, lines of thought, desires, come into collision, negotiate, interweave. And as we have already intimated, this is the space where meaning is made possible but cannot be made: meaning in movement, 'never able to reach its point of closure and finality' (1998b, 28).

Unfortunately, my dogged pursuit of the patterns in Bowie's thought and writing do justice neither to the broad sweep and gracefulness of that thought, nor to the sumptuousness of the writing, nor indeed to the tireless and exhilarating penetration of the critical mind. Given the consummateness of his art, it seems something of an impertinence to ask about Bowie's critical persuasions. Our final formulation of his achievement, at least within the terms of this epilogue, might be words he applied to Proust: 'an "interdisciplinarist" beyond the dreams of the modern university' (1998c, 18).

Notes

INTRODUCTION

1. The use of the acronyms ST, TT, SL, TL, for 'source text', 'target text', 'source language', 'target language' respectively, may strike some readers, to begin with, as rebarbative. I would defend the terms themselves ('source text', 'target text', etc.) on the grounds that they are standard currency in the literature of translation studies, and that they avoid the ambiguities and unwanted implications of alternatives such as 'original', 'translation', 'translated text', 'language of the original'. And I would defend the use of acronyms both because, again, they are standard practice in the field, and because, once accustomed to them, the eye instantly identifies them, without their repetition becoming cumbersome. From time to time in the text, readers are reminded of the keys to the acronyms.

2. Malcolm Bowie (5 May, 1943 – 28 January, 2007) was, from July 2002 until his premature death, Master of Christ's College, Cambridge. He had previously been a Fellow of Clare College, Cambridge (1969–1976), Professor of French Language and Literature, University of London (Queen Mary College) (1976–1992) and Marshal Foch Professor of French Literature, University of Oxford (1992–2002). He was the Founding Director of the Institute of Romance Studies (London) (1989–1992), Co-director, then Director, of the European Humanities Research Centre (Oxford) (1996–2002), and President of the BCLA (1998–2006); and he acted as General Editor of *French Studies* (1980–1987) and of Cambridge Studies in French (1980–1995). His principal publications include: *Henri Michaux: A Study of His Literary Works*, 1973; *Mallarmé and the Art of Being Difficult*, 1978; *Freud, Proust and Lacan: Theory as Fiction*, 1987; *Lacan*, 1991; *Psychoanalysis and the Future of Theory*, 1993; *Proust among the Stars*, 1998 (Truman Capote Award for Literary Criticism, 2001). He was elected Fellow of the British Academy (1993) and Fellow of the Royal Society of Literature (1999).

1 READING AND TRANSLATION

1. With its talk of the embodied and the experiential, it might seem that cognitive poetics is equally concerned with the phenomenology of reading. But this an

illusion. It is an interpretative mode which does not, as it might claim, heal the Cartesian rift between mind and body. Its concern is with underlying general and abstract conceptual structures – models, frames, maps, schemas – with norms, and with readerly conditioning; and by 'embodiment', the cognitive analyst means the embodiment of these conceptual structures in the act of reading, rather than the activation, by reading, of the body of the reader, or the elicitation of kinaesthetic response by text. An underlying danger of its approach is that it attributes to the consciousness of the reading mind what it describes as happening linguistically within the text. Peter Stockwell states, in his introductory guide to cognitive poetics, apropos of metaphor: 'cognitive linguistics is interested in the conceptual level primarily' (2002, 106). The translational approach pursued here is perhaps best represented by the fascinating collection of versions contained in *One Poem in Search of a Translator: Rewriting 'Les Fenêtres' by Apollinaire* (ed. Eugenia Loffredo and Manuela Perteghella, 2009). The idea of collecting a range of experimental accounts of a particular poem deserves to be much repeated and developed.

2. The *Collins English Dictionary* (Glasgow: HarperCollins, 2000) gives, as the etymology of 'rampage': '[C18: from Scottish, of uncertain origin; perhaps based on RAMP]' (1276). 'Ram' is from '[Old English *ramm*; related to Old High German *ram* ram, Old Norse *ramr* fierce, *rimma* to fight]' (1275–6), while 'page' has, as its twin etymologies: '[C15: via Old French from Latin *pāgina*]' and '[C13: via Old French from Italian *paggio*, probably from Greek *paidion* boy, from *pais* child]' (1115).

3. Proust defines the readerly equivalent of humming thus: 'En réalité, chaque lecteur est quand il lit le propre lecteur de soi-même. L'ouvrage de l'écrivain n'est qu'une espèce d'instrument optique qu'il offre au lecteur afin de lui permettre de discerner ce que sans ce livre il n'eût peut-être pas vu en soi-même' (1989, 489–90) [In reality every reader is, while he is reading, the reader of his own self. The writer's work is merely a kind of optical instrument which he offers to the reader to enable him to discern what, without this book, he would perhaps never have perceived in himself (1983b, 949)]. Proust also provides a more specific account of readerly humming, and a glimpse of the kind of consideration which might produce its distortions, in the narrator's response to the fictional writer, Bergotte: 'D'après ses livres j'imaginais Bergotte comme un vieillard faible et déçu qui avait perdu des enfants et ne s'était jamais consolé. Aussi je lisais, je chantais intérieurement sa prose, plus *dolce*, plus *lento* peut-être qu'elle n'était écrite, et la phrase la plus simple s'adressait à moi avec une intonation attendrie' (1987a, 95–6) [From his books I had formed an impression of Bergotte as a frail and disappointed old man, who had lost some of his children and had never got over the loss. And so I would read, or rather sing his sentences in my mind, with rather more *dolce*, rather more *lento* than he himself had perhaps intended, and his simplest phrase would strike my ears with something peculiarly gentle and loving in its intonation (1983a, 104)].

4. When I became critically involved with translation and began to practise it in the mid-1990s, I took much heart from Rob Pope's 1995 *Textual Intervention:*

Critical and Creative Strategies for Literary Studies, with its watchword: 'Reading is a form of re-writing. Every interpretation is an act of intervention'; and I took heart, too, from its programme of such interventions: production of parallel, alternative and counter-texts; 're-centering', 're-genreing' and cross-media adaptation; exercises in imitation, parody and collage (see headpages blurb). In a short article for *The European English Messenger* (1999), Pope punchily summarised his position, including among the tenets of his 'manifesto for re-writing': '7. *Translation* always involves transformation as well as transference: between different languages and between different varieties of the same language – between "creative" and "critical" discourses, for instance' (1999, 43). Pope's interests and objectives are not exactly the same as mine: his is an interpretative approach, mine an anti-interpretative one; for him, the ST, or base text, remains the critical objective, for me the path forward from the ST is paramount. But his work continues to be extremely stimulating.

5. Emily Apter expresses this paradox thus: 'while translation is deemed essential to the dissemination and preservation of textual inheritance, it is also understood to be an agent of language extinction. For translation, especially in a world dominated by the languages of powerful economies and big populations, condemns minority tongues to obsolescence, even as it fosters access to the cultural heritage of "small" literatures' (2006, 4).

6. I say 'as I adapt it', because, as Venuti (2011, 129) points out, McGann's account of the 'constructivist' is still coloured – certainly too much for my taste – with semiological thinking, and an interpretative vocabulary of coding/decoding/deciphering. The distinction that I want to make between hermeneutic and constructivist reading has close affinities with Roland Barthes's distinction between 'readerly' and 'writerly' texts (1970, 10–11). With readerly texts, according to Barthes, the reader has access only to signifieds, is 'plongé dans une sorte d'oisiveté, d'intransitivité' [is plunged into a kind of idleness, of intransitivity], and treats the text as product rather than as process of production. With writerly texts, on the other hand, the reader accedes 'pleinement à l'enchantement du signifiant, à la volupté de l'écriture' [fully to the enchantment of the signifier, to the pleasure of writing]; he does not consume, but produces. The writerly text 'est un présent perpétuel, sur lequel ne peut se poser aucune parole *conséquente* (qui le transformerait, fatalement, en passé)' [is a continuous present, on which no *consequential* language can settle (which would transform it, unavoidably, into the past)].

7. Medial-axis, or *Mittelachse*, verse is most commonly associated with Arno Holz's cycle of poems *Phantasus*. Holz began the cycle in the late 1890s and by the time of his death in 1929, it had reached something over 60,000 lines. His work bears out that principle of addition *into*, of expansion from within, of infinite embedding, that *Mittelachse* verse seems to be driven by. With this sense of a world oozing out of a cleft in the middle of the paper, it is not surprising that *Mittelachse* verse should attract processes of agglutination and compounding, of morphemes and lexemes fusing together, so that *scriptio continua* seems an almost natural consequence. It is often suggested that this verse-structure, with

its symmetries developing long arabesques, is perhaps an inevitable product of *fin-de-siècle* cultivations of sinuous, organic forms.

8. In borrowing McGann's term 'radial reading', I must again take a certain distance from his use of it. For McGann, radial reading is primarily a need-driven process of consultation (checking meanings, references) (1991, 116), the decoding of the contexts 'that interpenetrate the scripted and physical text' (1991, 119) and the reconstruction of the text's socio-historical field and modes of production (1991, 120, 125). My radial reading is not necessarily invoked by the text; it is more reader-orientated and also includes involuntary associations, uncontrollably triggered intertexts, random memories and fantasies.

2 READING: VOICE AND RHYTHM

1. See, for example, Patsy Rodenburg (1998, xi): 'To speak a heightened text clearly to hundreds of people requires a huge vocal extension. To express passion and charged ideas takes enormous vocal range and energy whatever the size of the playing space. And to sustain this kind of work again and again over years takes a combination of consummate craft and dedication.' And with a slightly wider purview, see Michael McCallion (1998, xxi): 'Your voice must be capable of conveying all the nuances of meaning your work demands; it must be a completely flexible and accurate instrument of expression and communication which remains absolutely under your control.' See also Colette Lecourt (1999).

2. For further reflections on the relationship between the inner and outer voice, see Berry, 2000, 22–4.

3. Tim Ingold describes this supplementation of sense by sense thus: 'If hearing is a mode of participatory engagement with the environment, it is not because it is opposed in this regard to vision, but because we "hear" with the eyes as well as the ears. In other words, *it is the very incorporation of vision into the process of auditory perception that transforms passive hearing into active listening*' (2000, 277; original emphasis).

4. Nancy Perloff reminds us of the earlier history of this gradual post-humanising of the voice: 'the invention of the phonograph (1877), radio (1891), and tape recorder (1934–35) accelerated these developments by broadening the repertoire of sounds and, in the case of magnetic tape, enabling poets and composers to manipulate recorded sounds through splicing, speed modification, and the superimposition of sound layers' (2009, 98).

5. I need to underline this inseparability of the cognitive and performative in rhythm, so as not to run athwart the distinction made by Tim Ingold between cognition and performance as processes connected, respectively, with script and score (2007, 11–12). In effect, there is, I think, little difference between our positions: the reading of rhythm that I canvass coincides with Ingold's classical and medieval modes of reading, in which cognition and performance are 'aspects of the same thing' (2007, 17).

6. Ford's dictum will remind us of Laforgue's words in his notes on Impressionism of 1883: 'Chaque homme est selon son moment dans le temps, son milieu de race et de condition sociale, son moment d'évolution individuelle, un certain clavier sur lequel le monde extérieur joue d'une certaine façon. Mon clavier est perpétuellement changeant et il n'y en a pas un autre identique au mien. Tous les claviers sont légitimes' (Dottin, 1988, 172–3) [Each individual is, according to his moment in time, his ethnic milieu and that of his social condition, his stage of personal evolution, a certain keyboard on which the external world plays in a certain manner. My keyboard is constantly changing and there is no other identical to mine. All keyboards are legitimate].

7. 'In typing and printing, the intimate link between the manual gesture and the inscriptive trace is broken. The author conveys feeling by his choice of words, not by the expressiveness of his lines' (Ingold, 2007, 3).

8. On this subject in modern verse more generally, see Dworkin, 2003.

9. We should, however, acknowledge that several typefaces flirt dangerously with illegibility. I think particularly of the highly condensed typefaces, and of mavericks such as Contacta, Gala Quadra and Syrup.

10. We have associated handwriting with the voice, each sharing an inimitable individual signature. If handwriting has peculiar access to the physiological voice, we can perhaps allow that typefaces can enact the expressive voice. The handbook of *1000 Fonts* (Gordon, 2009) informs us that: 'Spoken language is so rich in its ability to express and communicate the myriad conditions of the human experience that it seems fitting that designers should seek to squeeze every conceivable nuance and emotion from the characters that make up the written word – in order to give visual speech greater feeling, depth, and power' (6). But it also makes claims that take typefaces in the direction of the physiological: 'It is no coincidence that individual letterforms are called characters and, like human characters, letters have their own unique vocal identities' (8). This latter claim may relate particularly to typefaces derived from scripts; certainly they sometimes, quite explicitly, have ambitions to catch individual hands/voices: da Vinci and Cézanne, for example. They also imitate different ethnic accents: Bagel (Hebrew), Chineze, Falafel (Arabic), for instance.

11. We might look to Kurt Schwitters's musical instructions for the voice in performances of his 'Ursonate' (1922–32), as an early example of this enterprise (2002, 52–80, 233–7).

12. But we need to be aware of a certain paradoxicality. If our argument is that phonemes and morphemes, even if fake, deserve to recover their innate energies, their full acoustic personalities as sources of pronunciation, as phonetics rather than phonology, that is, as raw primary sounds rather than as elements in an established sound system, then we must at the same time recognise that isolated phonemes and morphemes are artifices, if not fictions, of the written language. The bucking bronco of speech flow does not allow the disentanglement of its individual constituents. Speech cannot be adequately transcribed; and the spoken cannot be analysed other than in written form.

3 TRANSLATING THE TEXTUAL ENVIRONMENT (1)

1. Georges Perec puts it thus: 'lire, ce n'est pas seulement lire un texte, déchiffrer des signes, arpenter des lignes, explorer des pages, traverser un sens; ce n'est pas seulement la communion abstraite de l'auteur et du lecteur, la noce mystique de l'Idée et de l'Oreille, c'est, en même temps, le bruit du métro, ou le balancement d'un wagon de chemin de fer, ou de la chaleur du soleil sur une plage et les cris des enfants qui jouent un peu plus loin, ou la sensation de l'eau chaude dans la baignoire, ou l'attente du sommeil . . . ' (2003, 119) [Reading is not only to read a text, to decipher signs, to follow lines back and forth, to explore pages, to make one's way through meaning; it is not only the abstract communion of author and reader, the mystic marriage of Idea and Ear; it is, at the same time, the noise of the metro, or the swaying of a railway carriage, or the heat of the sun on the beach and the cries of the children playing a little way off, or the sensation of warm water in the bath-tub, or the anticipation of sleep].

2. For a recent treatment of 'primal scenes' of reading in Proust's novel – Marcel's mother reading George Sand's *François le Champi* to him; Marcel reading alone in the garden at Combray – see Watt, 2009, 17–44.

3. Bonnefoy has waged a running battle for a long time with Mallarmé's literary ethos (see Scott, 1998b). Many would argue that Bonnefoy does scant justice to the hold that Mallarmé's so-called abstraction has on the vivid sensuousness of lived existence.

4. Barthes expresses it in these terms: 'Ne vous est-il jamais arrivé, lisant un livre, de vous arrêter sans cesse dans votre lecture, non par désintérêt, mais au contraire par afflux d'idées, d'excitations, d'associations? En un mot, ne vous est-il pas arrivé de *lire en levant la tête*?' (1984, 33; original emphasis) [Has it never happened to you, reading a book, to interrupt your reading incessantly, not through loss of interest, but, on the contrary, because of a rush of ideas, of stimuli, of associations? In a word, has it not happened to you *to read by lifting your head*?].

5. We are principally concerned with the textual and aesthetic effects of collage, but we should not forget that it has an ethical and ideological dimension. Jerome Rothenberg makes this declaration: 'Accordingly my work has involved not only translation but the use of techniques such as collage and appropriation as ways of opening our individual or personal poetry to the presence of other voices and other visions besides our own. I came to think of all of that – appropriation, collage, translation – in ideological terms' (2004, xv–xvi). Collage is a handy safeguard against ethnocentrism and dogmas of any hue.

6. Nuckolls observes: 'Speakers engaging in an ideophonic performance become agents immersed in the process, event, or action they are bringing about with sound' (2004, 71).

4 TRANSLATING THE TEXTUAL ENVIRONMENT (2)

1. Henry Sayre expresses and extends this shift of emphasis thus: 'A good way to think of performance is to realize that in it the potentially disruptive forces of the

"outside" (what is "outside" the text – the physical space in which it is presented, the other media it might engage or find itself among, the various frames of mind the diverse members of a given audience might bring to it, and, over time, the changing forces of history itself) are encouraged to assert themselves. This is different from traditional performance, in which, for instance, an unruly audience might completely wreck one's enjoyment of a symphony or in which, more subtly, bad acting might ruin *Hamlet*. It is, instead, upon the dynamics of such intrusions that performance has come to focus its attention' (1995, 94).

2. For a general history of twentieth-century performance, see Goldberg (2001).

3. Schafer describes the aim of the World Soundscape Project, established in 1970, as: 'to study the acoustic environment in order to determine how sounds affected our lives and from this information to try to design healthier and more beautiful soundscapes for the future' (1988, 158). Schafer's soundscape project had, as its principal progeny, CRESSON (Centre de recherche sur l'espace sonore at l'environnement urbain), located in the School of Architecture at the University of Grenoble, a research enterprise initiated by Jean-François Augoyard in 1979, the year in which he published *Pas à pas: Essai sur le cheminement quotidien en milieu urbain*. Augoyard and his fellow-researchers have adopted a methodology and terminology around the notion of sonic effects ('effets sonores') (see Augoyard and Torgue, 2005), which grow from a conciliatory critique of Pierre Schaeffer's 'sound objects' ('objets sonores') (too meticulous and laborious for purpose) and Schafer's 'soundscape' (too broad and blurred). Augoyard looks to occupy the middle ground between these (polarised) modes of investigation. We shall turn to the work of CRESSON in Chapter 8. What is important for our present purposes is that all three approaches are preoccupied with sound in its phenomenological dimension.

4. In the first stanza, MacBeth has put one too many l's in line 3; and in the fifth stanza, there are too few n's in the first line, and too few l's in the third.

5. A further implication of this first step, an implication which only came to fruition in the twentieth century, was the practice of keyboard writing (typewriter, computer), a topic briefly to be discussed in Chapter 8.

6. As Johanna Drucker puts it: '*The Yellow Pages* are not poetry, and certainly they are not derived from song, but they can be rendered poetical through vocal performance' (2009, 243).

7. Particular typefaces, or families of typeface, also have their own *histories* of shifting expressive values: 'The sanserif look that Tschichold and his contemporaries took to be a self-evident zeitgeist evocation of radical modernity had originally been revived, at the end of the eighteenth century, as the signifier of the classical, conservative past. For the romantic-era reader, the sanserif – in marked and diametric contrast to a mechanized modernity – possessed unmistakable "associations of rugged antiquity"' [James Mosley, 'The Nymph and the Grot: The Revival of the Sanserif Letter', *Typographica*, 12 (1965), 2] (Dworkin, 2003, xx).

8. 'Übersetzungen, die mehr als Vermittlungen sind, entstehen, wenn im Fortleben ein Werk das Zeitalter seines Ruhmes erreicht hat . . . In ihnen erreicht das Leben des Originals seine stets erneute späteste und umfassendste Entfaltung' (Benjamin, 1972, 11) [Translations that are more than transmissions of subject matter come into being when in the course of its survival a work has reached the age of its fame . . . The life of the originals [*sic*] attains in them to its ever-renewed latest and most abundant flowering (1992, 73)]. We should emphasise, however, that by 'survival', we refer not so much to 'Fortleben', the mere continuation of the work (ST) in time, but to another word that Benjamin uses in the same context, namely 'Überleben', the accession of the work (ST), through translation, to a higher plane. For a discussion of the distinction between 'Fortleben' and 'Überleben' in Benjamin's 'Die Aufgabe des Übersetzers' [The Task of the Translator], see Berman, 2008, 76–86.

9. It is indeed worth emphasising that this book is also about the displacement of the literary, in two principal senses: (i) the literary is not a fixed value as many would perhaps wish it, measurable in metaphors, or instances of acoustic patterning, or whatever. The literary has a migratory capacity and alights where the reader finds it, or the translator puts it. A punctuation mark, a font, a tone of voice, can as much activate the literary as an image, or a rhyme, or a rhythm. If the literary is an excess of the signifier, which no signified can do justice to, then it obtains wherever that condition obtains. (ii) We are moving beyond literature as a body of writing with a set of inherent qualities which identify it as literature, a set of technical features even, to a notion of the literary as a matter for the reader. Just as we might say that imagination, a faculty, has been replaced by the imaginary, a dimension of perception, so literature, a separate category of writing, has been replaced by the literary, a certain response triggered by any kind of device in any writing (for a fuller discussion of these matters, see Chapter 7).

10. Something of the same idea is expressed by Walter Benjamin: 'Seine volle Bedeutung erwinnt er [der Begriff der Übersetzung] in der Einsicht, daß jede höhere Sprache (mit Ausnahme des Wortes Gottes) als Übersetzung aller anderen betrachtet werden kann. Mit dem erwähnten Verhältnis der Sprachen als dem von Medien verschiedener Dichte ist die Übersetzbarkeit der Sprachen ineinander gegeben. Die Übersetzung ist die Überführung der einen Sprache in die andere durch ein Kontinuum von Verwandlungen. Kontinua der Verwandlung, nicht abstrakte Gleichheits- und Ähnlichkeitsbezirke durchmißt die Übersetzung' (1977, 151) [Translation attains its full meaning in the realization that every evolved language (with the exception of the word of God) can be considered a translation of all others. By the fact that, as mentioned earlier, languages relate to one another as do media of varying densities, the translatability of languages into one another is established. Translation is removal from one language into another through a continuum of transformations. Translation passes through continua of transformation, not abstract areas of identity and similarity (1996, 69–70)]. Put another way, one might say that, once language is involved in a particular linguistic purpose, all languages are

involved. In its individual inadequacy, any language is implicitly pleading with other languages to come to its aid.

11. For an illuminating discussion of the anthropology of perceptual and existential embedding in environment, see Ingold 2000, particularly Parts I and II.

5 TRANSLATING THE ACOUSTICITY OF VOICE

1. This question is perhaps rendered less implausible by the fact that, although a sequence of alexandrines is isosyllabic (i.e. has the same number of units, of the same metrical value), these same units, in the speaking of the line, will all clearly have different values (of pitch, intensity, duration); isosyllabicity does not entail isochronicity. Cornulier himself concedes: 'Le comptage métrique des syllabes est largement mental ("abstrait", comme aimeraient dire certains). Que m'importe qu'on prononce à peu près l'*i* consonne ou qu'on ne prononce pas l'*e* dans *Ariane*, du moment que je reconnais intérieurement la possibilité d'interprétation 6-syllabique de *Ariane, ma sœur*' (1982, 130) [The metrical counting of syllables is largely mental ('abstract', as some would like to say). What does it matter if the *i* is pronounced almost as a consonant and the *e* is not pronounced in *Ariane*, provided that I recognise in my mind the possibility of a hexasyllabic reading of *Ariane, ma sœur*].

2. In his *The Phonetic Description of Voice Quality*, for example, John Laver confesses that 'we know now only a little more about the factors that give rise to different qualities of voice than Quintilian did' (1980, 1).

3. This is not, of course, to say that the comma does not fulfil its usual syntactic functions at the same time.

4. For example, 'J'implorai d'elle un rendez-vous, / Le soir, sur une route obscure. / Elle y vint! – folle créature!' ('Le Vin de l'assassin'). 'Ô toi qui de la Mort, ta vieille et forte amante, / Engendras l'Espérance, – une folle charmante!' ('Les Litanies de Satan').

5. It is not clear if Baudelaire himself perceived the relationship between the two marks in this way. An example which would deserve comment if such an argument were pursued would be lines 13–14 of 'Le Poison', which, in the 1861 edition, run: 'Lacs où mon âme tremble et se voit à l'envers... / Mes songes viennent en foule.' In the 1857 *Revue française* version, 'Mes songes' is preceded by a dash.

6. The removal of the apostrophe ('Ô Beauté'), and the scare-quotes around 'unyielding scourge of souls', are both measures of dissociation from rhetorical grandiloquence and from the ceding of voice to ready-made formulation.

6 FREE VERSE AND THE TRANSLATION OF RHYTHM

1. 'Periodicity' I would define as the recurrence of linguistic units of the same length and the same structuring principle. Because it can only be ascertained in retrospect, at the end of the unit, periodicity belongs to the spatial rather than temporal, to units immobilised and juxtaposed. 'Rhythmicity', on the other hand, is a principle of modulation in time, the way in which a sequence characterises itself in movement, constructs a particular dynamic for itself.

2. The only accents in French which might be said to be metrically motivated are the accents at the ends of syllabic sequences whether of line or hemistich. However, in a sequence of octosyllables, for example:

```
- - - - - - - /
- - - - - - - /
- - - - - - - / etc.
```

it would be foolish to say that the line-terminal metrical accents do any more than endorse periodicity. They do not create a rhythm. But see Roger Pensom (2009) for a recent argument that accent is metrically constitutive of French verse.

3. Writing about the poetics of performance, Jerome Rothenberg notes: '. . . the value of a work isn't inherent in its formal or aesthetic characteristics – its shape or its complexity or simplicity as an object – but in what it does, or what the artist or his surrogate does with it, how he performs it in a given context' (1994, 642).

4. Murat later (2002, 421–37) tackles the problem of 'vers blancs' in prose in rather more extended and byzantine fashion. Are they examples of actual verse-lines, of *mètres virtuels*, or of *modules rythmiques*? That this question of nomenclature might be crucial is indicative of the corner that French verse-analysis has boxed itself into. *Mètres virtuels* take us in the direction of a prose derived from *vers libres classiques*, *modules rythmiques* in the direction of a prose affiliated to *vers libre*. But what this taxonomic puzzle does not take into consideration is the potential collisions between linguistic differentiation and the perceptions of the ear, where the perceptions of the ear are inextricably related to the education of reading. What is the point of reading if it does not make more options available to us, by sheer dint of our greater knowledge of more intertextual instances? Rhythmic intertextuality remains a peculiarly uninvestigated area of readerly experience. The defence of categories leads Murat to hedge the 'vers blancs' to be found in *Illuminations* with exclusion clauses: they cannot be less than eight syllables long, and if eight must be 4+4, 5+3 or 3+5 (otherwise they will be *modules rythmiques*); they cannot be *impairs*; they must be syntactically autonomous; they must follow a pattern already attested to in verse; they cannot be created by the application of the syllabic conventions of verse – these can only be applied when the metrical model has been identified (!). What conception of verse is being so strenuously defended here? What is at stake? Might not Rimbaud have adopted the prose poem precisely because of the different degrees and pedigrees of verse that it encrypts and makes available as part of the psychopathology of reading?

5. At this point, it would be as well to remember the words of Pierre Joris: 'In my years spent in the practice of poetry, both writing and translating it, a sense has gropingly emerged suggesting that a poem is not only the one version printed in a book or magazine, but is also all its other (possible) printed versions, plus all the possible oral and/or visual performances as well as the totality of translations it allows. The printed poem thus functions only as a score for all

subsequent readings (private or public) and performative transformations, be they through music, dance, painting or linguistic translation. Such a view is bound to destabilize a concept of the poem as fixed, absolute artefact, readable (understandable, interpretable) once and for all. Celan says as much in the Meridian: "The absolute poem – no, it certainly does not, cannot exist"' (1995, 34–5).

6. Laforgue made this declaration in a letter to Gustave Kahn in July 1886: 'J'oublie de rimer, j'oublie le nombre de syllabes, j'oublie la distribution des strophes, mes lignes commencent à la marge comme de la prose' (1941, 193) [I forget to rhyme, I forget the number of syllables, I forget the distribution of stanzas, my lines begin at the margin like prose].

7. In the words of Albert Mockel: 'car si sa position en évidence la doue d'une importance spéciale, la rime n'a pourtant pas, dans le vers moderne, un rôle indépendant du rôle des autres sons. Elle doit, pour acquérir toute sa valeur, s'allier avec les tons syllabiques voisins ou se fondre en leur rumeur qu'elle peut alors synthétiser par sa note vive' (1962, 129) [for if its prominent position endows it with a special importance, rhyme does not however enjoy, in modern verse, a role independent of the role of the other sounds. It must, to acquire a maximal value, ally itself with adjacent syllabic tones or blend into their music, which it can then synthesise by the vividness of its note].

7 THE REINVENTION OF THE LITERARY IN LITERARY TRANSLATION

1. The version of this passage in the Loeb Classical Library translation, by H. Rushton Fairclough, revised by G.P. Goold, runs as follows: 'But he does not recognize himself as he runs, nor as he moves, as he raises the mighty stone in his hand or throws it; his knees buckle, his blood is frozen cold. The very stone, whirled by the hero through the empty air, did not traverse the whole distance, nor drive home its blow. And as in dreams, when languorous sleep has weighed down our eyes at night, we seem to strive in vain to press on our eager course, and in mid effort collapse helpless: our tongue lacks power, our wonted strength fails our limbs, and neither voice nor words will come: so to Turnus, however bravely he sought to win his way, the dread goddess denies fulfilment' (Fairclough and Goold 2000, 365; capitals in original).

2. What assessment criteria are called upon in these reconstructive enterprises? Allen invokes the following types of data: '(1) specific statements of Latin grammarians and other authors regarding the pronunciation of the language; (2) puns, plays on words, ancient etymologies, and imitations of natural sounds; (3) the representation of Latin words in other languages; (4) developments in the Romance languages; (5) the spelling conventions of Latin, and particularly scribal or epigraphic variations; and (6) the internal structure of the Latin language itself, including its metrical patterns' (1965, vi).

3. For Allen (1965, 92–3) and Geoffrey Nussbaum (1986, 20–1), ictus is a relatively unproblematic reality. Brooks, for his part, reports: 'Recent scholars, especially

in Italy, have questioned the existence of this "ictus" altogether, while British scholars, though paying due regard to word accent, have been reluctant to abandon the concept altogether' (2007, 49), and concludes: 'It then became a matter of some importance to relate the stress patterns of the Latin language to the metrical patterns inherited from the Greeks, and I would contend that the problem of "ictus" versus word accent is not merely a problem which exercises modern academics but was one with which Roman poets were themselves actively engaged' (2007, 51).

4. Gasparov is presumably here referring to long and short syllables rather than to long and short vowels.

5. The 'plain' version of Fitzgerald's text is as follows:

> Just as in dreams when the night-swoon of sleep
> Weighs on our eyes, it seems we try in vain
> To keep on running, try with all our might,
> But in the midst of effort faint and fail;
> Our tongue is powerless, familiar strength
> Will not hold up our body, not a sound
> Or word will come: just so with Turnus now.

6. This is an idea that Borges returns to with some consistency, e.g.: 'To assume that every recombination of elements is necessarily inferior to its original form is to assume that draft nine is necessarily inferior to draft H – for there can only be drafts' (2001: 69); 'The Cervantes text and the Menard [*sic*] text are verbally identical, but the second is almost infinitely richer' (2000: 40).

7. '[E]n raison que le vers est tout, dès qu'on écrit. Style, versification, s'il y a cadence et c'est pourquoi toute prose d'écrivain fastueux, soustraite à ce laisser-aller en usage, ornementale, vaut en tant qu'un vers rompu, jouant avec ses timbres et encore les rimes dissimulées' (Mallarmé, 2003, 64) [the truth is, verse is everything, as soon as one writes. Style, versification, if there is cadence, and that is why any page by a sumptuous writer, using language withdrawn from its habitual haphazardness, ornamental, works like a broken line of poetry, playing with its sounds and hidden rhymes (Johnson, 2007, 183)].

8. For reflections on the discourses of urban perambulation, see Certeau (1984, 91–110) and Solnit (2002: 171–246).

9. For accounts of Situationism, see Plant (1992), Sadler (1998), McDonough (2002, 2009) and Ford (2005).

10. The French text of these opening lines runs:

> À la fin tu es las de ce monde ancien
> Bergère ô tour Eiffel le troupeau des ponts bêle ce matin
> Tu en as assez de vivre dans l'antiquité grecque et romaine
> Ici même les automobiles ont l'air d'être anciennes.

11. The French text runs:

> J'ai vu ce matin une jolie rue dont j'ai oublié le nom
> Neuve et propre du soleil elle était le clairon
> Les directeurs les ouvriers et les belles sténo-dactylographes
> Du lundi matin au samedi soir quatre fois par jour y passent

Le matin par trois fois la sirène y gémit
Une cloche rageuse y aboie vers midi
Les inscriptions des enseignes et des murailles
Les plaques les avis à la façon des perroquets criaillent
J'aime la grâce de cette rue industrielle
Située à Paris entre la rue Aumont-Thiéville et l'avenue des Ternes.

12. For a full and substantiated argument about the relationship between the street-photographic and the documentary, see Scott, 2007.

13. The French text runs:

Tu regardes les yeux pleins de larmes ces pauvres émigrants
Ils croient en Dieu ils prient les femmes allaitent des enfants
Ils emplissent de leur odeur le hall de la gare Saint-Lazare
Ils ont foi dans leur étoile comme les rois-mages
Ils espèrent gagner de l'argent dans l'Argentine
Et revenir dans leur pays après avoir fait fortune
Une famille transporte un édredon rouge comme vous transportez votre cœur
Cet édredon et nos rêves sont aussi irréels
Quelques-uns de ces émigrants restent ici et se logent
Rue des Rosiers ou rue des Écouffes dans des bouges
Je les ai vus souvent le soir ils prennent l'air dans la rue
Et se déplacent rarement comme les pièces aux échecs
Il y a surtout des Juifs leurs femmes portent perruque
Elles restent assises exsangues au fond des boutiques.

8 WRITING AND OVERWRITING THE SOUND OF THE CITY

1. 'The Letter as Such', a manifesto of 1913, signed by Khlebnikov and Kruchenykh, is more explicit about the functions of handwriting within the Cubo-Futurists' aesthetic vision: 'But ask any wordwright and he will tell you that a word written in individual longhand or composed with a particular typeface bears no resemblance at all to the same word in a different inscription' (Lawton and Eagle, 1988, 63); '*There are two propositions*: 1. That mood changes one's longhand during the process of writing. 2. That the longhand peculiarly modified by one's mood conveys that mood to the reader, independently of the words. Also, one has to pose the question of graphic signs, visual signs, or simply tactile signs as if felt by the hand of a blind man' (63–4).

2. 'A continuation of sound that is no longer heard. After the extinction of both emission and propagation, the sound gives the impression of remaining "in the ear" . . . [I]t is simply the mnestic trace of barely subsided sound signals' (Augoyard and Torgue, 2005, 87).

3. 'A perceptive effect describing the unstable and changing relations between elements of a sound ensemble' (Augoyard and Torgue, 2005, 73).

4. 'An effect linked to spatio-temporal conditions that expresses the difficulty or impossibility of locating a sound source. In the major variant of this effect, the sound seems to come from everywhere and nowhere at the same time. In a

minor variant, sound seems to come simultaneously from a singular source and from many sources' (Augoyard and Torgue, 2005, 130).

5. I have quoted at length from the Notes simply because Bonney's fascinating work is not as easily available for consultation as it deserves to be.

6.
           Her motion elastic, her furbelows Stygian –
           Marooned on a refuge, by the din of the street,
           My whole self convulsed as she passed callipygian,

           Her figure as svelte as her cadence was Phrygian
           And legs statuesque and galbous and fleet.
           Her motion elastic, her furbelows Stygian,

           An hypnotic *douceur* and Salome's religion
           Were locked in her look which I drank till replete;
           My whole self convulsed as she passed callipygian,

           Her eyes full of storm and so hauntingly strygian.
           Was she grieving *grande dame* or a whore on her beat,
           Her motion elastic, her furbelows Stygian?

           And then she was gone, slick-fast as a widgeon,
           To beyond all beyond, to where none ever meet.
           My whole self convulsed as she passed callipygian,

           Too late, but she knew, this canny Parisian,
           That love at last sight puts the city on heat,
           Her motion elastic, her furbelows Stygian.
           My whole self convulsed as she passed callipygian.

7.
           The street. Pandemonium. Hell let loose in the ear
           Tall and slim and regal,
                           all in black, a woman grieving

           What loss? Her cultured hand
                           raises her dress's hem.

           My dazed eyes will not let
                           her go, cling
           To *her* eyes, pale with a coming storm
           Which breaks. The street crashes round me.

           What did I see? Of course the tenderness
                           which holds you very still
           And the headlong suicides of the flesh.
           Her hand reveals a lithe, well-moulded leg.

           Then she was gone. Nowhere to be seen.
           Yet I've been jolted
                           back to life.
           Somewhere the traffic rumbles on and on.

           Missed trains, missed friends,
                           and other chances missed.
           These little pains disturb,
                         whip up the blood,

And still the street-noise dins inside my head
And still her hand lifts up her swinging hem.

8. As Augoyard and Torgue put it: 'In this way, there exists, between the sound and the sonic effect, not a relation of similarity but rather a set of mutual references between the sound, physically measurable although always abstract, and its interpretation, the particular fashioning by which it enters into perceptive development' (2005, 11).

EPILOGUE

1. Bowie's forebears in a humanist stylistics are Leo Spitzer, Stephen Ullmann, Richard Sayce, Jean-Pierre Richard.
2. As Bowie himself puts it: 'Literary theory can prosper, I would suggest, only by attending to the active sense of futurity that is internal to literary language and to the as yet unrealized zones of meaning that inhabit works of literary art' (1993b, 47).
3. Valéry's actual words are: 'J'observai que cette figure était décasyllabique, et je me fis quelques réflexions sur ce type fort peu employé dans la poésie moderne; il me semblait pauvre et monotone. Il était peu de chose auprès de l'alexandrin, que trois ou quatre générations de grands artistes ont prodigieusement élaboré. Le démon de la généralisation suggérait de tenter de porter ce *Dix* à la puissance du *Douze*' (1957, 1503) [I observed that this figure was decasyllabic and I engaged in some reflections on this verse-type so little used in modern poetry; it seemed to me poor and monotonous. It was a paltry thing when put beside the alexandrine, which three or four generations of great artists have prodigiously developed. The demon of generalisation suggested that I should try to raise this *Ten* to the power of *Twelve*].
4. In his Winnicott chapter (2000b, 28), Bowie is able confidently to declare: 'Winnicott's bare but highly inflected theoretical language is compatible with the craft languages appropriate to each discipline or art or technique. It is compatible, for example, with the language of draughtsmanship, narrative theory, rhetoric, Viennese sonata form, versification, *pointillisme* in the manner of Seurat, or paint-dripping in the manner of Jackson Pollock.'

Bibliographical references

Abbott, Helen, 2009. *Between Baudelaire and Mallarmé: Voice, Conversation and Music* (Farnham: Ashgate).

Ahl, Frederick (trans. and ed.), 2007. *Virgil: 'Aeneid'* (Oxford University Press).

Allen, W. Sidney, 1965. *Vox Latina: The Pronunciation of Classical Latin* (Cambridge University Press).

Apollinaire, Guillaume, 1965. *Œuvres poétiques*, ed. Marcel Adéma and Michel Décaudin (Paris: Gallimard).

  1991. *Œuvres en prose complètes II*, ed. Pierre Caizergues and Michel Décaudin (Paris: Gallimard).

Apollonio, Umbro (ed.), 1973. *Futurist Manifestos* (London: Thames and Hudson).

Apter, Emily, 2006. *The Translation Zone: A New Comparative Literature* (Princeton University Press).

Artaud, Antonin, 1964. *Le Théâtre et son double suivi de Le Théâtre de Séraphin* (Paris: Gallimard) (1st edn 1938).

  2003. *Pour en finir avec le jugement de dieu* (Paris: Gallimard).

Augoyard, Jean-François, 2007. *Step by Step: Everyday Walks in a French Urban Housing Project*, trans. David Ames Curtis (Minneapolis: University of Minnesota Press) (1st French edn 1979).

Augoyard, Jean-François, and Henry Torgue (eds), 2005. *Sonic Experience: A Guide to Everyday Sounds*, trans. Andra McCartney and David Paquette (Montreal and Kingston: McGill-Queen's University Press).

Barthes, Roland, 1970. *S/Z* (Paris: Seuil).

  1982a. 'Le grain de la voix', in *L'Obvie et l'obtus: Essais critiques III* (Paris: Seuil), 236–45.

  1982b. 'Écoute', in *L'Obvie et l'obtus: Essais critiques III* (Paris: Seuil), 217–30.

  1984. 'Écrire la lecture', in *Le Bruissement de la langue: Essais critiques IV* (Paris: Seuil), 33–6 (1st edn 1970).

  1995. 'Le degré zéro du coloriage', in *Œuvres complètes III: 1974–1980*, ed. Éric Marty (Paris: Seuil), 821.

Baudelaire, Charles, 1975. *Œuvres complètes I*, ed. Claude Pichois (Paris: Gallimard).

Beardsley, Monroe C., 1977. 'Aspects of Orality: A Short Commentary', *New Literary History*, 8, 521–30.

Benjamin, Walter, 1972. *Gesammelte Schriften IV. I*, ed. Tillman Rexroth (Frankfurt am Main: Suhrkamp).

    1977. *Gesammelte Schriften II. I*, ed. Rolf Tiedemann and Hermann Schweppenhäuser (Frankfurt am Main: Suhrkamp).

    1992. 'The Task of the Translator', trans. Harry Zohn, in Rainer Schulte and John Biguenet (eds), *Theories of Translation: An Anthology of Essays from Dryden to Derrida* (University of Chicago Press), 71–82.

    1996. 'On Language as Such and on the Language of Man', in Marcus Bullock and Michael W. Jennings (eds), *Walter Benjamin: Selected Writings I: 1913– 1926* (Cambridge, MA: Harvard University Press), 62–74.

Berger, John, 2008. *Berger on Drawing*, ed. Jim Savage, 3rd edn (Aghabullogue: Occasional Press).

Bergson, Henri, 1984. *Œuvres*, ed. André Robinet and Henri Gouhier, 4th edn (Paris: Presses Universitaires de France).

Berman, Antoine, 2008. *L'Âge de la traduction: 'La Tâche du traducteur' de Walter Benjamin: Un commentaire*, ed. Isabelle Berman, with Valentina Sommella (Saint-Denis: Presses Universitaires de Vincennes).

Bernard, Oliver (trans. and ed.), 2004. *Guillaume Apollinaire: Selected Poems* (London: Anvil Press Poetry).

Berry, Cicely, 2000. *Your Voice and How to Use It*, 2nd rev. edn (London: Virgin).

Bök, Christian, 2009. 'When Cyborgs Versify', in Marjorie Perloff and Craig Dworkin (eds), *The Sound of Poetry / The Poetry of Sound* (University of Chicago Press), 129–41.

Bonnefoy, Yves, 1979. 'On the Translation of Form in Poetry', *World Literature Today*, 53/3, 374–9.

    1992. 'Lever les yeux de son livre (1988)', in *Entretiens sur la poésie (1972–1990)* (Paris: Mercure de France).

Bonney, Sean, 2008. *Baudelaire in English* (London: Veer Books).

Borges, Jorge Luis, 2000. 'Pierre Menard, Author of the *Quixote*', in *Fictions*, trans. Andrew Hurley (London: Penguin), 33–43.

    2001. 'The Homeric Versions', in *The Total Library: Non-Fiction 1922–1986*, ed. and trans. Eliot Weinberger, trans. Esther Allen and Suzanne Jill Levine (London: Penguin), 69–74.

Bowie, Malcolm, 1973. *Henri Michaux: A Study of His Literary Works* (Oxford University Press).

    1987. *Freud, Proust and Lacan: Theory as Fiction* (Cambridge University Press).

    1990. 'Genius at Nightfall: Mallarmé's "Quand l'ombre menaça de la fatale loi . . ."', in Christopher Prendergast (ed.), *Nineteenth-Century French Poetry: Introductions to Close Reading* (Cambridge University Press), 225–42.

    1991. *Lacan* (London: Fontana [HarperCollins]).

    1993a. 'Comparison between the Arts: A Psychoanalytic View', *Comparative Criticism*, 15, 81–102.

    1993b. *Psychoanalysis and the Future of Theory* (Oxford: Blackwell).

1994. 'Towards a Poetics of Mallarmé's Late Prose', *Yearbook of Comparative and General Literature*, 42, 29–37.

1998a. 'Lacan and Mallarmé: Theory as Word-Play', in Michael Temple (ed.), *Meetings with Mallarmé in Contemporary French Culture* (University of Exeter Press), 67–80.

1998b. 'Proust and Psychoanalysis', *Publications of the English Goethe Society*, n.s. 68, 20–8.

1998c. *Proust among the Stars* (London: Fontana [HarperCollins]).

1999. 'What Is Literature?', review article on Denis Hollier, *Absent without Leave: French Literature under the Threat of War*, Raritan, 19/2, 14–26.

2000a. 'Mallarmé's Last Things', *Journal of the Institute of Romance Studies*, 8, 1–11.

2000b. 'Psychoanalysis and Art: The Winnicott Legacy', in Lesley Caldwell (ed.), *Art, Creativity, Living* (London: Karnac Books), 11–29.

2001. 'Postlude: Proust and the Art of Brevity', in Richard Bales (ed.), *The Cambridge Companion to Proust* (Cambridge University Press), 216–29.

2003. 'Part III: The Modern Period 1789–2000', in Sarah Kay, Terence Cave, Malcolm Bowie, *A Short History of French Literature* (Oxford University Press), 193–314.

2004a. 'Introduction', to Gustave Flaubert, *Madame Bovary*, trans. Margaret Mauldon (Oxford University Press), vii–xx.

2004b. 'Proust and Italian Painting', *Comparative Criticism*, 25 ('Lives of the Disciplines: Comparative Biography'), 97–122.

2007. 'Is Music Criticism Criticism?', in Gillian Beer, Malcolm Bowie and Beate Perrey (eds), *In(ter)discipline: New Languages for Criticism* (London: Legenda), 67–73.

Brooks, Clive, 2007. *Reading Latin Poetry Aloud: A Practical Guide to Two Thousand Years of Verse* (Cambridge University Press).

Cage, John (ed.), 1969. *Notations* (New York: Something Else Press).

Catach, Nina, 1996. *La Ponctuation: Histoire et système*, 2nd edn (Paris: Presses Universitaires de France).

Caws, Mary Ann (ed.), 2001. *Mallarmé in Prose* (New York: New Directions).

Certeau, Michel de, 1984. *The Practice of Everyday Life*, trans. Steven Rendall (Berkeley, CA: University of California Press).

Cohen, Edward H., 2000. 'Private and Public, Life and Art, in W.E. Henley's Hospital Poems', in Sabine Coelsch-Foisner and Holger Klein (eds), *Private and Public Voices in Victorian Poetry* (Tübingen: Stauffenberg), 227–36.

Cohn, Stephen (trans.), 1992. *Rainer Maria Rilke: 'Neue Gedichte'/'New Poems'*, intro. John Bayley (Manchester: Carcanet Press).

Cooper, G. Burns, 1998. *Mysterious Music: Rhythm and Free Verse* (Stanford University Press).

Cornulier, Benoît de, 1982. *Théorie du vers: Rimbaud, Verlaine, Mallarmé* (Paris: Seuil).

1994. 'Illuminations métriques: Lire ou faire des vers dans la prose à Rimbaud', in André Guyaux (ed.), *Rimbaud 1891-1991* (Paris: Champion), 103–23.

Cox, Christoph, and Daniel Warner (eds.), 2004. *Audio Culture: Readings in Modern Music* (New York: Continuum).

Cranston, Philip (trans.), 2008. *Jules Supervielle: Les Amis inconnus/Unknown Friends* (Potomac, MD: Scripta Humanistica).

Curtay, Jean-Paul, 1974. *La Poésie lettriste* (Paris: Seghers).

Davis, Lydia (trans. and ed.), 2003. *Marcel Proust: 'The Way by Swann's'* (London: Penguin).

Day Lewis, Cecil (trans.), 1966. *The Eclogues, Georgics and Aeneid of Virgil* (London: Oxford University Press).

Dickens, Charles, 1949. *A Tale of Two Cities*, ed. Sir John Shuckburgh (Oxford University Press) (1st edn 1859).

1953. *Great Expectations*, ed. Frederick Page (Oxford University Press) (1st edn 1860–1861).

Dottin, Mireille (ed.), 1988. *Jules Laforgue: Textes de critique d'art* (Lille: Presses Universitaires de Lille).

Drucker, Johanna, 2009. 'Not Sound', in Marjorie Perloff and Craig Dworkin (eds), *The Sound of Poetry/The Poetry of Sound* (University of Chicago Press), 237–48.

Dworkin, Craig, 2003. *Reading the Illegible* (Evanston, IL: Northwestern University Press).

Eliot, T.S., 1978. 'Reflections on *Vers Libre*', *To Criticize the Critic and Other Writings* (London: Faber and Faber), 183–9 (1st edn 1917).

Fagles, Robert (trans.), 2006. *Virgil: 'The Aeneid'*, ed. Bernard Knox and Michael Putnam (London: Penguin).

Fairclough, H. Rushton, and G.P. Goold (trans.), 2000. *Virgil: Aeneid VII–XII, Appendix Vergiliana* (Cambridge, MA: Harvard University Press; London: William Heinemann) (1st edn 1918).

Fitzgerald, Robert (trans.), 1992. *Virgil: 'The Aeneid'*, ed. Philip Hardie (New York: Everyman's Library) (1st edn 1981).

Flint, R.W. (ed.), 1972. *Marinetti: Selected Writings*, trans. R.W. Flint and Arthur A. Coppotelli (London: Secker and Warburg).

Fónagy, Ivan, 1971. 'The Functions of Vocal Style', in Seymour Chatman (ed.), *Literary Style: A Symposium* (London: Oxford University Press), 159–76.

1991. *La Vive Voix: Essais de psycho-phonétique* (Paris: Payot).

Fongaro, Antoine, 1993. *Segments métriques dans la prose d'' Illuminations'* (Toulouse: Presses Universitaires du Mirail-Toulouse).

Ford, Ford Madox, 1966. *Thus to Revisit: Some Reminiscences* (New York: Octagon Books).

Ford, Simon, 2005. *The Situationist International: A User's Guide* (London: Black Dog Publishing).

Fowlie, Wallace, 1993. *Rimbaud and Jim Morrison: The Rebel as Poet: A Memoir* (Durham, NC: Duke University Press).

Fresnault-Deruelle, Pierre, 1971. 'Aux frontières de la langue: Quelques réflexions sur les onomatopées dans la bande dessinée', *Cahiers de Lexicologie*, 18, 79–88.

Garrard, Greg, 2004. *Ecocriticism* (London: Routledge).

Gasparov, M.L., 1996. *A History of European Versification*, ed. G.S. Smith and L. Holford-Strevens, trans. G.S. Smith and Marina Tarlinskaja (Oxford: Clarendon Press).

Ginsberg, Allen, 1994. 'Notes for *Howl and Other Poems*', in Paul Hoover (ed.), *Postmodern American Poetry: A Norton Anthology* (New York: W.W. Norton), 635–7 (1st edn 1959).

Goldberg, RoseLee, 2001. *Performance Art: From Futurism to the Present*, rev. edn (London: Thames and Hudson).

Goody, Jack, 2000. *The Power of the Written Tradition* (Washington: Smithsonian Institution Press).

Gordon, Bob (ed.), 2009. *1000 Fonts* (Lewes: Ilex).

Goulbourne, Russell, 1999. 'The Sound of Silence . . . *points de suspension* in Baudelaire's *Les Fleurs du Mal* ', *Australian Journal of French Studies*, 36, 200–13.

Gruaz, Claude, 1980. 'La ponctuation, c'est l'homme . . . emploi de signes de ponctuation dans cinq romans contemporains', *Langue Française*, 45, 113–24.

Gullentops, David, 2003. 'Présences de l'alexandrin dans *Embarcadères*', in Monique Bourdin (ed.), *Jean Cocteau 4: Poésie critique et critique de la poésie* (Paris/Caen: Minard), 155–82.

Harvey, Anne (ed.), 1999. *Adlestrop Revisited: An Anthology Inspired by Edward Thomas's Poem* (Stroud: Sutton Publishing).

Heaney, Seamus (trans.), 1999. *Beowulf* (London: Faber and Faber).

Heidsieck, Bernard, 2001. *Notes convergentes: Interventions 1961-1995* (Romainville: Éditions al dante).

Henley, W.E., 1904. *Poems*, 7th edn (London: David Nutt).

Hervey, Sándor, and Ian Higgins, 1992. *Thinking Translation: A Course in Translation Method: French to English* (London: Routledge).

Hughes, Ted (trans.), 1997. *Tales from Ovid* (London: Faber and Faber).

Hugo, Victor, 1971. *Œuvres complètes VI*, ed. Jean Massin (Paris: Le Club Français du Livre).

Ihde, Don, 1976. *Listening and Voice: A Phenomenology of Sound* (Athens, OH: Ohio University Press).

Ingold, Tim, 2000. *The Perception of the Environment: Essays in Livelihood, Dwelling and Skill* (Abingdon: Routledge).

2007. *Lines: A Brief History* (Abingdon: Routledge).

Iser, Wolfgang, 1974. *The Implied Reader: Patterns of Communication in Prose Fiction from Bunyan to Beckett* (Baltimore, MD: Johns Hopkins University Press).

1978. *The Act of Reading: A Theory of Aesthetic Response* (London: Routledge and Kegan Paul).

Jackson Knight, W.F. (trans. and ed.), 1958. *Virgil: 'The Aeneid'* (Harmondsworth: Penguin) (1st edn 1956).

Jakobson, Roman, 1987. *Language in Literature*, ed. Krystyna Pomorska and Stephen Rudy (Cambridge, MA: Belknap Press of Harvard University Press).

1992. 'On Linguistic Aspects of Translation', in Rainer Schulte and John Biguenet (eds), *Theories of Translation: An Anthology of Essays from Dryden to Derrida* (University of Chicago Press), 144–51 (1st edn 1959).

Jandl, Ernst, 1985. *Das Öffnen und Schließen des Mundes: Frankfurter Poetik-Vorlesung* (Darmstadt and Neuwied: Luchterhand).

Jauss, Hans Robert, 1981. *Towards an Aesthetic of Reception*, trans. Timothy Bahti (Minneapolis: University of Minnesota Press).

Johnson, Barbara (trans.), 2007. *Stéphane Mallarmé: 'Divagations'* (Cambridge, MA: Belknap Press of Harvard University Press).

Joris, Pierre (ed. and trans.), 1995. *Paul Celan: 'Breathturn'* (Los Angeles: Sun and Moon Press).

Kirkman, Robert, Charlie Adlard and Cliff Rathburn, 2005. *The Walking Dead V: The Best Defense* (Berkeley, CA: Image Comics).

2008. *The Walking Dead VIII: Made to Suffer* (Berkeley, CA: Image Comics).

Kristeva, Julia, 1974. *La Révolution du langage poétique: L'Avant-garde à la fin du XIXᵉ siècle: Lautréamont et Mallarmé* (Paris: Seuil).

1977. *Polylogue* (Paris: Seuil).

Laforgue, Jules, 1941. *Lettres à un ami 1880-1886*, ed. G. Jean-Aubry (Paris: Mercure de France).

Laver, John, 1980. *The Phonetic Description of Voice Quality* (Cambridge University Press).

Lawrence, D.H., 1967. 'Introduction to *New Poems*', *Selected Literary Criticism*, ed. Anthony Beal (London: Heinemann), 84–9 (1st edn 1920).

Lawton, Anna, and Herbert Eagle (trans. and eds), 1988. *Russian Futurism through Its Manifestoes, 1912-1928* (Ithaca, NY: Cornell University Press).

Lecourt, Colette, 1999. *La Voix de la réussite ou la parole maîtrisée* (Paris: Marabout).

Lefebvre, Henri, 2004. *Rhythmanalysis: Space, Time and Everyday Life*, ed. and trans. Stuart Elden and Gerald Moore (London: Continuum).

Leishman, J.B. (trans. and ed.), 1964. *Rainer Maria Rilke: 'New Poems'* (London: Hogarth Press).

Loffredo, Eugenia and Manuela Perteghella (eds), 2009. *One Poem in Search of a Translator: Rewriting 'Les Fenêtres' by Apollinaire* (Bern: Peter Lang).

Longley, Edna (ed.), 2008. *Edward Thomas: The Annotated Collected Poems* (Tarset: Bloodaxe Books).

Lorenceau, Annette, 1980. 'La ponctuation chez les écrivains d'aujourd'hui: résultats d'une enquête', *Langue Française*, 45, 88–97.

Ma, Ming-Qian, 2009. 'The Sound Shape of the Visual: Toward a Phenomenology of an Interface', in Marjorie Perloff and Craig Dworkin (eds), *The Sound of Poetry/The Poetry of Sound* (University of Chicago Press), 249–69.

MacBeth, George, 1968. *The Night of Stones* (London: Macmillan).

McCallion, Michael, 1998. *The Voice Book: For Everyone Who Wants to Make the Most of their Voice*, 2nd edn (London: Faber and Faber).

McDonough, Tom (ed.), 2002. *Guy Debord and the Situationist International: Texts and Documents* (Cambridge, MA: MIT Press).

(ed.), 2009. *The Situationists and the City* (London: Verso).

McGann, Jerome, 1991. 'How to Read a Book', *The Textual Condition* (Princeton University Press), 101–28.

McKerrow, Ronald B. (ed.), 1958. *The Works of Thomas Nashe III* (Oxford: Blackwell).

MacShane, Frank (ed.), 1964. *Critical Writings of Ford Madox Ford* (Lincoln, NE: University of Nebraska Press).

Mallarmé, Stéphane, 2003. *Œuvres complètes II*, ed. Bertrand Marchal (Paris: Gallimard).

Melville, A.D. (trans.), 1986. *Ovid: 'Metamorphoses'*, ed. E.J. Kenney (Oxford University Press).

Merleau-Ponty, Maurice, 2004. *The World of Perception*, trans. Oliver Davis (London: Routledge).

2010. *Phénoménologie de la perception* (Paris: Gallimard) (1st edn 1945).

Mills, A.D., 1998. *A Dictionary of English Place-Names*, 2nd edn (Oxford University Press).

Mockel, Albert, 1962. 'Propos de littérature', *Esthétique du symbolisme*, ed. Michel Otten (Brussels: Palais des Académies), 69–173 (1st edn 1894).

Morley, Simon, 2003. *Writing on the Wall: Word and Image in Modern Art* (London: Thames and Hudson).

Murat, Michel, 2000. 'Rimbaud et le vers libre: Remarques sur l'invention d'une forme', *Revue d'Histoire Littéraire de la France*, 2, 255–76.

2002. *L'Art de Rimbaud* (Paris: José Corti).

2008. *Le Vers libre* (Paris: Champion).

Nida, Eugene, 1964. *Toward a Science of Translating: With Special Reference to Principles and Procedures Involved in Bible Translating* (Leiden: E.J. Brill).

Nuckolls, Janis, 2004. 'Language and Nature in Sound Alignment', in Veit Erlmann (ed.), *Hearing Cultures: Essays on Sound, Listening and Modernity* (Oxford: Berg), 65–85.

Nussbaum, G.G., 1986. *Vergil's Metre: A Practical Guide for Reading Latin Hexameter Poetry* (Bristol Classical Press).

Olson, Charles, 1966. 'Projective Verse', in Robert Creeley (ed.), *Selected Writings* (New York: New Directions), 15–26 (1st edn 1950).

Parkes, M.B., 1992. *Pause and Effect: An Introduction to the History of Punctuation in the West* (Aldershot: Scolar Press).

Pensom, Roger, 2009. 'Accent et syllabe dans les vers français: Une synthèse possible?', *Journal of French Language Studies*, 19/3, 335–61.

Perec, Georges, 2003. 'Lire: Esquisse socio-physiologique', *Penser/classer* (Paris: Seuil).

Perloff, Nancy, 2009. 'Sound Poetry and the Musical Avant-Garde: A Musicologist's Perspective', in Marjorie Perloff and Craig Dworkin (eds), *The Sound of Poetry/The Poetry of Sound* (University of Chicago Press), 97–117.

Peureux, Guillaume, 2009. *La Fabrique du vers* (Paris: Seuil).

Phillips, Catherine (ed.), 1986. *Gerard Manley Hopkins* (Oxford University Press).

Plant, Sadie, 1992. *The Most Radical Gesture: The Situationist International in a Postmodern Age* (London: Routledge).

Pope, Rob, 1995. *Textual Intervention: Creative and Critical Strategies for Literary Studies* (London: Routledge).

1999. 'Critical-Creative Re-Writing: A Briefing', *The European English Messenger*, 8/2, 41–4.

Popin, Jacques, 1998. *La Ponctuation* (Paris: Nathan).

Poulet, Georges, 1969–1970. 'Phenomenology of Reading', *New Literary History*, 1, 53–68.

Prawer, Siegbert, 1952. *German Lyric Poetry: A Critical Analysis of Selected Poems from Klopstock to Rilke* (London: Routledge and Kegan Paul).

Proust, Marcel (trans. and ed.), 1916. *John Ruskin: 'La Bible d'Amiens'*, 6th edn (Paris: Mercure de France).

1983a. *Remembrance of Things Past: I*, trans. C.K. Scott Moncrieff and Terence Kilmartin (Harmondsworth: Penguin).

1983b. *Remembrance of Things Past: III*, trans. C.K. Scott Moncrieff, Terence Kilmartin and Andreas Mayor (Harmondsworth: Penguin).

1987a. *À la recherché du temps perdu I*, ed. Jean-Yves Tadié (Paris: Gallimard).

1987b. *On Reading Ruskin*, ed. and trans. Jean Autret, William Burford and Phillip J. Wolfe (New Haven: Yale University Press).

1988. *À la recherche du temps perdu III*, ed. Jean-Yves Tadié (Paris: Gallimard).

1989. *À la recherche du temps perdu IV*, ed. Jean-Yves Tadié (Paris: Gallimard).

Purnelle, Gérald, 2003. 'Camouflage et dislocation: De l'alexandrin au vers libre chez Breton et Cocteau', in Monique Bourdin (ed.), *Jean Cocteau 4: Poésie critique et critique de la poésie* (Paris/Caen: Minard), 113–53.

Pym, Anthony, 2010. *Exploring Translation Theories* (Abingdon: Routledge).

Quiller-Couch, Arthur (ed.), 1927. *The Oxford Book of English Verse 1250–1900* (Oxford: Clarendon Press).

Quirk, Randolph, Sidney Greenbaum, Geoffrey Leech and Jan Svartvik, 1985. *A Comprehensive Grammar of the English Language* (London: Longman).

Rainey, Lawrence (ed.), 2005. *Modernism: An Anthology* (Oxford: Blackwell).

Reynolds, Dee, 2008. 'Kinesthetic Rhythms: Participation in Performance', in Elizabeth Lindley and Laura McMahon (eds), *Rhythms: Essays in French Literature, Thought and Culture* (Bern: Peter Lang), 103–18.

Rilke, Rainer Maria, 1960. *Sonnets to Orpheus*, trans. C.F. MacIntyre (Berkeley: University of California Press).

1962. *Gesammelte Gedichte* (Frankfurt am Main: Insel).

Roche, Denis, 1968. 'Leçons sur la vacance poétique *(fragments)*', *Éros énergumène suivi du Poème du 29 avril 62* (Paris: Seuil), 9–17.

Rodenburg, Patsy, 1998. *The Actor Speaks: Voice and the Performer* (London: Methuen).

Rothenberg, Jerome, 1994. 'New Models, New Visions: Some Notes Toward a Poetics of Performance', in Paul Hoover (ed.), *Postmodern American Poetry: A Norton Anthology* (New York: W.W. Norton), 640–4 (1st edn 1977).

2004. *Writing Through: Translations and Variations* (Middletown, CT: Wesleyan University Press).

Sadler, Simon, 1998. *The Situationist City* (Cambridge, MA: MIT Press).

Sarantou, Ioulia-Marina, 2001. 'The Erodynamics of Punctuation in Baudelaire's "Les Bijoux"', *Australian Journal of French Studies*, 38, 213–27.

2004. 'The Punctuational Language of Dandyism in Baudelaire's "Épigraphe pour un livre condamné"', *Forum for Modern Language Study*, 40/1, 14–26.

Sauer, Theresa, 2009. *Notations 21* (New York: Mark Batty Publisher).

Sayre, Henry, 1995. 'Performance', in Frank Lentricchia and Thomas McLaughlin (eds), *Critical Terms for Literary Study*, 2nd edn (University of Chicago Press), 91–104.

Schafer, R. Murray, 1974. *The New Soundscape: A Handbook for the Modern Music Teacher* (London: Universal Edition).

(ed.), 1977a. *European Sound Diary* (Vancouver: A.R.C. Publications).

1977b. *The Tuning of the World* (New York: Alfred A. Knopf).

1988. Review of Jean-François Augoyard and Henry Torgue (eds), *À l'écoute de l'environnement: Répertoire des effets sonores* (Marseilles: Éditions Parenthèses, 1988), *Yearbook of Soundscape Studies*, 1, 158–63.

2005. 'Foreword', in Jean-François Augoyard and Henry Torgue (eds), *Sonic Experience: A Guide to Everyday Sounds*, trans. Andra McCartney and David Paquette (Montreal and Kingston: McGill-Queen's University Press), xi–xvi.

Schwitters, Kurt, 2002. *PPPPPP: Poems Performance Pieces Proses Plays Poetics*, ed. and trans. Jerome Rothenberg and Pierre Joris (Cambridge: Exact Exchange).

Scott, Clive, 1998a. *The Poetics of French Verse: Studies in Reading* (Oxford: Clarendon Press).

1998b. 'The Mirage of Critical Distance: The Mallarmé of Yves Bonnefoy', in Michael Temple (ed.), *Meetings with Mallarmé in Contemporary French Culture* (University of Exeter Press), 199–226.

2000. *Translating Baudelaire* (University of Exeter Press).

2002. 'Translating Free Verse: Jaccottet and Auden', *Channel Crossings: French and English Poetry in Dialogue 1550-2000* (Oxford: Legenda), 209–38.

2006. *Translating Rimbaud's 'Illuminations'* (University of Exeter Press).

2007. *Street Photography: From Atget to Cartier-Bresson* (London: I.B. Tauris).

2009. 'From Linearity to Tabularity: Translating Modes of Reading', *CTIS Occasional Papers*, 4, 37–52.

Scott, David H.T., 1977. *Sonnet Theory and Practice in Nineteenth-Century France: Sonnets on the Sonnet* (University of Hull Publications).

Shakespeare, William, 2005. *The Sonnets and A Lover's Complaint*, ed. John Kerrigan (London: Penguin).

Solnit, Rebecca, 2002. *Wanderlust: A History of Walking* (London: Verso).

Steele, Timothy, 1999. *All the Fun's in How You Say a Thing: An Explanation of Meter and Versification* (Athens, OH: Ohio University Press).

Stockwell, Peter, 2002. *Cognitive Poetics: An Introduction* (London: Routledge).

Storey, Graham, 1981. *A Preface to Hopkins* (Harlow: Longman).

Subramanyan, K.G., 1986. 'Tagore – The Poet Painter', in Ray Monk and Andrew Robinson (eds), *Rabindranath Tagore: A Celebration of His Life and Work* (Museum of Modern Art, Oxford), 55–62.

Supervielle, Jules, 1934. *Les Amis inconnus* (Paris: Gallimard).

Symons, Arthur, 1893. 'The Decadent Movement in Literature', *Harper's New Monthly Magazine*, 87, 858–67.

Tedlock, Dennis, 1977. 'Toward an Oral Poetics', *New Literary History*, 8, 507–19.

Toury, Gideon, 1980. *In Search of a Theory of Translation* (Tel Aviv University/The Porter Institute for Poetics and Semiotics).

Valéry, Paul, 1957. *Œuvres I*, ed. Jean Hytier (Paris: Gallimard).

Venuti, Lawrence, 2011. 'Introduction: Poetry and Translation', *Translation Studies*, 4/2, 127–32.

Watt, Adam, 2009. *Reading in Proust's 'À la recherche': 'Le Délire de la lecture'* (Oxford: Clarendon Press).

West, David (trans. and ed.), 2003. *Virgil: 'The Aeneid'* (London: Penguin) (1st edn 1990).

Woolf, Virginia, 1966. *Collected Essays II* (London: Hogarth Press).

Yeats, W.B. (ed.), 1936. *The Oxford Book of Modern Verse 1892–1935* (Oxford: Clarendon Press).

    1962. 'Literature and the Living Voice', *Explorations* (London: Macmillan), 202–21.

    1965. *Collected Poems* (London: Macmillan).

Index

Made in the USA
Middletown, DE
15 October 2016